Learning and Teaching for Enhanced Society

Learning and Teaching for Enhanced Society

Deepali Gupta

RANDOM

RANDOM PUBLICATIONS
NEW DELHI (INDIA)

Learning and Teaching for Enhanced Society

ISBN 978-93-5111-502-1

Published in 2015 in India by

RANDOM PUBLICATIONS

4376-A/4B, Gali Murari Lal, Ansari Road
New Delhi-110 002
Phone : +9111-43580356, 011-23289044, 011-43142548
e-mail: sales@randompublications.com,
info@randompublications.com, randomexports@gmail.com

Reprinted 2021

Type Setting by : Friends Media, Delhi-110089
Digitally Printed at : Replika Press Pvt. Ltd.

Preface

For more than 150 years a set of pedagogies reflecting the priorities of the Industrial Age has been embedded in the process of mass schooling. The hallmarks of these pedagogies are found in teacher-controlled learning where deconstructed and reconstructed information is presented to same-age cohorts of students in standardised classroom settings.

Globalisation has enabled rapid advancements in technology; we have entered the knowledge age where social networking technologies are changing business, media and political structures. Users can now access information wherever and whenever. However, it has had little impact on the processes of schooling. There is an urgent need for a new educational model; a rethinking of the nature of schooling – its purpose, pedagogies, curriculum, structures, assumptions and expectations.

The old pedagogies persisting into the 21st century are no longer relevant. They ignore the capacity for schooling to take place in both a physical and virtual learning space. If we are to embrace these new opportunities, we need a 21st century pedagogy – a paradigm which reflects a bold and creative commitment to relevance and quality learning and teaching.

This book argues that a physical and virtual schooling capacity, underpinned by social technologies, challenges us to fundamentally re-think our current pedagogies. A supporting pedagogical framework must go beyond connecting schools and providing hardware for students and teachers. It has to be built on the relational nature of learning and be relevant to all those interested in schooling in today's world. This book is designed for teachers and all educators who are currently working with, or who would like to know more about the reforms taking place in the educational sector.

Author

Contents

1

Teaching for Enhanced Learning

In the days when university classes contained highly selected students, at university by choice, the traditional lecture followed by tutorial seemed to work well enough. Today, when the student population is quite diversified, many students seem not to be coping, while teachers feel they are being unfairly put upon. Some believe that these students should not be at university at all.

Let us take two students attending a lecture. Susan is academically committed; she is bright, interested in her studies, and wants to do well. She has clear academic and career plans, and what she learns is important to her. When she learns she goes about it in an "academic" way. She comes to the lecture with relevant background knowledge and a question she wants answered. In the lecture, she finds an answer to that question; it forms the keystone for a particular arch of knowledge she is constructing. She reflects on the personal significance of what she is learning. Students like Susan virtually teach themselves; they need little help from us. The way Susan learns fits Marton and Saljo's description of a *deep* approach to learning, but in making this connection it is important to emphasise that "deep" describes how Susan usually goes about her learning, it does *not* describe a personality characteristic of Susan.

Now take Robert. He is at university not out of a driving curiosity about a particular subject, or a burning ambition to excel in a particular profession, but to obtain a qualification for a job. He is not even studying in the area of his first choice. He is less committed than Susan, and has a less developed background of relevant knowledge; he comes to the lecture wiuh no questions to ask. He wants only to put in sufficient effort to pass. Robert hears the lecturer say the same words as Susan heard, but he doesn't see a keystone, just another brick to be recorded in his lecture notes. He believes that if he can record enough of these bricks, and can remember them on cue, he'll keep out of trouble come exam rime. Robert appears to adopt a *surface* approach to learning, but again it must be emphasised that this is not to describe Robert as a person, but to describe the way he currently learns. The teaching challenge is precisely to change his usual way of learning, not to see it as an impediment to teaching him.

Students like Robert probably are in higher proportions in today's classes than was the case 20 years ago. They will need help if they are to achieve die same levels of understanding that their more committed colleagues achieve spontaneously. To say that Robert is "unmotivated" may be true, but unhelpful. What that really means is that he is not responding to the methods that work for Susan. The challenge we face as teachers is to teach so that Robert learns more in the manner of Susan.

Thus, at Point A, the "passive" end of the teaching method continuum, there is a large gap between Susan and Robert in terms of the their level of engagement, as in the lecture example described above. At point B, the "active" end of the teaching method continuum, the gap between Susan and Robert is lessened; both are now using the higher-level activities. Problem-based learning would be an example of an active method, because it *requires* Robert to question, to speculate, to generate solutions, to use the higher order cognitive activities that Susan uses spontaneously. The teaching has narrowed the gap between diem, at least in terms of the kind of cognitive activity engaged.

There may well be endogenous limits to what students can do diat arc beyond any teacher's control, but there arc learning-related aspects diat *are* controllable. Capitalising on diem is what good teaching is about. *Good teaching is getting most students to use the higher cognitive level processes that the more academic students use spontaneously.* Good teaching narrows die gap.

The problem is to describe a technology of teaching that maximises the chances of engaging students' learning processes in this way.

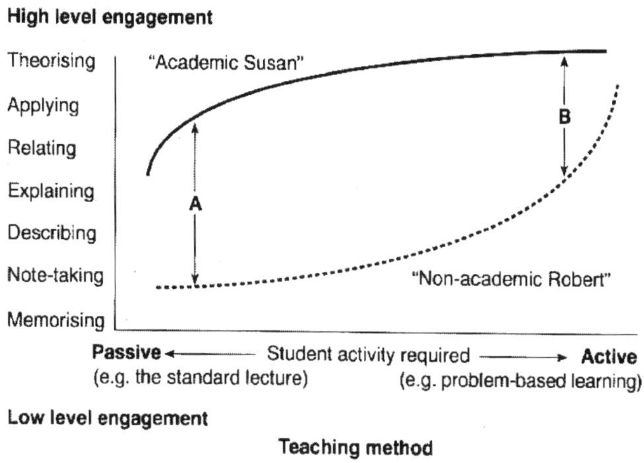

Figure 1. Student orientation, teaching method, and level of engagement.

Constructivism and Phenomenography

How do we derive such a technology? It seems reasonable to turn to the psychology of learning to derive a technology of teaching, but the track record is not encouraging. Learning has been die subject of research by psychologists for the whole of this century, but remarkably little has directly resulted in improved teaching. The reason is that, until recently, psychologists were more concerned with developing "The One Grand Theory of Learning" than in studying the contexts in which people learn, such as schools and universities. This focus has been rectified in the last 20 years or so, by focusing attention precisely on how students go about learning in formal, institutional contexts. Appropriately, this field of study is now designated as "student learning" research.

Student learning research originated in Sweden, with Marton and Saljo's study of surface and deep approaches to learning. They gave students a text to read, and told them they would be asked questions afterwards. Students responded in two different ways. The first group learned in anticipation of the questions, concentrating anxiously on the facts and details that might be asked. They "skated along the surface of the text", as Marton and Sal jo put it, using a surface approach to learning. What these students remembered was a list of disjointed facts; they did not comprehend the point the author was making. The second group on the other hand set out to understand the meaning of what die author was trying to say. They went below the surface of the text to interpret that meaning, using a deep approach. They saw the big picture and how the facts and details made the author's case. Note that the terms "deep" and "surface" as used here describe ways of learning a particular task, not, as many subsequently used the terms, as describing characteristics of students.

This series of studies struck a chord with ongoing work in other countries; in particular with that of Entwistle in the UK, and that of Biggs in Australia. The conceptual frameworks of these workers were originally quite different from that of the Swedish group; the former from individual differences psychology and the latter from cognitive psychology. However, there was a common focus on students being active in a learning context, and some strong implications for teaching could be drawn. There arc two main theories of learning within the student learning paradigm: phenomenography, and constructivism. "Phenomenography" was a term coined by Marton to describe the theory that grew out of his original studies with Sal jo, and has developed considerably since then. Constructivism has a long history in cognitive psychology, Jean Piaget being a crucial figure, and today it takes on several forms: individual, social, cognitive, postmodern.

While there are differences in flavour between constructivist-driven and phenomcnologically driven teaching, my own assumption is that helping teachers improve their teaching is best done using a theory that helps teachers reflect on what they are doing. For that they need a framework to aid reflection: a theory of learning that is broad based and empirically sound, that easily translates into practice, and that is readily understandable. To my mind this means constructivism, although there is a lot in common between the constructivist and phenomenological positions.

The most basic commonality is that meaning is not imposed or transmitted by direct instruction, but is created by the student's *learning activities,* well summarised in die term "approaches to learning". A surface approach refers to activities of an inappropriately low cognitive level, which yields fragmented outcomes that do not convey the meaning of the encounter. The deep approach refers to activities that arc appropriate to handling the task so that an appropriate outcome is achieved. The surface approach is therefore to be discouraged, the deep approach encouraged— and that is my working definition of good teaching. Learning is thus a way of interacting with the world. As we learn, our conceptions of phenomena change, and we see the world differently. The acquisition of information in itself does not bring about such a change, but the way we structure that information and think with it does. Thus, education is about *conceptual change,* not just the acquisition of information.

Such educative conceptual change takes place when:

1. It is clear to students (and teachers) what is "appropriate", what the objectives are, where all can see where they are supposed to be going, and where these objectives are buried in the assessment tasks.
2. Students experience the felt need to get there. The art of good teaching is to communicate that need where it is initially lacking. "Motivation" is a product of good teaching, not its prerequisite.
3. Students feel free to focus on the task, not on watching their backs. Often, attempts to create a felt need to learn, particularly through ill-conceived and urgent assessments, arc counter-productive. The game then becomes a matter of dealing with the test, not with engaging the task deeply.
4. Students can work collaboratively and in dialogue with others, both peers and teachers. Good dialogue elicits those activities that shape, elaborate, and deepen understanding.

These four points contain a wealth of implication for the design of teaching, and for personal reflection about what one is really trying to do.

Levels of Teaching Competence

What one sees as good teaching, and how one teaches, depends on what conception of teaching one has. There has been a great deal of research on conceptions of teaching, and there is some consensus on the broad picture. Prosser and Trigwell distinguish basically two conceptions, based on two strategies of teaching: teacher-focused and student-focused. Teacher-focused strategies are transmission theories of teaching; that is knowledge is conceived as being transmitted from expert teacher to inexpert learner, and the teacher's task it to "get it across". The lowest conceptions sees "it" as information, a higher conception sees transmission as being about important concepts needed to understand the discipline. But, in either event, the focus is on what the teacher docs. Student-focused strategics see the focus as being on bringing about conceptual change in students' understanding of the world, and it is what students do to achieve understanding that is important, not what teachers do.

Learning outcomes are determined by a whole complex of factors: fixed student-related factors such as ability; teaching-related factors such as curriculum, and methods of teaching and assessing; and the approaches to learning that students use while engaging in any particular task to achieve an outcome. All these factors affect each other, forming an interactive *system*. Any system, such as an eco-system, has to be understood as a whole. Components have to be considered as they affect each other, not as acting separately or additively.

Using this systems model, it is possible to formulate the assumptions underlying three common theories of teaching:

1. Learning is primarily a direct result of individual differences between students.
2. Learning is primarily the result of appropriate teaching.
3. Learning is the result of students' learning-focused activities which are engaged by students as a result both of their own perceptions and inputs and of the total teaching context.

The first two arc additive models, the third systemic. These different "theories" of teaching are parallel to the Prosser and Trigwell conceptions and are hierarchical or developmental as they seem to follow the growth of teacher competence. It is likely that teachers tend to hold diem at different points in their teaching career.

Level 1. Focus: About Students

Teachers at Level 1 focus on student differences. They are struck, as most beginning teachers arc, with the fact that there arc the good students and the poor students. Their own responsibility as teachers is to know the content well and to expound it clearly. Thereafter, it's up to the student to attend lectures; to listen carefully; to take notes; to read the recommended readings; and to make sure it's taken on board and unloaded on cue. At Level 1, the purpose of teaching is to transmit information, usually by lecturing, as in the lowest of the Prosser and Trigwell tcachcr-focuscd conception.

Basically, this conception holds teaching constant, so that variability in student learning is accounted for by individual differences between students, which makes this a *blame-ihe-siudent* theory of teaching. When students don't lcam, it is due to a deficit: ability; attitude; study skills; motivation; even a student's ethnicity. It is not considered that the teaching might have been the problem.

Level 2. Focus: About Teachers

The focus of teaching at the next level is more clearly on what the teacher does. It is still conceived as a transmission process, but of concepts and understandings, not just of information, as in Prosser and Trigwell's second teacher-focused strategy. Getting complex understandings across requires much more than chalk-and-talk, so the responsibility now rests to a significant extent on what the teacher does. The teacher who operates at Level 2 works at obtaining an armoury of teaching skills. Traditional approaches to stall development often worked on what the teacher does, as do "how to" courses, and books that provide prescriptive tips on getting it across more effectively:

- establish clear procedural rules at the outset, such as signals for silence;
- ensure clarity: project the voice, clear visual aids;
- eye-contact students while talking;
- don't interrupt a large lecture with handouts: chaos is likely.

This advice, useful as it is, is concerned with *management^* not with facilitating learning. Good management is important for setting the stage for good learning to take place—not as an end in itself.

Level 2 is also a deficit model, the "blame" this time on the teacher. It is a view of teaching often held by administrators because it provides a convenient rationale for making personnel decisions. Teaching is seen as a bag of competencies; the more competencies you have, the better a teacher you are.

Level 3. Focus:Students Role

The focus of teaching at Level 3 is on whether student activities leading to appropriate learning are being supported. No longer is it possible to say: "I taught them, but they didn't learn." Expert teaching certainly includes mastery of a variety of teaching techniques, but unless learning takes place, they have not achieved their purpose. The Level 3 teacher focuses on what the student docs; on what learning is or is not going on. Level 3 teaching is systemic, taking into account all components in die system.

This implies a view of teaching that is not just about facts, concepts and principles to be covered and understood, but about:

1. What it means to *understand* those concepts and principles in the way we want them to be understood.
2. What kind of *TLAs* (teaching/learning activities) are required to reach those kinds of understandings.

The first two Levels did not address these questions. Even Level 2, with its concern for concepts and principles, does not address the question of what it might *mean* to understand something at the desired levels. Getting students so to understand requires that they undertake the appropriate learning activities. This is where a Level 3 student-centred theory of teaching departs from the other models. It's not what *teachers* do, it's what *students* do that is the important thing. Shuell puts all this together dius:

> If students arc to learn desired outcomes in a reasonably effective manner, then the teacher's fundamental task is to get students to engage in learning activities that are likely to result in their achieving those outcomes.... It is helpful to remember that what the student docs is actually more important in determining what is learned than what die teacher does.

The Design of Teaching

ShuelPs statement may seem "motherhood", but it in fact contains a blueprint for the design of teaching and criterion-referenced assessment that is radically different from that which I would guess prevails in most institutions.

The fundamental assumption, that it is what the *student* does that is the important thing, may have entered the constructivist-typc rhetoric of many teachers, but it remains aloof from practice. During teaching, a great majority of teachers focus their awareness on what they are doing, not on what they are teaching, or on what their students are learning.

When we take this fundamental assumption of the centrality of student activity on board, we face three steps:

1. Saying what the "desired outcomes" are. In so doing, we specify our objectives.
2. Deciding if the outcomes are learned in a "reasonably effective manner". In so doing, we use assessment tasks tliat are criterion-referenced to our objectives.

3. Getting students to "engage in (appropriate) learning activities". In so doing, we use TLAs that encourage students to go about learning in a way that is likely to achieve our objectives.

We have first to be clear about what we want students to learn, and then teach and assess accordingly in an *aligned* system of instruction. It is a fully criterion-referenced system, where the objectives define what we should be teaching; how we should be teaching it; and how we could know how well students have learned it. In aligned teaching, there is maximum consistency diroughout the system. The curriculum is stated in the form of clear objectives which state the level of understanding required rather than simply listing the topics to be covered. The teaching methods chosen are those that are likely to realise diose objectives; you get students to do the things that the objectives nominate. Finally, the assessment tasks address the objectives, so mat you can test to see if the students have learned what the objectives state they should be learning. All components in the system address the same agenda and support each other. The students are "entrapped" in this web of consistency, optimising the likelihood diat they will engage the appropriate learning activities. I call this network *conslniciive alignment.*

The curriculum objectives arc at the centre. Decisions as to how they are to be taught, and how they may be assessed, follow. We express the objectives in terms of what constructive activities are most likely to achieve the desired outcomes for the topic or unit in question. Practically speaking, we specify the verbs which describe the behaviours which we want students to enact in the context of the content discipline being taught, specifying levels of understanding that can be used for awarding grades. The level of understanding required for a Pass is obviously less than that required for a High Distinction. The first step is, therefore, to arrange these levels of understanding in a hierarchy that corresponds to the grading system used. Teaching/learning activities are chosen that would be likely to encourage students to engage the optimal verbs, and that are practicable within the resources available. Objectives, teaching, and assessment, are now aligned, using the verbs in the objectives as markers for alignment. It remains to elaborate on alignment at the diree main stages of teaching, and to point to some examples of aligned teaching.

Aligning Objectives, Teaching, and Assessment

Stating objectives in terms of the nature of understanding. In a criterion-referenced system, the criteria must be clear. But while most teachers would agree they teach for "understanding", that word has many values. We frequently express one meaning of understanding but assess another. In making our objectives clear it is essential that we unpack and make explicit the meanings we want our students to address. The very highest levels of understanding that we want students to display by the end of a degree program—and in some cases very much before the end—are "performative"; that is, students *act differently* when they really understand. Students need to understand to the extent that a particular sector of their world has changed, and is now coming under their control. They behave differently towards that which they truly understand. Capturing that difference in an assessment task is what Perkins and Blythc mean by "performances of understanding".

The initial task in teaching any unit is therefore to clarify the kind of understanding that is wanted, and if the unit is to be graded (A, B, C, D, etc.), the objectives need to be stated in such a way as to allow the information from the assessments to specify the level of pass. Various models can be used to define the hierarchical nature of understanding in order to derive such a framework. One such is the SOLO taxonomy, which is represented schematically in Figure 2.

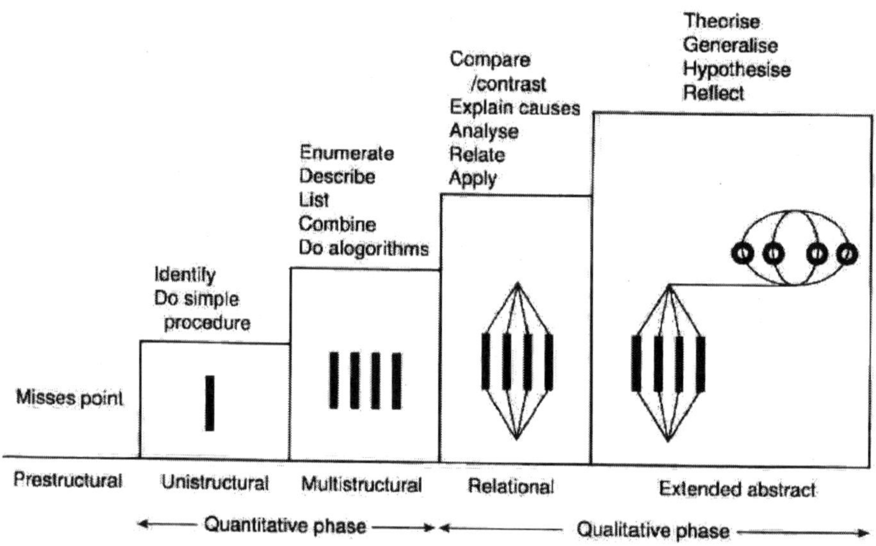

Figure 2. SOLO Taxonomy: Schematic represention

The diagram is intended to depict the cumulative nature of learning, and the nature of some major transitions. Some verbs typical of each level are suggested on top of the boxes. Usually, a major idea or procedure is learned (unistructural), then extended quantitatively (multistructural). Some curriculum targets or objectives might address these lower levels, but not important ones. Major objectives would refer to at least relational levels of understanding, where students are not only expected to know facts and information, but to structure them in forms that can be applied to common problems and domains. By the end of professional training, students should be extending knowledge to hitherto unseen problems and domains.

It is not intended that the SOLO levels exactly parallel grade levels: that "D" is unistructural, "A" extended abstract. Rather, the intention is that the SOLO levels provide a hierarchical framework within which specific levels may be defined to suit the unit and grade level in question.

Selecting TLAs. The next step is to set up the teaching/learning context so that students have every encouragement to react with the level of cognitive engagement that the objectives require. For example, most tertiary objectives require students to use knowledge, but much tertiary teaching is not about using knowledge but telling students about using knowledge. Such declarative knowledge—knowledge that can be talked about meaningfully—does not necessarily imply that it can be used functionally. Certainly, students need to know about important concepts, and lecturing is not a bad way of letting them know, but there arc better ways.

Teachers of large classes often sec little option but to lecture. However, the lecture can easily be turned into a session in which the student is also an active participant. Other and more generative TLAs can be peer-directed or self-directed, both of which take the heat off the teacher. Class size, although constraining, is no reason to abandon the principle of alignment. *Assessment tasks.* Assessment in practice has two functions: to tell us whether or not the learning has been successful, and in conveying to students what we want them to learn, as stated by Ramsden:

> From our students' point of view, the assessment always defines the actual curriculum.

Backwash from assessment is not a problem, it is the solution. In a criterion-referenced system, the objectives arc embedded in the assessment tasks. So, if students focus on the assessment, they will be learning what the objectives say they should be learning. It is only when the assessment tasks elicit lower level cognitive activities than the objectives nominate that backwash gets a bad name. Unfortunately, that is most of the time, as seen by the psychology student quoted in Ramsden:

> I hate to say it, but what you have got to do is to have a list of "facts"; you write down the important points and memorise those, then you'll do all right in the test.... If you can give a bit of factual information—so and so did that, and concluded that—for two sides of writing, then you'll get a good mark.

You shouldn't get a good mark, but you do, because the assessment is not aligned to the objectives, unless that teacher really did think memorisation was adequate.

Lack of alignment is a major reason why students adopt a surface approach to learning. Poor alignment often results from such institutional policies as requiring assessment results to be reported in percentages or "marks", or requiring results to be distributed along a pre-determined curve. The first can be mitigated by assessing qualitatively but reporting quantitatively, but the second is crippling. There can be no *educational* justification for grading on a curve.

Such practices exist for two reasons, which feed each other: administrative convenience, and genuinely confused thinking about assessment. The confusion arises because two quite different models of summative assessment co-exist:

1. The *measurement* model was developed by psychologists to study individual differences. It is designed to assess personal characteristics of individuals, for the purpose of comparing them with each other or with general population norms. Such assessment is norm-referenced (NRA). The model requires reducing performances to numbers along a scale, so that comparisons between individuals can be made. It assumes that the characteristic being measured is stable, and frequently that it is normally distributed.
2. The *standards* model is designed to assess changes in performance as a result of learning, for the purpose of seeing what, and how well, something has been learned. Such assessment is criterion-referenced (CRA). This model is the relevant one for summative assessment at university. The point is not to identify *students* in terms of some

characteristic, but to identify *performances* that tell us what has been learned, and how well.

None of the assumptions of the measurement model apply to the assessment of learning:

- quantifying performances gives little indication of the *quality* of the performance. Identifying only the quantitative aspects of learning sends the wrong messages to students, and guarantees unaligned assessment;
- teaching is concerned with change, not stability;
- teachers shouldn't want a "good spread" in grade distributions. Good teaching should *reduce* the gap between Robert and Susan, not widen it.

Marking quantitatively, constructing tests to "get a spread", and allocating grades along the curve, are all very common practices, but they make criterion-referencing of higher cognitive level performances all but impossible.

Criterion-referenced assessment in the constructive alignment model requires assessment tasks that are likely to elicit the learning verbs that are stipulated in the objectives.

Assessment modes are in four groups: extended prose, such as the conventional essay; objective format, which can be assessed rapidly; performance assessment,which assesses understanding as put to work (performances of understanding); and rapid assessments suitable for large classes. Each of these groups has its own advantages and disadvantages as do individual assessment tasks within each group. It would be impractical to discuss each of these assessment tasks here, beyond simply pointing out that alternatives to the traditional quantitative approaches to assessment exist—even for assessment in large classes. Further details may be found in Biggs.

Aligned Teaching

Alignment can be achieved in a variety of successful teaching "methods". In fact, I would argue that the extent to which any teaching is successful is at least in part due to the extent to which it exemplifies alignment between objectives, TLAs, and the assessment tasks. Two very successful methods, in the sense that they engage students at a high level of cognitive activity, are problem-based learning (PBL), and the learning portfolio (LP).

Problem-based Learning (PBL)

Problem-based learning is alignment itself. The objectives are to get students to solve problems they will meet in their professional careers—the teaching method is to present them with problems to solve; the assessment is based on how well they solve them.

It seems so obvious. Yet for years, education for the professions followed a proactive model, where the disciplines are taught first, independently of each other, and armed with all that declarative knowledge, and with some skill training, the student is accredited as ready to practise as a professional. However, many are not. Their declarative knowledge has been framed by examination requirements, its range of application slopping at the final exam. Their ability to solve unseen problems is often untested. Professional practice requires knowledge that can be put to work immediately. If the objectives nominate professional competence on graduation, but declarative knowledge is the output, something has been missed. Curriculum, teaching, and assessment are not aligned. The reason why this model persists is not educational but institutional. Universities are usually organised by content departments, to which academics arc appointed, and it is much easier to deliver programs on a content basis than on a multi-disciplinary basis.

In PBL, the problems arc carefully selected so that, by the end of the program, the learner is expected to cover much of the same content as is covered in a traditional program, but the *nature* of the knowledge so gained is different. It is acquired in a working context and is put back to use in that context.

The TLAs follow from the presented problems. Learners are assigned to small problem-solving groups and begin interacting with teachers, peers and clients; they build up a knowledge base of relevant material and learn where to go to seek out more. Students meet with a tutor and discuss the case in relation to the knowledge they have obtained. The knowledge is applied, the case is treated.

The assessment is in terms of the original case studies. For example, medical PBL developed the "Triple Jump", a three-step exercise where the student is evaluated at each step:

1. *Dealing zoith the problem or case:* diagnosing, hypothesising, checking with the clinical data base, use made of information, reformulating.

2. *Review of independent study:* knowledge gained, level of understanding, evaluating information gained.
3. *Final problem formulation:* synthesis of key concepts, application to patient's problem, self-monitoring, response to feedback.

The alignment is evident. To practise as a particular professional requires solving problems that belong to that profession. Thus, professional skill is the goal, professional practice comprises the TLAs, professional skill is what is assessed (amongst other things).

The Learning Portfolio

The final illustration is a case study involving the use of the learning portfolio. Although this started out simply as portfolio assessment in a unit in a part-time 13. Ed. programme, the backwash took over, and in effect dictated the TLAs. In this case, alignment was created bottom-up.

The general aim of the unit was to get the students, who were practising teachers, to demonstrate that they could drive their classroom decision-making with their psychological knowledge, based on reflective practice. Such an aim would be applicable to advanced units in most professional programs.

The objectives. These were expressed as grading categories, the level of activity defining the category.

A: Students *reflect* on their own teaching, *evaluate* their classroom decisions in terms of theory, and thereby *improve* their teaching, *formulate* a theory of teaching that demonstrably drives decision-making and practice, *generate* new approaches to teaching on that basis.

B: Students *apply* course content, *recognise* good and poor applications of principles. "B" includes a "missed 'A'": the student had a good try at reflecting but didn't quite make it. C: Students *understand* declarative; *discuss* content meaningfully, *know about* a reasonable amount of content. Also include "missed 'B"\ D: Students *understand* in a minimally acceptable way: essentially "missed 'C'", or "badly missed 'B"\

If students could unequivocally demonstrate in a portfolio item the level of performance indicated by the verbs in the category, basically the highest category grade successfully addressed would be awarded.

The TLAs. The TLAs were negotiated with the students when they realised what they had to do, which was to decide on die evidence for their learning, and to explain why they thought it met the objectives. The following dialogue, condensed from several sessions, illustrates how this happened (S = students, T = teacher):

S: What sort of items do we select?

T: That's up to you. Think hard about the objectives. Here's a list of sample items.

S: Can we have a trial run?

T: Of course. You can submit that as an item if you're happy with my assessment of it. If you're not, have another go.

S: How do we show we can reflect?

T: Use your journal [the one compulsory item].

S: What do we put in it?

T: Talk it over with your colleagues. Why don't you form a learning partnership with one or two others? Sit next to them in class, get their phone number, discuss the course with them. You can help each other.

S: Wouldn't it be better if we had discussion groups of students teaching the same subjects as we do? Then we can share experiences on similar problems.

T: Certainly. The two neighbouring rooms are free *[booked in anticipation]*.

S: But we want to brush up on die topics. Will you lecture us?

T: Here's the schedule; there's a topic for each session. You have some pre-reading to do, just a few pages, before each session. *I'll* meet half the class at a time, while the other half is having discussion groups, and we can clarify each topic.

In short, the assessment tasks drove the students' learning activities, which became the TLAs. One student referred to the portfolio as "a learning tool". In fact, it is difficult to separate a TLA from an assessment task. For example, students used the learning journal to learn how to reflect, and it was used later as evidence of reflection. The same thing happens in PBL; it is a necessary consequence of alignment. Grappling with the task you want students to learn is automatically a learning process that becomes a learning outcome. When you are learning to drive a car, is the act of driving a learning process, or an outcome of learning?

In this case study, alignment evolved "bottom-up" in the course of negotiating with students struggling to cope with a new form of assessment. This might be contrasted with die "top-down" alignment of formally structured PBL. The important thing is that, however it came about, alignment with qualitatively and holistically defined objectives brings about quality learning in both cases.

In an aligned system of instruction, the teacher's task is to sec dial the appropriate verbs arc:

1. Nominated in the objectives.
2. Likely to be elicited in die chosen TLAs.
3. Embedded in die assessment tasks so that judgments can be made about how well a given student's level of performance meets the objectives.

Because the teaching methods and the assessment tasks now access the same verbs as arc in the objectives, the chances are increased that most students will in fact engage with the appropriate learning activities. This is, by definition, a deep approach.

Constructive alignment is common sense, yet most university teaching is not aligned. This is possibly because many academics, holding traditional transmission theories of teaching that ignore alignment, simply haven't seen the need to question dicir assumptions. Typically, the lecturer presents information throughout die semester. At the end of the semester a test is given, the main function of which is to "get a good spread" between students, to distinguish the good learners from the poor learners. This might seem reasonable at first sight, but our primary job is not to discriminate between students but to teach content to all students in our classes. Tests constructed to discriminate assume no *inherent* relation between what is taught and what is tested. A good criterion-referenced system of assessment could certainly change that, as long as the *need* for such a system is perceived. Some administrative requirements, such as reporting in percentages, make alignment difficult, while grading on the curve makes alignment impossible. Resource limitations are often seen to limit large-class teaching to "passive" methods such as mass lecturing, and non-aligned assessments such as multiple choice testing, but while resource limitations do limit the options, there arc ways of rethinking teaching and assessment in large classes that at least acknowledge alignment. One advantage of the emerging top-down management of universities—possibly the only advantage educationally speaking—is that more enlightened educational policies could be required throughout institutions. Some certainly are going in that direction. It seems more likely, however, that as managcrialism is itself a highly quantitative outlook, it is possibly even less likely now than ever that the major decision-makers in universities would appreciate the need for qualitative and holistic approaches to criterion-referenced assessment.

At all events, the current revolution in universities is putting teaching under the spotlight, which at least provides an opportunity for some reflection on current practice. Certainly, students are not learning as well as they might be. Aligning practice on the basis of what students should be doing is likely to be more fruitful than focusing only on what teachers and administrators do.

References

Biggs, J.B.. *Student approaches to learning and studying.* Melbourne: Australian Council for Educational Research.

Entwistij, N. & Ramsdkn, P.. *Understanding undent learning.* London: Croom Helm.

Martin, E. & Bai.ia, M. An expanding awareness: How lecturers change then-understanding teaching. *Research and Development in Higher Education, 13,* 298-304.

Taylor, C.. Assessment for measurement or standards: The peril and promise of large scale assessment reform. *American Educational Research Journal, 31,* 231 262. Tricaviut, K. & Prosshr, M.. Towards an understanding of individual acts of teaching and learning. *Higher Education Research & Development, 16,* 241-252.

2

Pedagogies for the 21st Century

An urgent question demands the attention of every educator: How well does today's schooling prepare students for the 21st century? This question deserves an answer based not on what worked in the past but on what is a relevant schooling experience today. The past can only inform, not determine the future of schooling.

For more than 150 years a set of pedagogies reflecting the priorities of the Industrial Age has been embedded in the process of mass schooling. The hallmarks of these pedagogies are found in teacher-controlled learning where deconstructed and reconstructed information is presented to same-age cohorts of students in standardised classroom settings.

> ...educators and systems spent the 20th century perfecting the 19th century model of schooling. (Heppell)

Many have worked very hard at making improvements to schooling within the confines of this paradigm. Stephen Heppell wryly observed that educators and systems spent the 20th century perfecting the 19th century model of schooling.

Globalisation has enabled rapid advancements in technology; we have entered the knowledge age where social networking technologies are changing business, media and political structures. Users can now access information wherever and whenever. It is what Jimmy Wales, the founder of Wikipedia describes as the 'democratisation of knowledge'.

However, it has had little impact on the processes of schooling. There is an urgent need for a new educational model; a rethinking of the nature of schooling – its purpose, pedagogies, curriculum, structures, assumptions and expectations. The old pedagogies persisting into the 21st century are no longer relevant. They ignore the capacity for schooling to take place in both a physical and virtual learning space. If we are to embrace these new opportunities, we need a 21st century pedagogy – a paradigm which reflects a bold and creative commitment to relevance and quality learning and teaching.

Strands of Relevance

A relevant education for the 21st century must have two essential strands. These strands must be tightly woven together to ensure that the schooling experience is relevant to the life each student chooses to pursue and the skills required to live in today's world.

First, it must be truly humanising in that it must enhance the learners' humanity, improving their competence as managers of their own lives, members of society (both local and global), effective participants in the workforce and active contributors to a changing environment. Its overarching aim is to enable them to pursue wisdom.

Second, it must be truly socialising in that it must enhance the learners' communal and global consciousness and foster responsible citizenship.

To this end, it must be socio-critical, deepening awareness of the nature of society and its need for development. And it must be transformative, enabling learners to make a difference to the lives of individuals, communities and the changing world in which they live. The learning we are talking about is lifelong learning which prepares for future, ongoing engagement in solving real problems, dealing with real events and competently coping with the dynamics of real life. The skills that are essential for achieving these outcomes include collaborative teamwork, problem-solving, communicating, making connections, creating, and expressing oneself in a variety of ways. These skills will be future-focused but based on successful experience and sound evidence. They will lead the way, tapping into the incredible potential of the Web 2.0 technologies.

A supporting pedagogical framework must go beyond connecting schools and providing hardware for students and teachers. It has to be built on the relational nature of learning and be relevant to all those interested in schooling in today's world.

The Web 2.0 World

It would be hard to find a better example of rapid and dynamic change than the development of the worldwide web. In less than five years we have seen the web morph from being a place to access information to being a network of social interaction.

> .... seen the web morph from being a place to access information to being a network of social interaction.

Web 2.0 has captured this change. Web 1.0 was characterised by static read-only sites where information could be searched for and retrieved. It was all about content and publishing. Web 2.0 has been dubbed the read/write web or social networking software. Its sites are all about people and communities as well as content and publishing; they encourage communication, collaboration and connection in every area.

Grossman expresses the potential of this very aptly when he says that Web 2.0 is an 'opportunity to build a new kind of international understanding, not politician to politician, great man to great man but citizen to citizen, person to person'. The digital generation who has been online since birth is as comfortable in the Web 2.0 world as they are in the physical world. Marc Prensky states that, 'Today's students have mastered a large variety of tools that we will never master with the same level of skill. From computers to calculators to MP3 players to camera phones, these tools are like extensions of their brains.' The attraction of using social software is the ease and speed with which they can communicate either one-to-one through instant messaging, one-to-many through blogs, or many-to-many through wikis. In September 2006, 60% of Australian internet users visited MySpace, and 50% visited YouTube. The Hitwise survey notes that these sites have become the 'first online destination for Internet users as they integrate social networking into their other daily web activities, such as email, search engine use and research'.

Challenge to Today's Models of Schooling

The obvious challenges posed to schooling as a result of the technological revolution are becoming widely recognised. In its 2001 report, Schooling for Tomorrow (Learning to change: ICT in schools), the OECD's Centre for Educational Research and Innovation questions existing models of schooling in the strongest terms:

> 'As information-rich technology diffuses pervasively into homes and workplaces, it increasingly calls into question the relevance of much within the knowledge-based curricula. In a world with easy access to huge stores of information, the skills of accessing, handling and using data and materials become more important than the ability to recall in detail ever greater amounts across many fields of knowledge. The young people who inhabit this technology-rich information society already question the relevance of the traditional approach. Aspects of existing school practice are called into question, as ICT both underlines a need for curriculum change and affords the means whereby the desired change can be achieved.'

This challenge is repeated throughout the professional literature. According to David Warner, for instance, the emergence of information communication technologies (ICT) and the development of Web 2.0 (e.g. YouTube, Flickr, MySpace, del.icio.us) have transformed the social and economic landscape. These changes have a profound impact on schooling as educators prepare students for life beyond the classroom – a transition which should be seamless and familiar.

Mitchel Resnick refers to the new technologies as having 'the potential to fundamentally transform how and what people learn throughout their lives. Just as advances in biotechnologies made possible the "green revolution" in agriculture, new digital technologies make possible a "learning revolution" in education'.

> If we are to ensure that teaching remains an 'art' for enabling the acquisition of powerful learning in the 21st century, we need to question the continuing use of old pedagogies that belong in other times and circumstances.

The message is clear: If we are to ensure that teaching remains an 'art' for enabling the acquisition of powerful learning in the 21st century, we need to question the continuing use of old pedagogies that belong in other times and circumstances. Fundamental rethinking is necessary. Relevant 21st century pedagogy is not something that can be tacked or massaged onto the pedagogies of the 20th century.

Calls to Transformation

Schools are experiencing strong pressures to go beyond simple change and to radically transform themselves so that they might reflect the reality of their social and technological context. They are certainly at a watershed, often confused, overwhelmed and seeking relevance.

Admittedly, various initiatives are in place to improve the quality of schooling. An example is Education Queensland's New Basics program which seeks to link content, pedagogy and assessment in a more productive way. At their best these productive pedagogies focus on connectedness and knowledge integration within an inquiry-based curriculum. But so often such initiatives remain locked in old patterns of thinking and do not bring about the necessary transformation. When that happens we are left with new wine in old wineskins!

Competing Narratives

Attempts to conceptualise and shape schooling reflect the dominant educational narrative of those seeking to set the agenda. The term 'educational narrative' is used here to encompass the story, map or paradigm we use in describing the nature of education as we understand it, including the pedagogies we employ. It provides us with a structure for shared reflection, conversation, evaluation, planning, the clarification of mission and the devising of strategies for development and change. It connects our beliefs, our values and our hopes.

> A strictly utilitarian narrative sees school basically as an instrument of the economy.

We must clarify and apply our own coherent and shared 21st century narrative in the context of competing narratives. The defining themes of these narratives challenge us. Let us look briefly at some of them. A strictly utilitarian narrative sees school basically as an instrument of the economy. A well-educated workforce produces national wealth. Effective schooling is a return on an investment. A consumerist narrative conceptualises school as a business selling a commodity called 'education' to individual customers which it attracts to itself in an open marketplace where it competes with other 'providers'. It draws heavily on the priorities, images and values of the commercial world.

A pragmatic narrative aims at measurable efficiency and acceptability. It is shaped by political and popular perceptions, and is highly responsive to the special agendas of ascendant groups. An individualistic narrative sees schooling as serving the interests and aspirations of individuals who pursue personal goals without regard for the common good of society. It has little concern for the communal nature of schooling, unless this facilitates achievement of the individual's purely personal goals. Such narratives overlap – each is reflected in the metaphors and other images used to describe schooling. These narratives govern curriculum constructs, learning environments and school cultures. They influence the pedagogies that are employed on a daily basis.

In Search of a New Narrative

New ideas about the nature of schooling, and its most relevant pedagogies, in the 21st century are taking shape. Canadian theorist, George Siemens, for instance, claims that students no longer learn only through traditional ways of constructing knowledge but by connecting with each other and technology.

'We are trying to use theories of learning from a predominantly physical era and force them to work in a digital era. We need a new pedagogy, a new view of learning, a new view of knowledge or interacting.'

Perhaps there has been no more relevant time for educators to re-visit the core questions of what and why, how and where – the rationale, content, methodology and location of their core concern: quality learning. This re-visiting must raise some vitally important questions about our understanding of the processes of knowing when the sheer quantity of knowledge is exploding around us. It must lead us, too, to reconsider our concept of curriculum and the appropriateness, or otherwise, of structuring learning and teaching within discrete disciplines.

A Challenge to the Imagination

New circumstances and new opportunities offer a prodigious challenge to the imagination, a challenge which must be probed if we are to develop the most appropriate. Effective pedagogies will always be based on a thorough understanding of how people learn. In general terms, they will be grounded in certain principles: quality relationships, respect for individual differences, focus on core processes of making meaning, active participation in relevant and authentic learning tasks, the development of autonomy, and so on. They will be informed by research, reflection and analysis. These principles remain at the core of effective learning and teaching. The great educational theorists proclaimed them and the best teachers apply them. The challenge now is to use the principles not only to support learning and teaching in the physical space but in a virtual space. Effective teaching will always be relational. However, in a virtual learning space, the role of a teacher will be to guide students in making the connections to resources, ideas and people; how to find and discern what they need "instead of depending on us to provide them.'

The essential principles of effective learning provide us with the foundations upon which to develop appropriate pedagogies that are creatively applied in ways which complement each other, maximise opportunities and respond to 21st century demands. In keeping with this sort of thinking, specific questions arise, such as how can we fully utilise the emerging relational technologies and social software in enriching these pedagogies and in facilitating the acquisition of new knowledge and skills? And how can the curriculum be most appropriately conceptualised and organised so as to tap into new capacities? These foundations can only be built on by a teaching profession which has truly come of age. Andy Hargreaves expresses this fact with blunt honesty:

> 'Teaching is not a place for shrinking violets, for the overly sensitive, for people who are more comfortable with dependent children than they are with independent adults. It is a job for grown-ups, requiring grown-up norms of how to work together.'

Key Propositions

I now wish to present five propositions which both tie together earlier observations and will lead to more precise descriptions of an appropriate range of pedagogies. Needless to say, all of these propositions overlap, combining to support an urgent appeal for radical change.

Proposition 1

'Curriculum', as it has been traditionally understood, has passed its used-by date. A more appropriate mindset leads us to speak of 'frameworks' that are constructed collaboratively and with imagination out of mutual respect for both learner and teacher.

Proposition 2

The skills that are appropriately learned and applied with a 21st century framework are not the same as those that served past eras: memorisation, specialisation, control/order, sameness/insularity. Rather, they the skills needed in a dynamic present and future: interconnectedness, managing meaning, living with paradox, working intelligently towards positive change, and maintaining a global perspective.

Proposition 3

Such skills require transforming pedagogies which will focus on the nurturing of clear-thinking, discerning, flexible and creative problem-solvers who will exercise their developed capacity to make the world a better place.

Proposition 4

The emerging technologies must be used to enrich these transforming pedagogies.

Proposition 5

To facilitate such learning and teaching, the use of learning spaces both within and beyond the immediate school plant, must be characterised by creativity and adaptability.

A Raft of Pedagogies

In attempting to answer the question, 'What are the pedagogies most likely to serve individuals and communities (both local and global) in the 21st century?', it is my intention not to supply a set of recipes or specific teaching formulas but suggest categories or directions which teachers might explore in their own search for approaches relevant to their students, to themselves, and to the settings within which they work. Here, then, is a raft consisting of four planks, four interconnected sets of pedagogies. When reflected upon and discussed in depth, these might well stimulate and facilitate learning experiences which will be relevant, timely and transformative.

Pedagogies which Personalise Learning

Our narrative reminds us that, at the centre of the process of education, is the individual student. Peters says, 'Teaching is about one and only one thing: Getting to know the child,' and Caldwell echoes this in his first theme in imagining the self-managing school: 'The student is the most important unit of organisation – not the classroom, not the school, not the school system.'

This commitment leads immediately to recognition of individual differences in the backgrounds, abilities, interests and learning styles of students. It underlies the importance of teachers' knowing their students as individuals and employing a range of flexible teaching and organisational strategies in responding to them. In other words: to personalise learning. Structures that reflect a one-size-fits-all approach to meeting students' needs and move students, lock-step, towards achieving narrow, easily-measured and strictly predetermined goals, do violence to the development of responsible, resourceful and self-directed learners.

Contribution of Social Technologies

The commitment of truly effective teachers to personalised learning can be wonderfully enhanced by skilful utilisation of the emerging social technologies. These essential tools of the 21st century pedagogies can be employed in creative, transparent and intuitive ways, as evidenced by application of the new social software in a Web 2.0 world of interactions.

Here individual students readily become active and contributing participants who are finding their own ways of applying learning and gaining control of the process. This personalising of learning can be both physical and virtual in nature – a possibility undreamt of by earlier generations of teachers. We are only beginning to realise the implications of this for lifelong learning. In the school context, the teacher has an important role to play in establishing structures that will facilitate learning of this kind, in demonstrating, mentoring, providing feedback and helping the student to make connections and construct deeper meaning.

The whole concept of a curriculum consisting of separate subjects or disciplines must certainly be challenged as students show themselves quite capable of using electronic networks to transcend old boundaries and learn in integrated ways. They become empowered to work, learn and think differently. At a most practical level, this personalising of learning requires students to have adequate access to the relevant technologies. If this is not sufficiently available or not maintained, the result is frustration and sometimes alienation. It also requires flexibility in both space and time. Students need to be able to move and rearrange themselves if they are to work collaboratively; flexible timetabling allows for tasks to be pursued extensively and in depth. A third pre-requisite is the teacher's ability and willingness to operate in a less rigid and controlling environment – one which demonstrates a genuine commitment to learning of this kind placing trust in the learner.

Pedagogies which Enable the Learner

One of our central educational aims is the development of the whole person: mind, body and spirit. This calls for pedagogies which enable the learner to develop and move towards becoming an independent, fully-functioning, contributing member of society. Such pedagogies must be fundamentally liberating in that they will help break the chains imposed by ignorance and inadequate opportunities. As Collins says we are "only good in relation to what we can become."

Enabling pedagogies encourage curiosity and a sense of wonder. They provide learning opportunities that are meaningful and relevant to students, encouraging learners to critique and question, to seek meaning, to make choices, and to create and express ideas with skill and confidence. The pedagogies will challenge students with ever-richer and more complex experiences and opportunities to deepen insights and improve skills. In so doing they will develop the metaskills necessary for lifelong learning. Pedagogies that are truly enabling are informed by sensitivity to the individual learner. Rather than attracting blame towards the student, they focus on the processes being used in the attempts to learn. A feature of a classroom culture of high and enabling expectations is the experience of personal and collective success. Success deprivation is devastating. 'Productivity thrives on success,' says researcher and clinician, Mel Levine.

'Individuals with chronic success deprivation feel like losers, and out of a sense of hopelessness they simply shut down their minds. Success and failure occur in spirals. Failure may lead to further failure, while success energises the system for more success.'

ASSUMPTIONS

We see the transforming possibilities of the social technologies in enriching these pedagogies and in engaging students in constructing personal meaning and taking responsibility for their own learning. Even the rigid scheduling of time for learning can be realistically questioned. The open-ended nature of education through these technologies can provide rich learning challenges which stimulate imagination, provoke deeper thinking and require the application of core learning skills. The possibilities are endless.

Resnick reminds us that 'children can now use computer simulations to explore the workings of systems in the world (everything from ecosystems to economic systems to immune systems) in ways that were previously not possible.' We need to transform curricula so that they focus less on 'things to know' and more on 'strategies for learning the things you don't know'. As new technologies continue to quicken the pace of change in all parts of our lives, learning to become a better learner is far more important than learning to multiply fractions or memorising the capitals of the world.'

Interpersonal Nature of Learning

Quality learning and teaching are grounded in powerful relationships that are built on mutual respect and trust. These relationships are strongly influenced by the core of shared beliefs. Such relationships amongst students themselves and between them and their teachers provide a supportive context for peer-tutoring, group work, modelling, and coaching, collaborative problem-solving and constructive risk-taking. This extends beyond school. The ability to learn and work as a member of a team becomes even more important in a society where knowledge expands at an incredible rate. Cooperation, shared learning and interdependence are taking their place amongst the most desired qualities for successful employees.

Social Networking

Web 2.0, or social networking software, can provide very effective ways of strengthening the impact of interpersonal learning. It can break down the sense of isolation – everything can become collaborative and social in nature. While Web 1.0 is static and read-only, Web 2.0 allows users to write as well as read. Today's students are global citizens, accessing and creating content on demand, usually from home. School systems can promote learning agendas that are engaging, social, personal and that link communities.

The social networking tools are now widely used by students in the out-of-classroom, collaborative construction and sharing of knowledge. Schools neglect this fact to their peril. MySpace, blogs, podcasts and wikis claim an important place in schools seeking to promote more profound and effective thinking and learning that refuses to be constrained by traditional subject boundaries. School systems can promote learning agendas that are engaging, social, personal and that link communities. As Hargreaves explains: 'We are only at the beginning of this transformation, which will not be simply about ICT in classrooms but about a new relationship between what happens in formal education and what happens in the home, the workplace and the community.'

An excellent example of how social networking software is being used for interpersonal learning in the 'flat classroom project'. This project links students from the International School Dhaka in Bangladesh with students from the computer science class at Westwood School in Georgia, USA. Students from each school are paired and use Web 2.0 tools such as wikis and podcasts to explain and discuss topics from Thomas Freidman's book *The World is Flat*. Teachers and students cooperate in designing meaningful interactive materials that link texts, images and sounds to structure and to illustrate and represent ideas.

Pedagogies which Contribute to Building the Learning Community

The communal nature of the school presents a core image and recurring theme of the educational narrative where the school is viewed essentially as a learning community as well as a community of individual learners. In such a community, knowledge is often constructed collaboratively; individuals learn from each other, with each other and, in a special sense, on behalf of each other. Appropriate pedagogies include facilitation of student teamwork, negotiation of learning tasks, and across-curriculum and across-grade learning and teaching initiatives. Students are conscious of belonging to networks both within and beyond the school where knowledge, resources and problem-solving initiatives are shared. In this manner, learning becomes a process of creating connections and networks of great variety.

In 2005, Dr Tim Tyson, Principal of Mabry Middle School, created a blog featuring the work of his staff and students. This blog is now a leading example of innovative educational practice using Web 2.0. However, Dr Tyson readily admits that technology is not a magic bullet but more a 'tool that when appropriately leveraged, brings people together so that they can collaboratively create and share with unprecedented ease and facility'.

Teachers as Learners

Teachers in the twenty-first century need to see themselves as co-learners and collaborators within the learning environment. In their role as learners teachers learn a great deal about – and often from – their students. They learn from each other, too. And, as a collaborative group, they learn together. This type of learning leads to new ways of understanding and applying existing knowledge.

Warner identifies a number of 'knowledge era' skills for effective teaching. These include:

- Collaboration
- Negotiation to arrive at shared expectations
- Engagement management (managing learning not classrooms)
- Creating and managing knowledge
- Developing individual learning programs
- Self-awareness and self-evaluation
- Self-management and self-directed learning

He stresses that these are not new skills but that they are key skills for the twenty-first century paradigm. A particular challenge facing teachers in the knowledge age relates to re-visiting their existing pedagogies. Experience suggests that, in the first instance, they simply adopt those elements of technology which serve their existing teaching style without exploring the full extent of new opportunities to develop interactive, searching and collaborative approaches for nurturing higher-order thinking skills and learning. 'While new digital technologies make a learning revolution possible, they certainly do not guarantee it. Early results are not encouraging. In most places where new technologies are being used in education today, the technologies are used simply to reinforce outmoded approaches to learning. Even as scientific and technological advances are transforming agriculture, medicine and industry, ideas about and approaches to teaching and learning remain largely unchanged.'

Learning Communities

The importance of schools becoming effective learning organisations with teachers engaged in productive dialogue, teamwork and shared learning is imperative as they rethink their assumptions about learning and teaching in the 21st century. Together as learning communities, teachers can reshape pedagogies that are relevant to today's learners. The learning community of the school is networked into other, more expanded, learning communities of schools and other community agencies where best practice is shared, information systems and links are developed and there is an expanding understanding of what is possible. An important partnership – the one which links home and school cannot be overlooked in bringing together the learning communities. The emerging technologies can make a major contribution to this in providing effective avenues of communication and collaboration. The new social technologies have a particular significance in developing transforming pedagogies within all these learning communities. Students become content creators, contributors, evaluators, communicators and collaborators both with and beyond their school, experiencing participatory membership in a global learning community.

Global Community

The most dramatic example of the extended – global – learning community is experienced in the Internet which is requiring educators to rethink the processes of teaching, collaborating and communicating. Because of its essential characteristic of being social and participatory, Web 2.0 can play a powerful role in building and sustaining the learning community. The composition of the educational narrative is, in the first instance, a work of the imagination.

And so, eventually, is its full implementation. This calls for nothing less than an exploration of the way we view schooling, along with a practical framework for possible change.

The assertion is made that those who work in and for schools will have to work differently if they are to serve their students and society in the knowledge age of the 21st century. They will need to imagine a new model of schooling to match the tools and capabilities, including Web 2.0, now available. For this to occur, transformational leadership needs to be dispersed throughout the school community. We stand together at the beginning of a transformation of schooling for life.

While we live in a digital age, the essential conversation is not just about technology in classrooms. Rather, it is about new relationships between teachers and learners, between learners and the process through which they grow in competence and wisdom, and between what happens in formal education and what happens in the home, the workplace and the community.

There are many forces seeking to re-shape the future of schooling. Essential contributors to this inevitable process must be the teachers and the learning communities to which they belong.

References

Caldwell, B. *Re-imagining educational leadership.* ACER: Melbourne

Collins, J. *Good to great and the social sectors,* Random House: London

Elmore, R. *School reform from inside out.* Harvard Education Press: Cambridge

Fullan, M. "Professional learning communities writ large" in Dufour, R. & Eaker, R. (eds) On common ground: the power of professional learning communities. Solution Tree: Bloomington, IN

Friedman, T *The world is flat: a brief history of the 21st century.* Farrar, Straus and Giroux: New York

Hough, M., Paine, J. and Austin, L. *Creating quality learning communities.* Macmillan Education: South Melbourne.

Siemens, G. What does it mean to know today? *Education Review* 16(08),13.

3

Authentic Learning for Enhanced Society

Students say they are motivated by solving real-world problems. They often express a preference for *doing* rather than *listening*. At the same time, most educators consider learning-by-doing the most effective way to learn. Yet for decades, authentic learning has been difficult to implement. Certain experiments are too dangerous, difficult, or expensive to conduct in the classroom; many are simply impossible to perform. After all, educators cannot expect their students to set the tectonic plates in motion, summoning up an earthquake at will, or to travel back in time and replay decisive moments in the American Civil War, can they? Well, perhaps they can.

Thanks to the emergence of a new set of technological tools, we can offer students a more authentic learning experience based on experimentation and action. With the help of the Internet and a variety of communication, visualization, and simulation technologies, large numbers of undergraduates can begin to reconstruct the past, observe phenomena using remote instruments, and make valuable connections with mentors around the world. With access to online research communities, learners are able to gain a deeper sense of a discipline as a special "culture" shaped by specific ways of seeing and interpreting the world. They begin to grasp the subtle, interpersonal, and unwritten knowledge that members in a community of practice use (often unconsciously) on a daily basis. "Learning becomes as much social as cognitive, as much concrete as abstract, and becomes intertwined with judgment and exploration," just as it is in an actual workplace.

Developmental psychologist Jerome Bruner reminds us that there is a tremendous difference between learning *about* physics and learning *to be* a physicist. Isolated facts and formulae do not take on meaning and relevance until learners discover what these tools can *do* for them. As George Siemens suggests, learning to be a physicist, a chemist, or an historian is all about forging concrete connections—interpersonal connections between apprentices and mentors, intellectual connections between the familiar and the novel, personal connections between the learner's own goals and the broader concerns of the discipline. Connection-building will require new forms of authentic learning—forms that cut across disciplines and bring students into meaningful contact with the future employers, customers, clients, and colleagues who will have the greatest stake in their success. Without a doubt, technology will play an essential supporting role.

Focus of Authentic Learning

Authentic learning typically focuses on real-world, complex problems and their solutions, using role-playing exercises, problem-based activities, case studies, and participation in virtual communities of practice. The learning environments are inherently multidisciplinary. They are "not constructed in order to teach geometry or to teach philosophy. A learning environment is similar to some 'real world' application or discipline: managing a city, building a house, flying an airplane, setting a budget, solving a crime, for example." Going beyond content, authentic learning intentionally brings into play multiple disciplines, multiple perspectives, ways of working, habits of mind, and community.

Students immersed in authentic learning activities cultivate the kinds of "portable skills" that newcomers to any discipline have the most difficulty acquiring on their own:

- The *judgment* to distinguish reliable from unreliable information
- The *patience* to follow longer arguments
- The *synthetic ability* to recognize relevant patterns in unfamiliar contexts
- The *flexibility* to work across disciplinary and cultural boundaries to generate innovative
  solutions

Learning researchers have distilled the essence of the authentic learning experience down to 10 design elements, providing educators with a useful checklist that can be adapted to any subject matter domain.

1. *Real-world relevance*: Authentic activities match the real-world tasks of professionals in practice as nearly as possible. Learning rises to the level of authenticity when it asks students to work actively with abstract concepts, facts, and formulae inside a realistic— and highly social— context mimicking "the ordinary practices of the [disciplinary] culture."
2. *Ill-defined problem*: Challenges cannot be solved easily by the application of an existing algorithm; instead, authentic activities are relatively undefined and open to multiple interpretations, requiring students to identify for themselves the tasks and subtasks needed to complete the major task.
3. *Sustained investigation*: Problems cannot be solved in a matter of minutes or even hours. Instead, authentic activities comprise complex tasks to be investigated by students over a sustained period of time, requiring significant investment of time and intellectual resources.
4. *Multiple sources and perspectives*: Learners are not given a list of resources. Authentic activities provide the opportunity for students to examine the task from a variety of theoretical and practical perspectives, using a variety of resources, and requires students to distinguish relevant from irrelevant information in the process.
5. *Collaboration*: Success is not achievable by an individual learner working alone. Authentic activities make collaboration integral to the task, both within the course and in the real world.
6. *Reflection (metacognition)*: Authentic activities enable learners to make choices and reflect on their learning, both individually and as a team or community.
7. *Interdisciplinary perspective*: Relevance is not confined to a single domain or subject matter specialization. Instead, authentic activities have consequences that extend beyond a particular discipline, encouraging students to adopt diverse roles and think in interdisciplinary terms.
8. *Integrated assessment*: Assessment is not merely summative in authentic activities but is woven seamlessly into the major task in a manner that reflects real-world evaluation processes.

9. *Polished products*: Conclusions are not merely exercises or substeps in preparation for something else. Authentic activities culminate in the creation of a whole product, valuable in its own right.
10. *Multiple interpretations and outcomes*: Rather than yielding a single correct answer obtained by the application of rules and procedures, authentic activities allow for diverse interpretations and competing solutions.

Educational researchers have found that students involved in authentic learning are motivated to persevere despite initial disorientation or frustration, as long as the exercise simulates what really counts—the social structure and culture that gives the discipline its meaning and relevance. The learning event essentially encourages students to compare their personal interests with those of a working disciplinary community: "Can I see myself becoming a member of this culture? What would motivate me? What would concern me? How would I work with the people around me? How would I make a difference?" Colleges and universities across the country are turning to authentic learning practices and putting the focus back on the learner in an effort to improve the way students absorb, retain, and transfer knowledge. Following are examples of authentic learning practices and their benefits.

Simulation-Based Learning

The Mekong e-Sim is an online learning environment that uses simulation and role-playing to immerse students in the complexities of authentic decision making, helping them develop the communication, collaboration, and leadership skills they will need to be successful practitioners in their fields. By asking students to assume the identities of stakeholders in the Mekong River Basin of Southeast Asia and debate the merits of a proposed development project, the Mekong e-Sim offers a structured method of exposing students to the wide range of social, political, economic, and scientific conflicts that affect complex engineering projects, particularly those that may be multinational in scope. Students from different disciplinary backgrounds (including civil, environmental, telecommunications, software, and mechanical) have used this learning tool to collaborate with others on authentic problems of global importance.

Student-Created Media

Students in The University of British Columbia's Department of Classical,

Near Eastern, and Religious Studies have created 3D virtual reconstructions of the ancient Athenian marketplace known as the agora and were required to present a rationale for the design choices they made as they built their replicas of the agora's theater, museum, and mint. Working from forensic evidence, including data from aerial photos, satellite images, surface surveys, topographic maps, structure measurements, and what is known as the "material culture assemblage"—or the accumulation of shards (pottery, stone tools, and so on) found on the occupation layers of the site—students employing the Ancient Spaces 3D model editor are able to learn by doing or, more precisely, learn by reconstructing key architectural and artistic environments of the ancient world.

Inquiry-Based Learning

At Carnegie Mellon University, cognitive scientists are teamed with expert faculty in a variety of disciplines to reach an understanding of where novices commonly run into trouble when introduced to unfamiliar material in a particular field. With this information in hand, the teams design Web-based courses that are "cognitively guided," providing students with the scaffolding they need at every stage of their development as preprofessionals. For example, an instructor teaching a course on the mathematics that underlie chemistry asks students to investigate a real-world problem: arsenic contamination of the water supply in Bangladesh.

Learners are introduced to key concepts and practice targeted skills while instructors, aware of common student misunderstandings, check for comprehension and provide feedback. Using additional "what if" questions, instructors help students continue to think flexibly about applying their newly acquired skills to other situations.

Peer-Based Evaluation

Calibrated Peer Review (CPR) is a free Web-based program that allows instructors to incorporate frequent writing assignments into their courses, regardless of class size, without increasing their grading workload. Students are trained to be competent reviewers and are then given the responsibility of providing their classmates with personalized feedback on expository writing assignments. Meanwhile, with access to all student work, instructors can monitor the class as a whole and assess the progress of each student.

Remote Instruments

Through a browser interface, MIT makes it possible for students around the world to conduct experiments with specialized equipment located on the MIT campus, including a shake table that simulates earthquakes and a sensor-equipped flagpole that measures meteorological parameters. Software agents oversee instrument usage, assigning priorities to individual experiments. For students without immediate access to expensive specialized equipment or extremely rare scientific instruments, this approach can open the door to active learning experiences that would otherwise be beyond their reach.

Research Data

In disciplines from ornithology to social history, students are becoming legitimate peripheral participants in virtual communities of practice, collecting data either first-hand or through remotely located smart sensors. In other cases, students use data collected by researchers (such as virtual sky data accessible through the National Science Digital Library Project) to conduct their own investigations. They are practicing higher-order analysis on real data sets while contributing to the common knowledge base.

Documenting Achievements

In 2001, the mechanical engineering faculty at UT Austin needed a way of documenting and sharing student projects, tracking the achievement of learning objectives, reinforcing the link between class work and real-world engineering concerns, and encouraging students to reflect on their own learning processes. Polaris, an in-house e-portfolio system, was created. UT engineering students not only use their e-portfolios to showcase their best work and evaluations for prospective employers; Polaris also supports the learning process. The system uses a "metacognitive" strategy that encourages students to study their own learning patterns in an effort to improve their performance over time. In addition, a feedback cycle allows students to post their individual work electronically, perform intra-group and extra-group reviews, question project assumptions, and learn to critique their peers constructively, as they must do throughout their engineering careers.

IT Support to Authentic Learning

Authentic learning is not new. It was the primary mode of instruction for apprentices who later took their places within established craft guilds. At one time apprenticeship was the most common form of learning. However, as the numbers of students grew in the 19th century, the logistics and economics of transporting large numbers of students to relevant work sites made large-scale apprenticeship programs impractical. Other risks emerge associated with managing the activities of novices in workplaces, opening institutions up to significant liability should student interns injure themselves or others. Significantly, educational researchers are coming to the conclusion that "the value of authentic activity is not constrained to learning in real-life locations and practice, but that the benefits of authentic activity can be realized through careful design of Web-based learning environments." Today's Web-based learning environments give students access to many of the same resources that professionals use in their research.

With Web-based access to radio astronomy data, for example, students have discovered stars overlooked by veteran researchers. History students with access to American Civil War archives are drawing their own conclusions about the history and sociology of the time. With online access to remote instruments, students are using rare or expensive equipment to run experiments and interpret data for themselves. In the process, they are dealing with incomplete and uncertain information, coming to grips with complex patterns, and realizing the messiness of real-life research where there may not be a single right answer. Technology is also providing access to phenomena that might otherwise remain opaque to many novices, particularly so-called experiential learners. Software visualizations, images, audio, and haptics bring abstractions to life. For instance, when scientific, mathematic, and engineering concepts require learners to build abstract mental models that involve invisible factors, such as intangible force fields and interactions among charged particles, visualization and haptic devices can be used to help learners feel force, pressure, and temperature.

However, access to digital archives, databases, instruments, or even haptic devices may not guarantee an authentic learning experience without the most important factor: community participation. In authentic learning situations, tasks are accomplished collaboratively, whether or not distance is involved. Educators can use Web-based communication tools to help students collaborate with one another, sharing and constructing knowledge. Social networking tools such as del.icio.us, or citation management tools for researchers such as Connotea, can help learners find a broader community willing to share information and references. And students can reflect on their learning and performance by taking "snapshots" of their group activities with the help of blogs, e-portfolios, quizzes, and video-capture tools.

Authentic learning can rely on educational software developed to simulate typical scenarios that professionals encounter in real-world settings. Along with communications tools, these online experiences often integrate intelligent tutoring systems, concept mapping, immediate feedback, and opportunities for reflection, including the chance to replay recorded events and adopt alternative decision paths. For example, when educational researchers reported that new teachers were having difficulty translating the theories they learned in graduate school into effective real-world practice, developers at the University of Wollongong, the University of Missouri, and Nanyang Technological University in Singapore devised educational software that would help them manage behavioral and learning issues in the classroom. The software taps into the various pressure situations and emotions teachers are likely to experience as they engage their students in a lesson. As the simulation unfolds, the new teacher plans and implements a lesson, views the effects of the lesson from multiple student perspectives, receives feedback and advice from online mentors, and explores alternatives by pausing or repeating the entire learning episode. The simulation also makes use of research data documenting the way exemplary teachers manage behavioral and learning issues in classroom settings.

Finally, some technologies allow students to cohabit the same persistent simulation (or "metaverse"), engaging in collaborative role-playing, grappling with multiple perspectives on the same set of issues, and responding to a dynamically changing situation. In the future, vivid simulations of clinics, schools, laboratories, and other workplaces may augment the conventional internship experience, but only if they offer learners immediate access to one another, to an extended family of mentors, and to the resources of the global network.

Technological support for today's authentic learning environments commonly includes:

- High-speed Internet connectivity for provision of multimedia information, including dynamic data and practical visualizations of complex phenomena and access to remote instrumentation in conjunction with expert advice.
- Asynchronous and synchronous communication and social networking tools for the support of teamwork, including collaborative online investigation, resource sharing, and knowledge construction.

- Intelligent tutoring systems, virtual laboratories, and feedback mechanisms that capture rich information about student performance and help students transfer their learning to new situations.
- Mobile devices for accessing and inputting data during field-based investigations.

Research and Authentic Learning

Authentic learning aligns with research into the way the human mind turns information into useful, transferable knowledge. Cognitive scientists are developing a comprehensive portrait of the learner. Three principles illustrate the alignment between learning research and authentic learning:

1. *Learners look for connections:* When we approach a subject for the first time, we immediately try to perceive the relevance of the new concept to our lived experience. When a new piece of information simply doesn't fit in any of our existing knowledge structures (or "schemas"), it is often rejected. This means that the more encouragement a learner has to become invested in material on a personal level, the easier it will be to assimilate the unfamiliar.
2. *Long-lived attachments come with practice:* Concepts need to be "aired" repeatedly and regularly, defended against attack, deployed in new contexts, and associated with new settings, activities, and people. Otherwise, the attachment is broken and the information lost.
3. *New contexts need to be explored:* The concepts being learned are always part of a much larger "learning event" and are directly linked in the learner's mind with social circumstances—the setting, the activities, the people.

Along with this emerging learner profile, cognitive scientists are studying the mind-set of the educator or subject matter expert, with some illuminating results.

1. *Experts have blind spots:1* Most faculty receive little or no training in the art and science of instruction and tend to rely on their intuitions about how novices learn. Current learning research demonstrates that those intuitions are commonly faulty simply because the instructor is an expert in the field. The longer experts continue to work in their discipline, the further removed they become from the perspective of the novice. Known as "the expert's blind spot," this inability to

recognize (or empathize with) beginning students' difficulties can lead expert instructors to teach in a manner that makes sense from their perspective but not necessarily from the student's perspective.

2. *Educators evoke feelings:* The teacher-as-facilitator can make or break a learning event. Learning methods evoke feelings in students that reinforce, support, or detract from knowledge construction. Since even the cleverest team of students dealing with complex, sustained investigations may have difficulty making good judgments in the absence of appropriate "scaffolding," it is the educator's role to design appropriate comprehension checks and feedback loops into the authentic learning exercise, preferably the very kinds of interventions commonly exhibited in real-world settings. For example, students engaged in publishing a peer-reviewed journal will evaluate each other over the course of the project and may receive additional guidance from the educator in the role of publisher or editorial board member.
3. *Higher education should include the conative domain:* Instructors that provide engaging activities supported by the proper scaffolding can help students develop expertise across all four domains of learning:

   Cognitive capacity to think, solve problems, and create

- Affective capacity to value, appreciate, and care
- Psychomotor capacity to move, perceive, and apply physical skills
- Conative capacity to act, decide, and commit

Researchers warn that higher education has focused for too long on inculcating and assessing those cognitive skills that are relatively easy to acquire—remembering, understanding, and applying—rather than the arguably more important skills of analyzing, evaluating, and creating. Moreover, in developing these lower-order thinking skills, educators have largely ignored the other major learning domains, particularly the conative, which determines whether a student has the necessary will, desire, commitment, mental energy, and self-determination to actually perform at the highest disciplinary standards. By engaging students in issues of concern to them, from global warming to world hunger, authentic learning awakens in learners the confidence to act.

Those who adopt innovative learning strategies must be ready to adjust their assessment strategies accordingly. Otherwise, the purpose of the entire enterprise may well be defeated. There are eight critical factors that researchers say must be aligned to ensure a successful learning environment:

- goals
- content
- instructional design
- learner tasks
- instructor roles
- student roles
- technological affordances
- assessment

An educator can introduce authentic content, replacing textbooks with historical documents and scientific data from remote sensors. She can design problem-based activities to replace lectures. She can expect students to collaborate with one another (despite student resistance to these active requirements). She can even surrender some of her own power as an expert to join students as a colearners. And she can support all this innovation with visualizations, simulations, and interactive technologies. Still, she may not achieve her goals if she neglects to rethink her assessment strategies. After all, what is the use of adopting loftier goals for yourself and your students if you continue to use multiple-choice tests that seek the "right" answer, capturing only the lower-level knowledge that is easiest to measure? Rather than relying on a single assessment method, instructors who adopt authentic learning methods must analyze multiple forms of evidence to measure student performance, including observations of student engagement and artifacts produced in the process of completing tasks.

Importance of Authentic Learning

Jean Lave and Etienne Wenger argue that all would-be scientists, mathematicians, engineers, and historians need to be "enculturated" into the discipline—and the earlier, the better. Along with memorizing facts and practicing technical procedures, beginning students should be learning what John Seely Brown calls the "genres" of the discipline—the schema through which full members of the disciplinary community "recognize whether a problem is an important problem, or a solution an elegant solution, or even what constitutes a solution in the first place." What's more, students should know what it feels like for actual stakeholders beyond the classroom to hold them accountable for their work products. So, whether the learning activity results in a business plan, a set of design specifications, a presentation to the city council, or a short film, evaluation occurs naturally over the course of the project, coming from several sources (as it would in real life), including peers, supervisors, and clients. The goal is to give learners the confidence that comes with being recognized as "legitimate peripheral participants" in a community of practice.

Authentic learning may be more important than ever in a rapidly changing world, where the half-life of information is short and individuals can expect to progress through multiple careers. According to Frank Levy and Richard Murnane, expert thinking and complex communication will differentiate those with career-transcending skills from those who have little opportunity for advancement. Expert thinking involves the ability to identify and solve problems for which there is no routine solution. This requires pattern recognition and metacognition. Another differentiator is complex communication, such as persuading, explaining, negotiating, gaining trust, and building understanding. Although foundational skills (reading, writing, mathematics, history, language) remain essential, a more complex set of competencies are required today. These go beyond being technically competent to being able to get things done, demonstrate ethics and integrity, and work well with others. According to employers, the most important skills in new hires include teamwork, critical thinking/reasoning, assembling/organizing information, and innovative thinking/creativity.

Why isn't authentic learning more common? The reliance on traditional instruction is not simply a choice made by individual faculty—students often prefer it. This resistance to active learning may have more to do with their epistemological development than a true preference for passivity. Entering freshmen are likely to use a right-or-wrong, black-or-white mental model. At this dualistic stage, students believe that the "right answer exists somewhere for every problem, and authorities know them. Right answers are to be memorized by hard work." By confronting students with uncertainty, ambiguity, and conflicting perspectives, instructors help them develop more mature mental models that coincide with the problem-solving approaches used by experts. Authentic learning exercises expose the messiness of real-life decision making, where there may not be a right or a wrong answer per se, although one solution may be better or worse than others depending on the particular context. Such a nuanced understanding involves considerable reflective judgment, a valuable lifelong skill that goes well beyond the memorization of content.

To be competitive in a global job market, today's students must become comfortable with the complexities of ill-defined real-world problems. The greater their exposure to authentic disciplinary communities, the better prepared they will be "to deal with ambiguity" and put into practice the kind of "higher order analysis and complex communication" required of them as professionals.

References

Dede, C., Korte S., Nelson, R., Valdez, G., & Ward, D. J. (2005). *Transforming learning for the 21st century: An economic imperative*. Naperville, IL: Learning Point Associates. R

Downes, S. (2007). *Emerging Technologies for Learning*. Coventry, U.K.: Becta.

Goleman, D. (1996). *Emotional intelligence: Why it can matter more than IQ*. London: Bloomsbury.

Lave, J., & Wenger, E. (1991). *Situated learning: Legitimate peripheral participation*. Cambridge: Cambridge University Press. Brown, op. cit.

Perry, W. G. Jr. (1981). Cognitive and ethical growth: The making of meaning. In A. W. Chickering (Ed.). *The modern american college* (p. 79). San Francisco: Jossey-Bass.

Reeves, T. C. (2006). How do you know they are learning?: The importance of alignment in higher education. *International Journal of Learning Technology*, *2*(4), 302–304.

4

21st Century Skills for Science Learners

The recommendations for the design of teacher preparation and professional development models that can sustain the career-long development of ambitious pedagogy—including approaches to instruction that can cultivate 21st Century skills in young learners. I begin by describing what it means to be a "reform-oriented teacher," articulating characteristic performances of advanced instruction with the kinds of 21st Century skills they foster in young learners.

Relationship with 21st Century Skills

Over the past five years, ideas about effective instruction in science classrooms have achieved new clarity through converging scholarship across the areas of science studies, student learning, assessment, and curriculum. The recent volume *Taking Science To School*, for example, identifies four strands of proficiency for students *and for teachers* who are responsible for guiding young science learners. Students and teachers should be able to:

- Understand, use, and interpret scientific explanations of the natural world
- Generate and evaluate scientific evidence and explanations
- Understand the nature and development of scientific knowledge, and
- Participate productively in scientific practices and discourse.

These proficiencies are embodied most clearly in classroom activities such as content-rich inquiries and non-routine problem-solving. What these proficiencies "look and sound like" in practice however, has not been well-translated into models for teacher performance (such as a Learning Progression for teachers), nor have underlying skills and understandings required for these performances been articulated.

The vision of how 21st Century skills play out in classrooms is closer to *studio-based science* rather than to laboratory–based science environments (in which "hands-on" activity often shapes the organization of teaching and learning, to the point of being valuable for its own sake). By studio science I mean that the primary focus of student work is to solve complex problems, and that multiple forms of learning activity by students (gathering relevant information, collecting data, testing models, learning new concepts needed to understand the problem, etc.) is always in the service of producing an evidence-based solution to a problem. The studio science approach is characterized by a focus on a few key science ideas, purpose-driven group work, student ownership of problems and problem-solving approaches, the on-going public vetting of multiple solutions and models as they are being developed, and the use of feedback to refine ideas and solutions. I should note here that the studio orientation to science learning involves students in *generating* and *re-framing* problems—a skill that is actually more fundamental than the five 21st Century skills listed currently.

Some explanation may be helpful for understanding how the features of reform-based teaching listed above lead to different 21st Century skills in students. In Row 1 of the table, the teacher's ability to identify big ideas in science is crucial to the development of problems and inquiries that are appropriately challenging and worth exploring in depth. Although the knowledge needed by teachers here does not correspond directly with a particular 21st Century skill, it lays the foundation for the design of extended engagements with problems that are pre-requisites for students to develop various 21st Century skills.

The elicitation of learners' current conceptions requires that students, individually or in groups, develop representations of their thinking to share with the teacher or other students. A teacher may, for example, ask students at the beginning of a unit of instruction to imagine what the key features of a pulley system are, including visible features and as well as what can't be seen. This requires students to identify salient features, make decisions about how to represent these, and how to present such a model to an audience (complex communication). It also requires them to interpret both representational conventions and the ideas behind the representations that other students have developed. Inevitably, students attempt to reason out how systems like pulleys (or cells in hypotonic solutions, or convection currents in the Earth's atmosphere) operate, and in particular how changes in one part of the system affect changes in other parts of the system (systems thinking).

The teacher prompts students to develop hypotheses or small-scale theory about what is happening to cause a natural phenomenon. What students learn here is to communicate in a disciplinary language. They learn not only "what counts" as hypotheses or explanations, but how these terms fit into a specialized rhetorical system of evidence-based argumentation (complex communication). Because the teacher asks students to move beyond describing a phenomenon to offering potential explanations that involve underlying events or processes, students are pressed to reason abstractly about how the elements—both tangible and theoretical—influence one another (systems thinking).

The teachers place partial responsibility on students to make decisions about what kinds of information resources and experiences they need to develop solutions to the central problem or develop an explanatory model for the central phenomenon (self-management). Because multiple sources of information, activities, and representations are now being brought into the mix, teachers must help students see patterns across broad spans of information (non-routine problem solving) and integrate these into sensible mental frameworks (systems thinking).

Both student self-monitoring and teacher awareness of what students' current state of understanding are. On the teachers' part this is accomplished by employing a range of formative assessment strategies. The teacher, however, has to have the skills to scaffold both the metacognition and self-regulation in students (self-management). Because reform science teaching is predicated on the regular pursuit of big questions or complex problems, students' ability (and habits of mind) to reflect on what they know and what they need to know is crucial. The self-management skill by students is almost never developed in traditional classroom settings, where students often exposed to multitudes of poorly connected concepts, are told what to use as information resources, told how to conduct activities, and told how to interpret the significance of these activities. In short, *the common teacher-centered classroom and typically overfilled curriculum obviate the entire suite of 21st Century skills*. Advanced placement courses in high schools are notorious for this type of instruction.

The teacher supports students in coordinating all previous learning experiences in order to represent an argument for why a particular problem solution or an explanatory model is best supported by evidence. This again requires complex communication among students who are working in small groups, and requires communication by groups of students to their peers. No one solution is considered in isolation from the others. As in authentic science there are multiple possibilities that have unique trade-offs (in problem-solving tasks) or bodies of evidentiary support (in inquiry or research scenarios). These solutions or explanations require systems thinking and non-routine problem-solving as well as communication skills. The communication skills here again involve the specialized disciplinary rhetoric of science. Social perceptiveness, negotiating ideas with others, and even students teaching one another all play a role in the culminating phase of reform teaching (complex communication). Teachers must understand how to make explicit to students the ways in which these forms of argument unfold in group settings and "what counts" as viable solutions or valid explanatory models.

In the description above we have not mentioned the 21st Century skill of adaptability. Adaptability, in my opinion, is not explicitly fostered by reform-based teaching. While the tasks students engage in could change substantially over the course of a unit of reform-based instruction, the types of change students would need to adapt to are not of the scope or character described in the outline of the 21st Century skills.

Classroom Teaching Today

Recent studies indicate that U.S. science students routinely engage in various forms of classroom inquiry without understanding connections to important scientific concepts, nor do they reason well about evidence and explanation. In an analysis of the TIMSS video data from science classrooms, Roth and Garnier note that in American classrooms "almost one-third of the lessons narrowly focused students' attention on performing activities with no attempt on the teachers' part to relate these activities to science ideas". In a study of 180 science lessons collected from a national sample, Weiss et al. noted that only a quarter of these lessons were judged to include adequate sense-making.

In another international study (PISA), American students fell significantly below the average on two subscales: explaining phenomena scientifically and using scientific evidence. Related findings from the *Inside the Classroom* study show that few lessons engaged students with concepts in a way that allowed them to understand the nature of science, specifically how scientific knowledge is generated, enriched, and changed.

Fewer than 10% of science lessons required students to use data or examples as evidence in supporting or critiquing conclusions.

Banilower, Smith, Weiss, and Pasley found that only 14 percent of all lessons in a national sample exhibited intellectual rigor, and that questioning was among the weakest elements of instruction. This apparent inattention to how classroom discourses influence learning is compounded by the fact that only about half of all science teachers can adequately interpret students' level of understanding and adjust instruction accordingly. A national survey of over 2,500 science teachers indicates that only about one in six lessons included pre-assessments to determine what students understood about a topic before instruction. A later study indicated that 35 percent of lessons contained some form of elicitation, however in some cases the prompt was not well-aligned with the learning goal stated by the teacher and was therefore unlikely to bring out relevant student ideas. Clearly American science teaching does not do a good job of developing ideas in depth, connecting ideas with material activity, or attending to student thinking as a way to shape instruction. It is noteworthy that the most problematic features of science teaching *do not* involve lab work, experiments or otherwise engaging students in material activities. Rather, it is the ineffective use of *classroom discourse* to probe students' ideas, to press students for explanation, or to encourage sense-making.

Teacher Skills Required for Reform-based Learning

While there are many skills and understandings one needs to teach science well, four broad abilities are crucial to reform-based teaching and teaching 21st Century skills.

1. *Deep interconnected content knowledge, ability to "see" big ideas in curriculum and understand how to teach these as big ideas.* Teachers'

content knowledge is related to the science teaching strategies they use and to student learning. Teachers with stronger content knowledge are more likely to teach in ways that help students construct knowledge, pose appropriate questions, suggest alternative explanations, and propose additional inquiries. Inquiry science teaching also demands that teachers have specific knowledge of *how to support students* in developing researchable questions, planning an investigation, collecting and interpreting data and presenting results. There is extensive support for both a focus on content knowledge in general and *specific forms of content knowledge* that best support teaching practice. Our own research further indicates that specific forms of reasoning with content knowledge are critical to reform teaching, the most important being the ability to identify fundamentally important science ideas underlying common curriculum topics. Because the context of teaching of 21st Century skills depends so heavily upon students' sustained engagement with complex problems, it stands to reason that teachers can only organize such high-quality curricular challenges if they themselves have deep and well integrated understandings of the content and the practices of science. I address these ideas in more detail later.

2. *Ability to engage students in specialized classroom discourses aligned with reform goals*. In considering the knowledge and skills necessary for laboratory work, it may seem intuitive to focus on the abilities of the teacher to design and manage *activities* for students. Recent scholarship, however, has emphasized that meaningful learning is a product *not of activity per se*, but of *sense-making discourse* aimed at developing conceptual understanding and the links between theory and observable phenomena. In this view, learning is not accomplished through the transmission of knowledge from person to person, but rather through an ongoing process of comparing and checking one's own understandings with those that are being rehearsed on the social plane of the classroom.

   In addition to using dialogue to facilitate conceptual understanding, other researchers have employed classroom discourse as a way to engage learners in the canonical practices of science—that is, "to formulate questions about phenomena that interest them [students], to build and criticize theories, to collect, analyze and interpret data, to evaluate hypotheses through experimentation, observation, measurement, and to communicate findings". Language, in the form of purposeful talk, reading, and writing, mediates all these activities (for examples of teachers reflecting on their own use of discourse in middle school settings. This emphasis on sense-making discourse is echoed in the policy literature aimed at clarifying what it means to get students to "think" in classrooms. Thompson and Zeuli state that "By think, we mean that students must actively try to solve problems, resolve dissonances between the way they initially understand a phenomena and new evidence that challenges their understanding, put collections of observations or facts together into patterns, make and test conjectures, and build lines of reasoning about why claims are or are not true. Such thinking is generative. It literally creates understanding in the mind of the learner". Because complex communications are fundamental to 21st Century skills, teachers' understanding of how language and other representations are used to create meaning in classroom contexts is crucial.

3. *Understanding the full range of assessment strategies, purposes and contexts within which they should be used.* Students' conceptual learning and sophisticated disciplinary performance are achieved in part by eliciting information from them through assessments as a means of gauging where they are in their progress toward a goal, and by providing ongoing targeted feedback to them. Research also suggests that understanding is supported when learners are asked to take an active part in determining what they understand and how they came to that understanding. Classroom practices that aid this kind of metacognition include peer and self assessment, reflection on one's progress and determining what needs further improvement, and activities geared toward allowing students to make sense of new concepts through talk or writing, which in turn allows teachers to gather information on student understanding to guide his or her next steps. All these pedagogical skills support the 21st Century skills of student self-regulation, self-monitoring, and metacognition.

4. *Understanding how to learn from one's practice.* There is a growing consensus within the field of teacher education that equipping novices with a repertoire of competent classroom practices is no longer considered an adequate professional preparation. Because initial training can only begin new educators on the long trajectory towards

expert teaching, it is equally important that these programs help novices develop strategies and habits of mind to *learn from practice* as they enter the profession, laying the foundations for career-long development. Broadly speaking, learning from teaching is best achieved through systematic cycles of inquiry into practice and using evidence generated by these inquiries to re-shape instruction. Some of the most promising of these types of inquiries draw upon records of practice from the participating teachers—in particular, samples of student work. Learning from one's practice should begin in teacher preparation and extend into one's professional career. Because the teaching of 21st Century skills is about *how* students learn, as well as *what* they learn, the regular examination of artifacts of student thinking or discourse may be the only way for teachers to ultimately judge and refine their own practice towards these ends.

Learning and Teaching of Science

Content Knowledge

To develop competence in subject matter instruction, teachers must have a deep foundation of factual and theoretical knowledge, and understand these facts and ideas in the context of a conceptual framework. These foundations begin with undergraduate work where subject matter knowledge and knowledge of the disciplinary activities of science are developed.

Unfortunately, research into undergraduate preparation indicates that the content knowledge gained is often superficial and not well integrated. The traditional didactic pedagogy to which teacher candidates are often exposed in university science courses provides only minimal conceptual understandings of their science disciplines. As a result, many pre-service teachers hold serious alternative conceptions about the science content, similar to those held by their students. In a year-long study of prospective biology teachers, participants reported never having thought about the central ideas of biology or the interrelationships among the topics. The teachers, all biology majors, could only list the courses they had taken as a way to organize their fields. They knew little about how various ideas were related to each other, nor could they readily explain the overall content and character of biology. These findings confirm those from a substantial literature on arts and sciences teaching in colleges and universities that has clearly documented both elementary and secondary teachers lacking a deep and connected conceptual understanding of the subject matter they are expected to teach.

Understanding Scientific Practice

With regard to prospective teachers' exposure to science as a knowledge-building enterprise, much of what new teachers learn about inquiry comes from their experiences as undergraduates, which are not unlike the confirmatory laboratory experiences found in secondary schools. In addition to the problem of being subjected to models of highly-structured inquiry, pre-service teachers are rarely exposed to ideas about science as a discipline at the college level and do not participate in discussions of how new knowledge is evaluated. Not surprisingly, the studies that have been done on inquiry in teacher education programs indicate that pre-service teachers lack basic knowledge of methodology and do not think in terms of theory as they attempt scientific investigations.

In multi-case studies of pre-service secondary science teachers' understandings of authentic inquiry practices during science methods courses most participants subscribed to a "folk theory" about scientific inquiry in which forms of knowledge and specialized disciplinary rhetoric that are crucial to reform-based teaching (e. g. model development, explanation, argument) had little or no role. The emphasis by these pre-service teachers was on collecting and analyzing data, but not on connecting this data to an underlying explanation. Two factors shaped participants' thinking about these inquiries. One was previous school-related research experience which influenced not only what they recognized as explanations or models but also the way they believed these could be incorporated into inquiry. The other was a widely-held simplistic view of "the scientific method" which constrained the procedures and epistemic frameworks they used for investigations.

Learning to Teach

We currently have limited understandings of how individuals develop the skills, knowledge, and habits of mind to become proficient teachers. Much of what we know comes from expert-novice studies, but these have not followed individuals over a period of years. Rather, these studies compare the thinking and practice of novices with separate groups of more experienced practitioners. Developmental pathways and a list of critical experiences that can advance the practice of novices over time have not been empirically validated. There are other kinds of research, however, that provide important clues to what might help or hinder teachers' learning throughout their careers. I outline these below.

One personal theory that many new teaching candidates hold about learning is that it amounts to a simple "transfer" of information from texts and teachers to students who acquire it from listening, reading, and memorization. This shapes their thinking about what kind of teaching is appropriate and possible in classrooms. When we consider the kinds of knowledge-building, problem-solving, metacognition, and collaboration that are part of 21st Century learning, such an oversimplified view of teaching seems a major impediment. These preconceptions, developed in teachers' "apprenticeship of observation", also condition what they then learn in training experiences. If this initial understanding is not engaged/confronted during teacher preparation, they may fail to grasp new concepts about teaching and learning or they may learn them for the purposes of a test, but revert to their preconceptions later.

We also know that even when novice teachers are exposed to powerful conceptual frameworks to help them think about organizing instruction and analyzing classroom events they will either not know how or when to enact these ideas when they enter the classroom, or, they will simply reject these frames and rely instead on conservative teacher-centered instruction. Reform-based teaching methods are often fundamentally different from how student teachers were taught and sometimes how teacher educators themselves learned as students. Short term interventions have shown little capacity to change teacher pre-conceptions. In contrast, longer term approaches that explicitly seek to elicit and work with novice teachers' initial beliefs have shown some success in fostering reform-based teaching.Although studies that follow novices from their preparation experiences into the first years of teaching are remarkably rare, the few that have been reported portray similar transitions into professional work: newcomers are willing to try out some non-traditional strategies when they enter their classrooms, but for a variety of reasons, they often bring few principled pedagogical practices with them from their pre-service training.

Part of the challenge in helping novices take up reform-based practices is that, as they begin their careers, they are not merely being apprenticed into a set of teaching strategies, but often into an intuitionist epistemology of professional knowledge and problem-solving. In his classic study of school teachers, Lortie noted that practitioners saw their pedagogy styled around personal preferences rather than grounded in an accepted body of knowledge. Teachers used—and still use—little more than informal observations of students to assess their own instructional efficacy and depend upon a kind of untested folk wisdom to deal with dilemmas of practice. Huberman has more recently characterized this approach to practice as "bricolage" or tinkering. In this view teachers develop as independent artisans, picking up a new activity here and a new technique there, choosing these to fit within their own styles and work settings. Both Huberman and Lortie suggest that these tendencies are reinforced by the everyday intellectual isolation of the classroom and by the absence of a shared and explicit vision of good teaching that could support conversations about how to improve practice.

Given the over-reliance on personal intuition, the isolation, and the lack of models for effective teaching, interventions designed to foster ambitious pedagogy in novice educators must consider new ways of making public "what counts" as accountable practice. Apprenticing teachers, and in particular novice teachers, into this type of teaching however, is complicated by the "hard wired" routines of low-level questioning in classrooms, by the lack of clear models of more sophisticated practice, and by inexperienced educators' limited understanding of students' capacities to engage in challenging work. This seems particularly problematic for reform-based science teaching and for developing the ability to cultivate 21st Century skills in young learners. Teaching for 21st Century skills is quite unlike the kinds of science teaching in today's classrooms. Reform-based teaching for example:

- demands a range of specialized discourses (both teacher-to-student discourse and student- to-student),
- relies on constant assessment of student thinking and subsequent "disciplined improvisation" by teachers to adapt to where students are/ need to go next, and
- requires a deeper understanding of both science content and of disciplinary practices than do traditional forms of instruction.

In a later section, we build upon this logic to suggest the development of a set of tools for teachers to support these kinds of transitions from traditional to reform-based instruction.

CHARACTERISTICS OF TEACHER PREPARATION

General features of effective teacher preparation programs. Some teacher preparation programs have graduates who report significantly greater feelings of preparedness, and are more highly-rated by employers who say they seek out these candidates because they are more effective in the classroom from the first days of teaching. A study of seven such programs found these common features:

- "A shared vision of good teaching that is consistent in courses and clinical work.
- Well-defined standards of practice and performance that are used to guide the design and assessment of coursework and clinical work.
- A common core curriculum grounded in substantial knowledge of child or adolescent development, learning, and subject matter pedagogy, taught in the context of practice.
- Extended clinical experiences (at least 30 weeks) that reflect the program's vision of good teaching, are interwoven with coursework, and carefully mentored.
- Strong relationships, based on common knowledge and beliefs, between universities and reform-minded schools.
- Extensive use of case study methods, teacher research, performance assessments, and portfolio examination that relate teachers' learning to classroom practice."

The same program features and pedagogical tools are noted in other studies of strong programs. Other studies indicate that a coherent science focused pre-service program and the number of methods courses positively relate to the implementation of reform-based science instruction. Luft, Roehrig, and Patterson say *multiple* methods courses, coordinated with an extended student teaching experience, may be critical to providing novice teachers with practices for reform-based teaching.

Coherence of a vision for good teaching throughout all early learning-to-teach contexts is important. When student teaching placements, for example, are *consistent with the programs' vision* of teaching and learning, and when a *shared understanding* of the purposes and activities of student teaching exists between student teachers, cooperating teachers and university supervisors, more powerful learning takes place. Novices have also benefited from repeated chances to try out high-leverage practices in real classrooms with mentoring that focuses on learning. When a well-supervised student teaching experience precedes or is jointly conducted with coursework (the coherence theme again), students are more able to connect theoretical learning to practice, become more comfortable with the process of learning to teach, and are more able to enact what they are learning in practice. Other studies show that when teachers learn content-specific strategies and tools that they are *immediately able to try and continue to refine with a group of colleagues* in a learning community, they are more able to enact new practices effectively.

Both student teaching and induction experiences should maintain a focus on student learning. This includes time to plan and debrief lessons together with a mentor. Mentoring (this was not conclusive data) can be an effective strategy to reduce teacher attrition and improve teacher quality. This research, however, refers to "being mentored" as seeing a more experienced colleague only once a month, at maximum.

Science-specific teacher preparation features. Subject matter knowledge clearly influences how and how well teachers teach. Teachers' academic preparation in science has a positive influence on students' science achievement. One study found that having an advanced degree in science was associated with increased student achievement from the 8th to 10th grade. The NRC Committee on Science and Mathematics Teacher preparation stated that "studies conducted over the past quarter century increasingly point to a strong correlation between student achievement in K-12 science and the teaching quality and level of knowledge of their K-12 teachers." However, Wilson, Floden, & Ferrini-Mundy conclude that "...we know next to nothing about *high quality teaching* in subject matter courses that are part of the preparation of teachers". In addition, the mechanisms through which such knowledge enters teachers' thinking and practice are not well understood.

Teachers with limited subject matter preparation tend to emphasize memorization of isolated facts and algorithms; they rely on textbooks without using student understandings as a guide to planning lessons; they use lower-level questioning and rule-constrained classroom activities; furthermore, they employ only limited use of student questions or comments in classroom discourse which results in marginal student development of conceptual connections and misrepresentations of the nature and the structure of the discipline. Kennedy notes that some take a minimalist view of necessary content knowledge by requiring teachers to only know the subject mater actually covered by the curriculum, reasoning that this knowledge is exactly what the teachers will be teaching. Kennedy and others argue, however, that if students can ask questions that extend beyond the formal curriculum (our own research shows that this happens *frequently*) and if teachers must respond to those questions, teachers need knowledge that goes far beyond the curriculum being taught.

Induction Support

Induction refers to continuing support for novice teachers during their first two to three years of professional work. Induction support can include periodic mentoring, helping new teachers become adjusted to local school culture and routines, assistance with classroom management, and other forms of technical help. This is important from a practical standpoint because first-year teachers assume responsibilities similar to those of experienced teachers while learning their job with little preparation. In the absence of post graduate support in the form of induction, students can revert back to more traditional practices and beliefs. In their study of new secondary science educators, Adams and Krockover found cases where new teachers failed to use the constructivist forms of instruction they had been taught in pre-service education, until two years after they had become practicing teachers. They noted that the key influence for these changes was a professional development experience that provided these individuals time to reflect on their own teaching and consider how it compared with what they had learned in their pre-service experience.

There is little research in this area that indicates how induction affects teaching and learning. In one of these few studies, Luft, Roehrig, and Patterson compared groups of new teachers who experienced different kinds of first year support: one group had induction that attended to the specific pedagogical needs of science teachers, one group had induction that focused only on general pedagogical support, and one group had no formally structured induction. Teachers in the first two groups ended up using practices more congruent with standards-based reforms. Those in the science-specific group were also more likely to hold beliefs about student-centered practices, implement more student-centered inquiry practices and feel fewer constraints in their teaching. This inquiry into practice must be science-specific and focus on high-value types of student performance. Our own research, described in a later section, provides evidence that spending the first year of induction collaboratively analyzing student work can promote reform-based classroom practices in novices.

Analyzing learning artifacts has helped teachers generate and test hypotheses about instructional decisions, pushed them to think beyond routine, familiar activity in the classroom, and led to improved student learning. Sato et al. found, for example, that during preparation for National Board Certification, that collegial analysis, reflection, and constructive critique of videotaped lessons, sharing of teaching strategies, and the analysis of pupil work against performance standards as "tools for critique" allowed teachers to enact high teaching standards in specific classroom practices and gave them feedback about what they were doing and how well. The analyses of teaching practices form the core of professional development activities in several Asian countries whose students perform very well in international comparisons of math and science achievement. Hiebert et al. note that "Although many factors account for the apparent success of continued teacher learning in these countries, the relentless focus on analyzing classroom practice and testing hypothesized improvements clearly support the growth of expertise among these teachers." In contrast to this focus on student learning, many U.S. teachers think of instruction in terms of implementing activities. They focus often on repairing problems with these activities rather than analyzing effects of instruction on students' learning.

Effective Professional Development

As with teacher preparation and induction, there are general conditions that have been associated with effective professional development. I describe these below and then suggest how some of the 21st Century skills might be incorporated into professional development designs. There are some consistent findings with regard to how *structural elements* of professional development (the broad temporal, participatory, and instructional contexts associated with professional development) and *core features* (characteristics of the learning experiences within the professional development structure) influence change in teacher practice.

In a study Garet et al. identified the core features of professional development that have significant effects on teachers' self-reported increases in knowledge and skills and changes in classroom practices:

a) a focus on content knowledge;

b) opportunities for active learning; and

c) coherence with other learning activities.

It is primarily through these core features that the following structural features significantly affect learning:

a) the form of the activity;

b) collective participation of teachers from the same school, grade, or subject; and

c) duration of the activity.

In a longitudinal study of 207 science and mathematics teachers from 30 schools, Desimone et al. reported similar findings—that professional development is more likely to change teacher practice when it has:

a) the collective participation of teachers from the same school, department, or grade;

b) active learning opportunities such as reviewing student work or obtaining feedback on teaching; and

c) coherence, for example, linking to other activities or building on teachers' prior knowledge.

Reform-type professional development also had a positive effect.

With regard to activity type, there is broad consensus among teacher learning researchers that "reform-oriented" professional development (activities such as teacher study groups) tends to result in more substantive changes in practice than "traditional" (workshops or college courses) professional development. For example, professional development in which teachers have themselves engaged in science inquiry activities have resulted in changes in practice *and* positive student learning outcomes. Other reform-oriented professional development, according to Garet et al.'s definition, includes being mentored or coached, participating in a study group, or engaging in an internship. These predictors had been identified by others as contributing to the quality of professional development.

With regard to duration of professional development (in terms of both time span and total contact hours). Supovitz & Turner found that more extended time spans permitted learning opportunities for teachers to integrate new knowledge into practice and to create "investigative cultures" in science classrooms, as opposed to stimulating superficial changes in practice. In a curriculum implementation study of teachers served by 28 different professional development providers, Penuel, Fishman, Yamaguchi, and Gallagher found that the incorporation of time for teachers to plan for implementation and the provision of technical support were important for promoting changes in teaching. They hypothesize it is likely that there is an interaction between the duration of professional development and other structural and core features, such as the employment of reform-oriented professional development. Referring to Desimone et al., 2002 who found that the duration of the professional development had *no effect* on outcomes, Penuel et al. hypothesize that the factor of time is important only to permit the experiences of community, coherence, and experimentation with new practices to unfold in meaningful ways.

With regard to collective participation, evidence from a wide range of studies examining school reform suggest that those that make extensive use of teacher collaboration are particularly successful in promoting implementation, in part because reforms have more authority when they are embraced by peers. Gamoran et al., hypothesized about the underlying mechanisms behind the benefits of collective participation in their study of six school sites where science and mathematics teachers were collaborating with university researchers to teach for understanding. They found supporting evidence for the following:

1) the shift from conventional teaching to teaching for understanding makes teachers' uncertainty more salient in all areas of teaching: curriculum, instruction, assessment, and teacher knowledge about student reasoning; and
2) professional communities of teachers provide the social mechanisms through which uncertainty can be managed, allowing teachers to respond to one another's affect, beliefs, ideas, to provide support and encouragement to try out ideas in the classrooms, and help each other maintain the practices that resonate with newly developing ideas about how to teach for understanding.

Other professional development efforts have successfully utilized the dynamics of communities to initiate and sustain reform efforts among teachers. Among these are Looking at Student Work (LASW), Japanese Lesson Study, and the Coalition of Essential Schools.

With regard to coherence, this characteristic refers to teachers' perceptions of how well aligned the professional development activities are with their own goals for learning and their goals for students. Teachers filter policy demands and messages from professional development providers through their own interpretive frames. The social context of schools had strong influence on these interpretive frames and thus teachers' decisions on how to enact. Frequently, teachers assimilate only bits and pieces of new activity into their own repertoire with little substantive change, or they reject these changes suggested in professional development setting altogether. Curricular reforms are particularly difficult in this regard because they require most teachers to make systemic changes to implement them well.

Penuel et al. refer to a coherence-related construct—*proximity to practice* (the degree to which professional development coincides with actual curriculum and classroom conditions that teachers are familiar with) as a feature that results in learning outcomes for teachers most directly translatable to practice. A number of studies have focused on site-based or curriculum linked professional development. Site-based professional development for example provides assistance at school, in the context of teachers' enactment, using approaches such as coaching. Curriculum-linked professional development focuses specifically on how to enact pedagogical strategies, use materials, and administer assessments associated with particular curricula. There is growing consensus that to make changes, teachers need professional development that is interactive with their teaching practice, allowing for multiple cycles of presentation and assimilation of, and reflection on their developing knowledge. A large-scale study conducted in California found this type of professional development far more effective than workshops focused on general pedagogical strategies in promoting changes in teachers' practice.

In sum, the most important factors of professional development that can influence reform-based teaching and the understanding of how to cultivate 21st Century skills in learners are:

1. The collective and collaborative participation by teachers from the same school, grade, or subject areas.
2. The collective development of an evidence-based "inquiry stance" by participants towards their practice.
3. Active learning opportunities that focus on science content, scientific practice, and evidence of student learning.

4. Coherence of the professional development with teachers' existing knowledge, other development activities, with existing curriculum, and with standards in local contexts.

TEACHERS' LEARNING TRAJECTORY

Our own research progr am—the Teachers' Learning Trajectory Initiative—has investigated the question of how teacher preparation and early career support can be designed to foster reform-based instruction in novice educators. We completed a multi-case study of 15 secondary science pre-service teachers, following them for three years through their preparation program, into student teaching, and through this first full year of teaching. A major feature of their preparation program was a methods course which focused heavily on four aspects of reform teaching. These four aspects are part of what we refer to as "ambitious pedagogy"; more specifically it is teaching about and with model-based inquiry.

The first of these four elements of ambitious pedagogy was *teachers' selection and treatment of key ideas from the curriculum*, in which the goal was to help novices see fundamental ideas in common curricula. Ideally this teaching would place significant focus on unobservable and/or theoretical processes in the natural world or on the relationships among science concepts. The second of these elements was *working with students' ideas.* To achieve competence here, novices would elicit and use students' current conceptions of science ideas to inform the direction of classroom activity and conversation. They would engineer productive classroom conversations, or consciously re-shape students' lines of thinking across multiple lessons. The third aspect of reform teaching was *working with science ideas in the classroom.* The goal here was for novices to highlight with students tentative explanatory models as the basis for investigating a phenomenon. The novice uses models as a referential representation of ideas before, during and after an inquiry, building in background knowledge of key science concepts and models as the inquiry progresses. The fourth aspect of reform teaching was called *pressing for explanation,* in which the novice asks students to use theoretical or unobservable processes to tell a causal story of why a target phenomena unfolded in particular ways. The novice unpacks/scaffolds "what counts" as an accountable scientific explanations with students.

These elements of pedagogy were modeled in the methods class; participants then had opportunities to try out these approaches through lesson planning and micro-teaching in the methods course. We found all participants, to varying degrees, appropriated more sophisticated epistemological views of how models, theory and evidence are used in scientific inquiry. These ideas ultimately *supported a shift in their goals for scientific investigation*—from "proving" a hypothesis, to testing and revising generalizable models.

Other ideas and practices, however, were not unproblematically appropriated. Scientific argument, for example, was rarely incorporated into participants' day-to-day discourse. While the majority of participants were eventually able to conduct independent inquiries and construct scientific arguments that coordinated their data with conjectured theoretical mechanisms, the regular use of argument as a specialized form of rhetoric was not evident during the course. A second example of conceptual stasis involves participants who could not "let go" of the idea of the scientific method. Some of these individuals spoke in terms of the scientific method being a separate enterprise from model-testing, while others saw the scientific method as the data-gathering core of activity within the larger model-testing process. During student teaching, more than half prompted their own students to use models, explicitly or implicitly, to make predictions, connect observations with underlying explanatory processes, and refine scientific ideas. Their pre- and post-course ratings of understanding models were roughly predictive of the degree of sophistication they employed in using model-based instruction with young learners.

The second phase of our study involved induction, during their first year of professional work, that was focused on the collaborative analyses of pupil work. We tested the hypothesis that novices in their first year of teaching could take up forms of ambitious pedagogy under the following conditions: 1) that a defined set of reform-based pedagogical practices introduced in teacher preparation would be the focus of sustained self-inquiry throughout the first year of teaching, 2) that participants use the analysis of their own pupils' work as the basis of critique and change in practice, and 3) that special tools be employed that help participants use a common frame of reference for hypothesizing about relationships between instructional decisions and student performance.

These special tools included a rubric that defined increasingly sophisticated levels of student performance in key areas of reform-based learning, and a protocol for guiding discussions during the collaborative examination of pupil learning artifacts. Over the course of their first year of teaching, *more than a third of the participants developed elements of expertlike teaching*, with the greatest gains made in pressing their students for evidence-based scientific explanations— a practice that *they* chose as the focus of their regular examination of student work (buy-in was important here, we pressed them a bit in this direction). This subset of participants held to the most problematized (i.e. sophisticated) images of the relationships between teaching and learning. This orientation influenced how they selected and analyzed their students' work, how they framed dilemmas to peers, and the degree to which they were able to participate in pedagogically productive discussions of practice during the collaborative analyses of pupil work. Despite variances in participation, most individuals in the study regularly taught in more reform-based ways than their curricula required them to during student teaching and their first year of professional work.

For a majority of participants, the system of tools (rubrics and protocol) was critical in allowing deep analyses of students' work and supporting a shared language that catalyzed conversations linking "what counts" as scientific explanation with the re-calibration of expectations for students, which in turn helped them envision more specialized forms of scaffolding for learners. On one level, the structure and language of the rubric allowed participants to see evidence of understanding in pupil work and to mediate understandings with peers (and in some cases their own students) about high-level expectations for learning science. On another level, when used together with the protocol during the collaborative analysis sessions, these tools pressed participants to be accountable for understanding science ideas they were trying to teach and for understanding the thinking represented in student work. This research indicates that pre-service and first year teachers are capable of productively analyzing student work. Furthermore, these analyses can play a significant role in helping some early career teachers achieve expert-like classroom performances. We also found, however, that the nature of individuals' participation in systems of tool-based practices reflected their underlying assumptions of what counts as learning and what counts as good teaching. Those who held a more a problematized view of the relationships between teaching and learning were not only more likely to engage early in more skilled teaching, but also to benefit more from evidence-based collaborative inquiry into practice. This kind of "professional momentum" was more difficult to achieve for those beginning their careers with simplified conceptions of teaching and learning. Another clear finding from this study: *Unless participants were able to identify big ideas* (fundamental underlying models for phenomena) in common curricula and consider how to begin teaching these ideas as models, *all other elements of reform-based teaching were much less likely to be enacted.* This suggests that special forms of content knowledge are important to teaching 21st Century skills and the ability to reason pedagogically *with* these forms of content knowledge is equally important.

We are currently exploring the links between our findings and the emerging theoretical construct of *adaptive expertise for teachers*. The most sophisticated early career teachers in our study exhibited many of the characteristics of adaptive expertise listed in the literature (cognitive flexibility, monitoring their own learning, striving for innovation). Similarly, our struggling teachers fit the profile of routine practitioners (seeking efficiencies, satisficing, etc.). Whether or not this theory of expertise can be used as a tool to stimulate individuals to grow into an adaptive stance to teaching, it does appear that *teaching for 21st Century skills will require teachers to become adaptive experts* and become proficient at the skills themselves.

Recommendations

Despite the lack of a substantial knowledge base in teacher preparation and professional development, some recommendations are warranted by the evidence. Let us summarize and recommend a specific suite of tools that may help efforts at fostering reform-based teaching.

Teacher preparation. The broad characteristics of effective teacher education programs have already been articulated. The following recommendations relate to science-specific preparation.

1. Science content preparation should not simply be a sampling of undergraduate courses whose content has no unifying threads (i.e. not integrated). An undergraduate major should be a coherent, connected experience. This could be accomplished by identifying and coordinating fundamental ideas that tie together all the courses in the major and by requiring some capstone experience in the major that synthesizes not only the content of the major, but the methodological and epistemological framework that guides contemporary inquiry in that domain.

2. In teacher education programs, all secondary science teachers should participate in science-specific methods courses that include regular opportunities to engage in the kinds of reform pedagogy described by the *National Science Education Standards*, and the intellectual work characterized by the 21st Century skills.
3. During practice teaching, pre-service teachers should be placed in schools with cooperating teachers who practice reform-based instruction, are competent with meaningful inquiry work and fostering 21st Century skills, and understand how to use all forms of assessment to give feedback to students and modify instruction. Also, cooperating teachers should understand how to scaffold novices as they try out these practices themselves.

Induction. The first two years of teachers' professional work should be supported by subject-specific mentoring and collaborative work that focuses primarily on student learning and its connections to instruction, rather than focusing on management issues or locating classroom materials. There should be opportunities for the regular analyses of pupil work with a group of colleagues sharing the same reform goals. This analysis should focus on high-leverage, reform-based practices, such as supporting students' attempts at evidence-based explanations of scientific phenomena or other forms of non-routine problem solving.

Professional development. The following characterizes elements of high quality continuing support for science teachers:

1. The collective and collaborative participation by teachers from the same school, grade, or subject areas.
2. The collective development of an "inquiry stance" towards practice.
3. Active learning opportunities that focus on science content, scientific practice, and evidence of student learning.
4. Coherence of the professional development with teachers' existing knowledge, other development activities, with existing curriculum, and with standards in local contexts.

New forms of tools and resources for teaching 21st Century skills. In addition to the broad recommendations above, teacher preparation, induction, and professional development would benefit from whole suites of tools to get novices to purposefully move their practice towards new kinds of expertise.

I say this because, as mentioned previously, the kind of teaching required to foster 21st Century skills is a radical transformation of what is accepted as "good instruction" today. Specifically, 21st Century instruction:

- is unlike instruction that most teachers and teacher educators have participated in or witnessed
- is underspecified (i.e. lacks detailed performance language that can act as a guide for planning, execution and reflection on teaching)
- is discourse intensive, requiring understanding of different "genres" of productive talk that, taken as a system, facilitates problem-solving by students
- places many learning decisions and activities in the hands of students that were formerly determined by the teacher
- places equal emphasis on learning subject matter, learning how to problem-solve with others, and learning how to learn
- depends upon the skilled monitoring of student thinking about complex problems or inquiries and relies as well on on-going targeted feedback to students.

The tools we need include:

1. A set of *representations of practice* for what these reform-based teaching approaches look like, enacted in a variety of classrooms at different levels of sophistication. These representations could take the form of learning progressions for teaching 21st Century skills, and video cases that richly contextualize examples of reform-based teaching found in the learning progression.
2. Tools to help teachers understand *how to identify "big ideas"* in curricula and how to treat those ideas as testable, revisable, generalizable models with students. This might be a standalone tool or it could be incorporated into curricula itself. Davis & Krajcik have used the term "educative curriculum" to describe *teaching materials that teachers can learn from.* They maintain that it is crucial for curriculum developers to design materials that support science teaching practice by embedding features that are explicitly educative for teachers who use these materials. Davis and Krajcik found that educative curricula helped pre-service as well as experienced teachers learn to employ principles of inquiry-oriented science instruction over time and across settings.

3. *Rubrics that help teachers imagine and assess "cases of student performance"* in different areas of reform-based learning. These rubrics could describe student performances in several key 21st Century skill areas, for example, "students select key pieces of a complex idea to express in words, sounds, and images, in order to build shared understanding", "use expert thinking to examine a broad span of information, recognize patterns, and narrow the information to reach a diagnosis of the problem", or "understand how an entire system works, how an action, change, or malfunction in one part of the system affects the rest of the system; adopting a "big picture" perspective on work." These student activities currently are underspecified and lack the kinds of contextualization that would help teachers make sense of then as part of their imagined practice.
4. *Discourse tools to help teachers mediate new forms of learning* that go beyond transmitting information to students. These discourse tools could provide general sequences of questions or prompts that experienced teachers use, along with common patterns of students' responses, and schemes for capitalizing on these responses to help students achieve particular intellectual goals. Our own research has identified a lack of whole-class discourse skills as a major impediment for new teachers attempting reform-based instruction. For example, we are currently developing discourse tools for "eliciting students' conceptions about science ideas," "pressing students for evidence-based explanations," and others.
5. *Collaborative analysis routines and tools to help teachers learn with each other from their own practice.* These would include protocols for selecting and analyzing student work, relevant to reform science and/or 21st Century skills, and for meeting in groups to link evidence of student learning to one's practice.

These tools will likely work together in more powerful ways than they can work individually.

These are not recommendations, but reminders of the scope of the challenge of re-envisioning science education for the future.

1. Reform-based teaching practice or practices that can foster 21st Century skills are rare in classrooms in part because they are under-specified for practitioners—and rare on another level because they call for a

fundamentally different vision of "what counts" as learning than do traditional forms of instruction.

2. Learning to teach competently depends upon a years-long continuum of experiences that cohere conceptually and build upon one another.
3. Throughout this continuum, it is most productive for teachers to be focused on recognizing and strategically fostering student learning in the forms of deep conceptual understanding of core scientific ideas and engagement with authentic scientific practices—not merely managing classroom experiences (e.g. labs) for students or exposing them to well-defined scientific ideas.
4. Throughout early learning-to-teach contexts (coursework in teacher preparation programs, student teaching, the induction years), novices should be brought up within a culture of evidence-based decision-making about the design of instruction, using student performance artifacts and other records of practice as the basis for the refinement of teaching.
5. Preparing teachers to engage in reform-based instruction and foster 21st Century skills will require systemic changes in order to be successful, tying together new visions of undergraduate preparation, teacher preparation, professional development standards and the re-conceptualization of K-12 curricula.

References

Abd-El-Khalick, F., Bell, R. L., & Lederman, N. G.. The nature of science and instructional practice: Making the unnatural natural. *Science Education*, 82, 417 – 436.

Berliner, D.C.. Learning about and learning from expert teachers. *International Journal of Educational Research*, 35(5), 463-483.

Carlsen, W. S.. Effects of new biology teachers' subject matter knowledge on curricular planning. *Science Education*, 75, 631-647.

Fullan, M.. *Change forces: Probing the depths of educational reform*. Bristol, PA: Falmer Press.

Luft, J. (in press). Beginning science teachers in different induction programs: The first year of teaching. *International Journal of Science Education*.

Mortimer, E. & Scott, P.. *Meaning making in secondary science classrooms. Philadelphia*: Open University Press.

Veenman, S, & Denessen, E.. The coaching of teachers: Results of five training studies. *Educational Research and Evaluation*, 7(4), 385-417.

5

Transforming Education for Modern Society

The 21st century seems quite different than the 20th in the capabilities people need for work, citizenship, and self-actualization. In response, society's educational systems must transform their objectives, curricula, pedagogies, and assessments to help all students attain the sophisticated outcomes requisite for a prosperous, attractive lifestyle based on effective contributions in work and citizenship. As discussed later, this and similar initiatives towards transforming schooling for the 21st century can leverage large scale investments external to education in U. S. economic development for global competitiveness and federally funded "cyberinfrastructure" for advanced research.

What can scholars say to society and its educational systems about core "21st Century Skills" students must master? Clearly, this descriptor, used by many groups providing advice on the topic of schooling for the 21st century, is an attention-getting misnomer; we can not reasonably predict the capabilities people will routinely use in 2095 any more than a comparable group of scholars in 1907 could have accurately forecast the competencies central to the workplace, citizenship and self-actualization in 1995. Thus, what we are really attempting to discern is the core capabilities people will need in the first part of the 21st century – say fifteen to thirty years hence – to qualify for an attractive, prosperous job and lifestyle.

Many frameworks for educational objectives in the 21st century distinguish between *knowledge* and *skills* and list examples of each, using the overarching descriptor of "21st Century Skills." However, a distinction between knowledge and skills is problematic. Research in cognitive science has established that knowledge and skills are richly intertwined, rather than knowledge as content on which skills act as a process. For example, applying mathematics as a perspective on understanding the world requires recognizing situations in which mathematical models might apply. This is neither a process-free content nor a content-devoid process, but a complex knowledge-skill mixture, an "understanding." Categorizing what students need for the 21st century as *understandings* based on interwoven content knowledge and process skills is a more accurate depiction of how the mind works than the separation between these that current frameworks typically impose, and how students actualize those understandings in practice are *performances*. So, this study uses the terms understandings and performances rather than knowledge or skills.

Research to Incite Strategic Planning

The fundamental goal of futures research and strategic planning is to aid individuals and organizations in managing complexity and uncertainty in their external environments over time. Futures research is oriented to articulating the long-range external forces that affect individuals, organizations, and societies; strategic planning deals with internal institutional goal setting, resource allocation, and monitoring of progress across multi-year time horizons. "21st Century Skills" is a conceptual construct developed through futures research and used by advocacy groups to incite effective strategic planning among stakeholders in education.

Ultimately, the single future that occurs is invented through the interaction of structural certainties (e.g., demographic forces), social-contractual assurances (such as cultural patterns), wild cards (e.g., natural disasters, terrorist acts), human choices, and indeterminacies. The predictions below about the workplace in 2022 are conservative in that the future is seen as largely determined by major trends in the present; in this respect, the vision presented is less sophisticated than a forecast. A prediction portrays the future as like a train track leading us to a predestined outcome for which we must prepare. In contrast, a forecast depicts the future as like a tree: one trunk (the past and present), with many branches (alternative futures). In this model of the future, individuals and institutions are like ants crawling up the trunk toward the branches, moving through the present to the future. Decisions made in the present strengthen and weaken various branches (fortify and undermine possibilities) because the choices not made are constrained as alternatives; by the time our present becomes our future, only one branch is left (the new trunk). While more sophisticated than trend-based predictions as a basis for strategic planning, a forecast of civilization in 2022 is too complex both conceptually and politically to serve as a basis for conceptualizing 21st century understandings and performances. Using the predictions below is likely accurate enough to serve as a reasonable basis for educational decision making.

Impacts of ICT on Society

The first observation is that the capabilities of computers and related technologies have repeatedly expanded since these devices were first developed in the 1940s: from numerical calculators to data processors, to productivity enhancers, to information managers, to communications channels, to pervasive media for individual and collective expression, experience, and interpretation. The kinds of personal expression enabled by sites such as MySpace and YouTube, the rich array of entertainment experiences available through massively multi-player Internet games such as World of Warcraft and America's Army, and the types of collective knowledge creation enabled by wikis and social tagging tools such as Edtags.org all illustrate this ongoing evolution of ICT. Many sectors of the economy are now in the process of developing and actualizing business strategies based on how people now use ICT as a means of individual and collective expression, experience, and interpretation.

Lagging behind other sectors of society, current approaches to using technology in schooling largely reflect applying ICT as a means of increasing the effectiveness of traditional instructional approaches: enhancing productivity through tools such as word processors, aiding communication by channels such as email and threaded asychronous discussions, and expanding access to information via Web-browsers and streaming video. All these have proven worthy in conventional schooling, as they have in workplace settings; however, none draw on the full power of ICT for individual and collective expression, experience, and interpretation – human capabilities emerging as core work and life skills for the first part of the 21st century.

The second observation about the impacts of ICT on society is that cognition is now distributed across human minds, tools/media, groups of people, and space/time. Further, the types of representations available in mediated interaction (e.g., immersive simulations, non-linear conceptual maps) are richer and more nuanced than those possible in face-to-face settings without ICT. For example, a class can discuss geography using Google Earth as a common referent in a more sophisticated way than through utilizing paper maps. Because of advanced computers and telecommunications, the process of individual and collective thought in civilization is increasingly dispersed symbolically, socially, and physically.

For better or for worse, entertainment and human interaction are delocalizing as well. People who share the same dwelling may have very different personal communities as their major sources of sociability, support, information, a sense of belonging, and social identity, as contrasted to the historic pattern of lifestyles centered on face-to-face groups interacting with local resources. Our great-grandparents would see our lifestyle as bizarre – "electronic nomads wandering among virtual campfires" – yet in counterpoint many youth today see prior generations as hapless prisoners of geography, trapped in the limits of a single physical location. Given that distributed thought, action, and sociability show no signs of receding, formal education should prepare people to achieve their full potential as workers and citizens in this emerging, novel, intellectual and psychosocial context, avoiding its weaknesses and traps while maximizing its strengths and opportunities. The third observation about the impacts of ICT on society is that the types of work done by people as opposed to the kinds of labor done by machines are continually shifting as computers and telecommunications expand their capabilities to accomplish human tasks. Economists Frank Levy and Richard Murnane have documented a very important aspect of what constitutes 21st century understandings and performances:

Declining portions of the labor force are engaged in jobs that consist primarily of routine cognitive work and routine manual labor—the types of tasks that are easiest to program computers to do. Growing proportions of the nation's labor force are engaged in jobs that emphasize expert thinking or complex communication—tasks that computers cannot do. These economists go on to explain that "expert thinking [involves] effective pattern matching based on detailed knowledge; and metacognition, the set of skills used by the stumped expert to decide when to give up on one strategy and what to try next". What a skilled auto mechanic does when all diagnostic systems show normal functioning, but the car is still malperforming is expert decision making: inventing new problem solving heuristics when all standard strategies have failed. "Complex communication requires the exchange of vast amounts of verbal and nonverbal information. The information flow is constantly adjusted as the communication evolves unpredictably". A skilled teacher is an expert in complex communication, able to improvise answers and facilitate dialogue in the unpredictable, chaotic flow of classroom discussion.

Education should prepare students for a world in which almost all types of routine cognitive tasks are done by computers and in which expert thinking and complex communications are the core intellectual capabilities by which people attain prosperity and economic security individually, as a region, and as a nation. These higher order performances are based on fundamental knowledge about how to do simpler types of work, so the shift needed is not to remove the learning of routine cognitive skills (such as basic arithmetic operations) from the curriculum. Rather, the fundamental change involves deemphasizing fluency in simple procedures as an end-goal of preparation for work and life (e.g., counting bills as a bank teller), instead using these routine skills as a substrate for mastering complex mental performances valued in the future workplace, such as advising clients about global investment strategies tailored to their individual situations.

In this enterprise of predicting the mid-range future, I do not assume any major technological advances not yet achieved, such as a substantial leap forward in artificial intelligence. Instead, I build my analysis on the continued evolution of sophisticated ICT that are not creative or smart in comparison to humans, but are increasingly adept at accomplishing "routine" tasks. How difficult in 2007 is developing predictions about the effects on civilization of ICT in 2022 and beyond, a period during which today's students are assuming roles of responsibility in society? The equivalent in recent history would be describing in 1992 the impact of computers and telecommunications in 2007. In the early 1990s – before the WorldwideWeb, universal email, digital telephony, massively multi-user virtual environments, and similar civilization-wide advances – scholars did accurately articulate many of the shifts in society we see today. However, very few people predicted some important changes, such as sociosemantic networking, and many "futurist" forecasts were unrealized.

Early 21st Century Trends

Thus far, the 21st century has seen a dramatic shift in the economic model for industrialized countries. Systems of economic development based on geography, trade rules, and tariffs; slow dissemination of scientific and technological discoveries; and long cycles of product life have given way to global trade, rapid product innovation, the lowering of trade barriers, rapid dissemination of scientific and technological discovery, and rapid global deployment and movement of capital and the means of production. In the early 21st century, income and wealth come from applying technology and new ideas to create new products and processes. Adding value to products and processes is the key to growing jobs and incomes in this new economic environment.

Competitive advantage for a region, state, or nation is now built on the skills of its general workforce, as opposed to its geography, trade laws, research labs, and patents; and critical to that competitive advantage are the education and skills training adults acquire in primary and secondary schools. In this new economic environment—the New Economy—education plays a critical role in maintaining national prosperity and stimulating economic growth. The level of workforce skills and the periodic need to update those skills are both steadily rising, with no end in sight.

The New Economy is driven by entrepreneurs, technology, and innovation. Novel ideas, discoveries, and technologies have produced whole new industries and products; innovation is now the primary basis for income and wealth generation. Globalization has forced business to drive rapid technological change into the very core of business operations and processes. Early efforts to improve productivity in business were aimed at applying technology to administrative and processing applications, such as purchasing, accounting, and payroll. These applications of technology changed the speed of work, but not the fundamental nature of work. As the New Economy took hold, the complexity of business dramatically increased. Global markets, just-in-time manufacturing and product fulfillment, outsourcing, lean manufacturing, and other changes forced fundamental changes in the nature and complexity of work. ICT applied to the core functions of business resulted in huge gains in productivity and the ability to manage and solve complex problems.

Another way in which ICT are changing the nature of the jobs for which schooling prepares its graduates is the increasing importance of "offshoring":

geographic shifts of comparative advantage in various types of economic production. For example, over the last couple centuries comparative advantage in textile manufacturing has geographically shifted from England to New England to the Carolinas to China and other low-wage countries; with each change, workers and employers in the region losing jobs were surprised and angered. In the 21st century, as ICT grow in power, geographic regions are exporting with comparative advantage not just manufactured goods, but also services, such as being a call-center operator.

Whether or not employers can import a service from outside their local region is not determined by whether the job is high-skill, high-education (e.g., doctor) or low-skill, low education (such as a security guard). Rather, the determining factor is whether the service is deliverable electronically without substantial diminution in quality (for example, securities analysis), or not (e.g., taxi drivers, airline pilots). Blinder terms these "impersonally delivered services" and "personally delivered services"; over time, advances in ICT will increase the proportion of jobs falling into the former category. Thus, for students to select a career and for countries to choose an economic development path that will lead to a prosperous, secure lifestyle is much more complex now than in prior generations because the division of labor and the location of work are both rapidly shifting.

Because the predictions above are based on economic trends in the initial years of the 21st century, they likely underestimate the degree to which work skills and conditions will alter compared to the late 20th Century. In particular, as discussed later, the impacts of emerging ICT on society (individual and collective expression, experience, and interpretation; distributed cognition and action; erosion of routine tasks in favor of expert decision making and complex communications skills) are probably understated. Forecasts of technology-based paradigm shifts tend to overestimate how quickly change will occur and to underestimate the impact of the alterations. This precept likely applies to our attempt to predict the 21st century capabilities today's students will need in workplaces a generation from now.

Employers Seek in 21st Century Workers

Numerous reports on the global, knowledge-based economy and the "flat" world document that tomorrow's workers must be prepared to shift jobs and careers more frequently, to be flexible and adaptable in acquiring job skills, and to integrate and focus a changing mix of job-derived and education-based knowledge on business processes and problems. The application of information technology to the very core of business operations has caused a profound change in the needed skills and talents of New Economy workers. Markets in the New Economy are rewarding those who have high educational achievement and technical skill. The worker of the 21st century must have science and mathematics skills, creativity, fluency in information and communication technologies, and the ability to solve complex problems. As the global economy continues to evolve, predictions are that workers will change jobs seven or eight times during their work life. To be competitive in this constant churn, workers will have to engage in lifelong learning to update their education and job skills. Clearly, the future personal economic security and well-being of American workers is tied to educational achievement.

Yet much of U.S. education is still based on the premise that economic processes and institutions will mirror those in the 20th century. Students are prepared to be future employees of business organizations now rapidly becoming obsolete. Current trends suggest that more students will run their own businesses rather than work for others and as adults must constantly, quickly, and efficiently learn new skills and information to be effective entrepreneurs. In this respect, the workplace forecasts above likely overstate the importance of skills as employees and understate the creativity, flexibility, and strong sense of self-efficacy today's youth will need to assume roles of economic leadership, rather than serving as followers for a few "captains of industry."

Thus, a crucial challenge for U.S. education is to align curriculum and learning to a whole new economic model based on an emerging global, knowledge-based workplace. To accomplish this we must transform children's learning processes in and out of school and engage student interest in gaining 21st century skills and knowledge. Linking economic development, educational evolution, workforce development, and strengthened social services is essential to meeting this challenge.

However, all those other responsibilities are possible only if education succeeds in providing the foundation for a prosperous national future. This does not mean that education for economic development is privileged more than other objectives. Nonetheless, those who want education to succeed in resolving major concerns (e.g., equity, moral citizenship, self-realization) need to incorporate perspectives about preparation for 21st century work into their planning.

Conceptual Framework for 21st Century Skills

Before articulating 21st century understandings and performances that seem central in light of these workplace shifts, developing a contextualized conceptual framework for these core capabilities is necessary. Part of that framework requires stipulating the metrics by which we judge whether, to merit inclusion, a human performance is truly significant in its projected importance to attaining an attractive, prosperous job and lifestyle – and sufficiently different from "20th Century Skills" to merit special attention. Determining the *degree* to which the capability is valuable in work and citizenship is key to these metrics, as is distinguishing in *kind* between "perennial" and "contextual" performances.

For example, "collaboration" is a perennial capability, always valued as a trait in workplaces across the centuries; as such, the basic value of this interpersonal performance is not intrinsically special to our emerging economic context. Arguably, however, the *degree* of importance for collaborative capacity is growing in an era where work is increasingly done by teams of people with complementary expertise and roles, as opposed to individuals doing manual operations on an assembly line. Thus, even though perennial in nature, collaboration is worthy of inclusion as a 21st century performance because, for the context in which today's students will function as adults, the importance of cooperative interpersonal capabilities is substantially higher than in the prior industrial era.

In contrast, the ability to rapidly filter huge amounts of incoming data, extracting information valuable for decision making, is arguably a "contextual" capability. Due to the prevalence of ICT, for the first time in human history people are inundated by enormous amounts of data that they must access, manage, integrate, and evaluate. The ability to separate signal from noise in a potentially overwhelming flood of incoming data is arguably a 21st century performance not in degree – because this is novel in history as a valuable capability – but in *kind.* This distinction is important because, unlike perennial capabilities, new types of human performances are typically not part of the legacy curriculum inherited from 20th century educational systems.

A Framework of Omission as Well as Commission

Another part of the contextualized conceptual framework for 21st century performances is more politically controversial, yet vital: What do we deemphasize in current instruction and assessment to make room for 21st century understandings? At present the dominant model for what the curriculum should contain is the federal No Child Left Behind (NCLB) Act, supported by both major political parties and the general public and based on "test-to-standard" strategies. Under NCLB, state content standards are developed by disciplinary experts, professional organizations, and various forms of interest groups; high-stakes tests document whether or not students are learning some subset of that content; and individual students, teachers, schools, and districts are rewarded or punished based solely on test performance. In practice, because states' high-stakes psychometric tests are typically based on multiple-choice and short-answer items that have no mechanism for assessing attainment of higher order understandings and performances, 21st century competences embedded in state curriculum standards are buried in a mass of lower-level material and generally ignored in day-to-day teaching. The curriculum is crowded with low-level facts and recipe-like procedures (e.g., In what year did Columbus discover America? What are the seven steps of historical inquiry?), as opposed to nuanced understandings and performances (i.e., What confluence of technological, economic, and political forces led to the age of exploration around the end of the 15th century? By what process of interpretating of historical data did you reach this conclusion?).

Even though the concept of standards, assessments, and accountability makes sense at a fundamental level, current policies for improving educational achievement based on this concept have many problems from the perspective of preparing today's children for tomorrow's world (Dede, 2005a). For example, current content standards are based on disciplinary "silos" that do not incorporate metrics of contextual value based on degree and kind. Physics experts indicate what pre-college students need to know if they eventually plan to be physicists, historians determine what pupils must master if they are to become professional historians, and so on. This has led to a huge tangle of content and skills that U.S. educators are mandated to cover in just 12 years—an impossible task! Further, much of what is taught within a subject is only useful to the small subset of students who plan to focus on that particular field in college; state curriculum standards in each discipline are typically neither interrelated nor prioritized to emphasize core understandings and performances all students will need to succeed in the 21st century. While attempts at integration and prioritization are made in national standards from professional organizations like the American Association for the Advancement of Science or the National Council for the Teaching of Mathematics, in practice this level of understandings and performances is ignored in classroom teaching because the high-stakes tests provide no vehicle for measuring student progress on them.

Because of the accountability systems built into this model of educational reform, teachers are using weak but rapid instructional methods, such as lecture and drill-and-practice, to race through the glut of recipes, facts, and test-taking skills they are expected to cover. Despite research indicating that guided inquiry, collaborative learning, mentoring, and apprenticeships are far more effective pedagogical strategies, introducing these into school settings is difficult given the crowded curriculum and the need to prepare students for high stakes tests. Simply delivering required information for students' passive absorption takes every second of instructional time. Teachers have no means by which to prioritize what understandings and performances to emphasize in terms of 21st century citizenship; workplace capabilities for the global, knowledge-based economy; and lifelong learning.

Among all these problems, the biggest single issue is that the first generation of high-stakes tests that our nation is using to determine students' educational outcomes has substantial flaws. These are summative, "drive-by" tests, which provide no diagnostic, just-in-time feedback that could help teachers aid struggling students. In addition, while some assessments emphasize on core ideas and measure at least a few higher-order thinking skills, many state legislatures have allocated such limited resources for test development that the resulting instruments often measure only a random assortment of low-level skills and content, rather than core, higher-order 21st century understandings and performances. In addition, policies such as financial incentives for teachers and districts to raise test scores can exacerbate already troubling differences in educational outcomes, promoting the abandonment of the very at-risk students the NCLB legislation was intended to help.

Yet this reform movement still has strong bipartisan support and widespread backing from the public. Under these circumstances, a contextualized framework must take on the political challenge of arguing what to deemphasize in the curriculum – and why – in order to make room for students to deeply master core 21st century understandings and performances. This is not a situation in we must eliminate an equivalent amount of current curriculum for each 21st century understanding added, because better pedagogical methods can lead to faster mastery and improved retention, enabling less reteaching and more coverage within the same timeframe. However, what education should emphasize as its core outcomes is politically controversial even if substantial sections of the 20th century legacy curriculum are not eliminated.

Downgrading the importance of some material in the current curriculum is much harder than adding content and skills because omission involves "unlearning." A major challenge in professional development is helping teachers, policy makers, and local communities *unlearn* the beliefs, values, assumptions, and cultures underlying schools' standard operating practices, such as forty-five minute class periods that allow insufficient time for all but superficial forms of active learning by students. Altering deeply ingrained and strongly reinforced rituals of schooling takes more than the superficial interchanges typical in "make and take" professional development or school board meetings. Intellectual, emotional, and social support is essential for "unlearning" and for transformational relearning that can lead to deeper behavioral changes to create next-generation educational practices. Educators, business executives, politicians, and the general public have much to unlearn if 21st century understandings are to assume a central place in schooling.

21ST Century Understandings

If we use the conceptual framework delineated above to apply the three observations about impacts of sophisticated ICT on society (individual and collective expression, experience, and interpretation; distributed cognition and action; erosion of routine tasks in favor of expert decision making and complex communications capabilities) to predictions about the emerging global, knowledge-based economy, what insights emerge about 21st century understandings? In particular, which 21st century performances are most crucial to emphasize, from the perspective of both importance and relative neglect in the curriculum at present? In the current frameworks of the Partnership for 21st Century Skills and similar initiatives, which core understandings are omitted or underemphasized? Which parts of contemporary instruction should we deemphasize to make room for deep mastery of 21st century performances? Conducting a comprehensive analysis of the entire school curriculum from this perspective is beyond the scope of this chapter. What follows illustrates such an analysis on one aspect of the 21st century understandings and performances students should learn, including novel methods for teaching and assessing these competencies.

In current conceptual formulations and instructional practices a neglected cluster of 21st century performances relates to "collective problem resolution via mediated interaction." In 21st century work, knowledge is grounded in a setting and distributed across a community, rather than abstract and isolated within individuals. Problem *finding* (the front-end of the inquiry process: making observations and inferences, developing hypotheses, and conducting experiments to test alternative interpretations of the situation) is crucial to reaching a point where the work team can do problem solving. Individual and collective metacognitive strategies for making meaning out of complexity (such as making judgments about the value of alternative problem formulations) are vital.

Each person involved has strong strategies in effective pattern matching based on detailed knowledge and in judging when to give up on a particular problem solving strategy and what to try next. Individuals on the work team are adept at manipulating sophisticated ICT applications and representations utilized within the complementary perspectives they bring to bear (e.g., using a spreadsheet to examine financial hypotheticals). They also are skilled in expressing core insights from their knowledge to others who have different backgrounds and experiences. Richly interactive complex communication among team members is not limited to face-to-face dialogue, but frequently relies on mediated interaction across distance in which the team co-constructs and negotiates shared interpretive understandings and a problem resolution strategy.

For example, a school district might task a team of teachers, school administrators, parents, and local business executives to develop a plan for improving students' educational outcomes in mathematics. Potential factors leading to subpar educational performance include individual differences in native language, gender, culture, and socioeconomic status; teachers' experience and preparation in mathematical content, subject-specific pedagogy, classroom management, and student engagement; state and district policies related to educational reform, the curricular materials used in mathematics, and the capacity of the technology infrastructure at local schools, among others. Under these circumstances, individual and collective skills in problem finding, inquiry, metacognition, collaboration, expert decision making, complex communication, and use of ICT tools, communicative media, and representations are vital to the team's success.

Teaching 21st Century Understandings

The suite of interrelated 21st century understandings and performances described above is largely absent in current pedagogical practices. Conventional, 20th century K-12 instruction emphasizes manipulating pre-digested information to build fluency in routine problem solving, rather than filtering data derived from experiences in complex settings to develop skills in sophisticated problem finding. Knowledge is separated from skills and presented as revealed truth, not as an understanding that is discovered and constructed, resulting in learning about rather than learning to do. Also, problem solving skills are presented in an abstract form removed from their application to knowledge; this makes transfer to real world situations difficult. The ultimate objective of education is presented as learning a specific problem solving routine to match every work situation, rather than developing expert decision making and metacognitive strategies that indicate how to proceed when no standard approach seems applicable.

Little time is spent on building capabilities in group interpretation, negotiation of shared meaning, and co-construction of problem resolutions. The communication skills stressed are those of simple presentation, rather than the capacity to engage in richly structured interactions that articulate perspectives unfamiliar to the audience. As discussed earlier, ICT applications and representations are largely used to automate traditional methods of teaching and learning, rather to model complexity and express insights to others. Face-to-face communication is seen as the "gold standard," so students develop few capabilities in mediated dialogue and in shared design within a common virtual workspace.

The discussion above suggests the importance of embedding students' understandings in performances they can fluently accomplish. In the workplace, employees prove their worth through performances, based on understandings but instantiated in sophisticated behaviors. In effective job settings, performances are part of an organizational culture that includes the provision of requisite tools, respect for all occupational roles, rewards for leadership and innovation; employees are part of a sociocultural, situated community of practice. To prepare students for a prosperous and secure future, educators need to build not just understandings, but experiences in a community of practice that develops fluent, sophisticated behaviors – yet classrooms today typically lack this type of learning and teaching, in part because high-stakes tests do not assess these competencies.

Assessments and tests focus on measuring students' fluency in various abstract, routine skills, but typically do not assess their strategies for expert decision making when no standard approach seems applicable. Essays emphasize simple presentation rather than sophisticated forms of rhetorical interaction. Students' abilities to transfer their understandings to real world situations are not assessed, nor are capabilities related to various aspects of teamwork. The use of ICT applications and representations is generally banned from testing, rather than measuring students' capacities to use tools, applications, and media effectively. Abilities to effectively utilize various forms of mediated interaction are typically not assessed.

Beyond these deficiencies in conventional practices of instruction and assessment, current conceptual formulations of 21st century understandings tend to underemphasize the interrelated nature of the capabilities described above. In contrast to the analysis above, typical lists of "21st Century Skills" may mention each individual aspect described above somewhere, but the capabilities students need are typically not discussed in terms of degree and kind, not presented as understandings that interweave content knowledge and process skills, not clustered into related suites of performances, and not prioritized in terms of relative neglect in the typical curriculum at present. 21st century initiatives should demonstrate to other groups how to evolve "next generation" curriculum standards and assessments by modeling a sophisticated development process and contextual framework that includes advice about what to deemphasize in current instructional practice as part of the "road maps" presented about how to actualize these initiatives.

21st Century Understandings and ICT Tools

An easy way to understand the role of information technology in helping students learn a curriculum composed of understandings and performances, delivered via pedagogy, and evaluated through assessment is to see the tools, applications, media, and virtual environments used as instrumental. Information and communication technologies (ICT) aid with representing content, engaging learners, modeling skills, and assessing students' progress in a manner parallel to how a carpenter would use a saw, hammer, screwdriver, and wrench to help construct an artifact. The two key points in this analogy are (1) the tools make the job easier and (2) the result is of higher quality than possible without the tools. 20th century containers are insufficient for representing 21st century understandings and intellectual/ psychosocial performances.

Much of what distinguishes 21st century performances is that a person and a tool, application, medium, or environment work in concert to accomplish an objective unobtainable otherwise (e.g., remote collaboration via groupware among a problem finding team scattered across the globe). However, ICT are not mere mechanisms for attaining the desired behavior; through distributed cognition, the understandings they enable are intrinsic to the fluent performance. Frameworks that discuss new "literacies" that are based on the evolution of ICT help to illuminate this aspect of 21st century learning.

For example, Jenkins and his colleagues delineate a set of novel literacies based on new media:

Play — the capacity to experiment with one's surroundings as a form of problem-solving

Performance — the ability to adopt alternative identities for the purpose of improvisation and discovery

Simulation — the ability to interpret and construct dynamic models of real-world processes

Appropriation — the ability to meaningfully sample and remix media content

Multitasking — the ability to scan one's environment and shift focus as needed to salient details.

Distributed Cognition — the ability to interact meaningfully with tools that expand mental capacities

Collective Intelligence — the ability to pool knowledge and compare notes with others toward a common goal

Judgment — the ability to evaluate the reliability and credibility of different information sources

Transmedia Navigation — the ability to follow the flow of stories and information across multiple modalities

Networking — the ability to search for, synthesize, and disseminate information

Negotiation — the ability to travel across diverse communities, discerning and respecting multiple perspectives, and grasping and following alternative norms

While these are presented as knowledge-independent skills rather than understandings, they illustrate how 21st century behaviors, such as collective problem-resolution via mediated interaction, are based on the capabilities of emerging interactive media.

Dede describes the types of learning strengths, styles and preferences "neomillennial" students acquire from their use of immersive collaborative media, such as multiplayer online games:

- Fluency in multiple media, valuing each for the types of communication, activities, experiences, and expressions it empowers.
- Learning based on collectively seeking, sieving, and synthesizing experiences, rather than individually locating and absorbing information from some single best source.
- Active learning based on experience (real and simulated) that includes frequent opportunities for reflection.
- Expression through non-linear, associational webs of representations rather than linear "stories" (e.g., authoring a simulation and a webpage to express understanding, rather than a paper).
- Co-design of learning experiences personalized to individual needs and preferences.

As discussed later, using immersive collaborative simulations in classroom settings offers a powerful method for building on these learning strengths and preferences to nurture 21st century understandings and performances.

Leu and his colleagues (in press) describe four characteristics of the "new literacies" generated by ICT. First, emerging ICT tools, applications, media, and environments require novel skills, strategies, and dispositions for their effective use. Second, new literacies are central to full economic, civic, and personal participation in a globalized society. Third, new literacies constantly evolve as their defining ICT continuously are renewed through innovation. Fourth, new literacies are multiple, multimodel, and multifaceted.

Leu's third point raises important issues about stability: How durable are 21st century performances in their applicability to work, citizenship, and self-actualization? How quickly will additional, important 21st century understandings and behaviors emerge as ICT continue to evolve? Certainly, tools, applications, media and environments are changing rapidly, with no end in sight. Typically, despite predictions of paperless offices or the end of the book, this evolution involves adding additional literacies and understandings rather than new performances displacing previously useful behaviors. Examining predictions about the future of ICT helps to illuminate what these additional literacies may be and what knowledge and skills may become less useful over time, as well as showing how planned national investments in "cyberinfrastructure" can leverage transforming schooling for the 21st century.

Cyberinfrastructure in Learning and Teaching

In recent years, the National Science Foundation has championed a vision of the future of research that centers on "cyberinfrastructure": the integration of computing, data and networks, digitally-enabled sensors, observatories and experimental facilities, and an interoperable suite of software and middleware services and tools. Gains in computational speed, high-bandwidth networking, software development, databases, visualization tools, and collaboration platforms are reshaping the practices of scholarship and beginning to transform teaching (Dede, in press – a). Cyberinfrastructures developed for research purposes also create intriguing opportunities to transform work and education in ways that parallel the shifts advocated in this study.

During 2004-05, with NSF funding, four workshops attended by experts in education were convened by the Computing Research Association. The foci of these workshops were:

- Modeling, Simulation, and Gaming Technologies Applied to Education
- Cognitive Implications of Virtual or Web-enabled Environments
- How Emerging Technology and Cyberinfrastructure Might Revolutionize the Role of Assessment in Learning
- The Interplay between Communities of Learning or Practice and Cyberinfrastructure

Collectively, these groups envisioned a cyberinfrastructure that "provides: 1) unprecedented access to educational resources, mentors, experts, and online educational activities and virtual environments; 2) timely, accurate assessment of student learning; and 3) a platform for large-scale research on education and the sciences of learning... Moreover, the new educational cyberinfrastructure will make it possible to collect and analyze data continually from millions of educational activities nationwide over a period of years, enabling new advances in the sciences of learning and providing systematic ways of measuring progress at all levels".

The NSF Cyberinfrastructure Council provides a scenario of how advanced visualization and simulation capabilities could advance education:

> Imagine an interdisciplinary course in the design and construction of large public works projects, attracting student-faculty teams from different engineering disciplines, urban planning, environmental science, and economics; and from around the globe. To develop their understanding, the students combine relatively small self-contained digital simulations that capture both simple behavior and geometry to model more complex scientific and engineering phenomena. Modules share inputs and outputs and otherwise interoperate. These "building blocks" maintain sensitivity across multiple scales of phenomena. For example, component models of transportation subsystems from one site combine with structural and geotechnical models from other collections to simulate dynamic loading within a complex bridge and tunnel environment. Computational models from faculty research efforts are used to generate numerical data sets for comparison with data from physical observations of real transportation systems obtained from various (international) locations via access to remote instrumentation. Furthermore, learners explore influences on air quality and tap into the expertise of practicing environmental scientists through either real-time or asynchronous communication. This networked learning environment increases the impact and accessibility of all resources by allowing students to search for and discover content, to assemble curricular and learning modules from component pieces in a flexible manner, and to communicate and collaborate with others, leading to a deep change in the relationship between students and knowledge. Indeed, students experience the profound changes in the

> practice of science and engineering and the nature of inquiry that cyberinfrastructure provokes.

One could create comparable vignettes to illustrate educational opportunities in constellations of fields across the sciences and social sciences.

The Computing Research Association report on educational visions for cyberinfrastructure also presents a vignette of a "serious game":

> Learners cooperate in designing and conducting a mission to Mars, in the context of a game-based simulation. In the course of the project they carry out a variety of STEM-related learning activities, spanning physics, chemistry, biology, engineering and mathematics. These become springboards for seeking other learning resources outside the game, and collaborating with other learners in online working groups. Learners access online science and engineering data sets and models in order to compare their predictions against results from space scientists. They receive guidance in inquiry skills, metacognitive learning skills, and collaboration skills. The game itself is constructed and adapted through the collaborative efforts of the participating learners. In his earth sciences course, John, for example, studies terrain data from Mars Rover missions and creates a model of the Martian terrain to be explored by others. Manuela, in her high-school engineering class, designs an autonomous rover vehicle to collect geologic samples and constructs a simulation of her rover design for use in the mission. She can then compare her model's performance in the simulation against records of actual Mars Rover missions. Sherry, the teacher, is assisted by virtual assistant teachers (intelligent tutors) embedded in the game that help her monitor learner progress and offer guidance and challenges. One of Sherry's virtual assistants reports that Manuela is having difficulty getting the controller of her virtual robot to work, and is not availing herself of online resources, so Sherry suggests that she discuss her design with an online community of robot enthusiasts. Data collected from learner performance within and surrounding the game provide the teacher with documentation and evidence of learning progress relating to curriculum standards and goals. In some contexts this may replace the need for standardized tests, but in others the teacher already has sufficient evidence to predict that the learners will meet the required standards. These scenarios of educational cyberinfrastructure are "extreme" in the sense that every application of information and communications technologies (ICT) to learning is imagined as both effective and technologically/economically feasible. As such, these vignettes include a sophisticated set of competencies for the mid-range future.

These visions of cyberinfrastructure, set about fifteen years in the future, do not contain a discrepant set of 21st century understandings and performances from those discussed earlier in this chapter. The human capabilities envisioned for the evolution of high-level scientific research certainly are likely to encompass performances as advanced as any other 21st century work setting. If these predictions about emergent cyberinfrastructure are accurate, the sophisticated understandings described above that underlie 21st century work and citizenship will remain reasonably stable for the next generation of students. Moreover, the U.S. is committed to spending billions of dollars to implement ubiquitous technologies for research and education that will provide an infrastructure to aid in preparing students for 21st century society.

Emerging Technology for Classroom Settings

In classroom settings, sophisticated ICT capable of supporting the teaching of collective problem resolution via mediated interaction are now emerging. This is important, because until this point in history schools have lacked the capacity to inculcate 21st century understandings and performances best learned through situated participation in real-world communities of practice. Reports such as the National Research Council's *How People Learn* cite situated theories of learning (mentoring and apprenticeships in communities of practice) as powerful in life, but very difficult to achieve in school settings. Emerging interactive media now have the capability to redress this deficit.

Emerging Media for Situated, Immersive, Collaborative Simulation

Three complementary technological interfaces are currently shaping how people learn, with multiple implications for K-12 education:

- The familiar *"world- to- the- desktop"* interface provides access to distributed knowledge and expertise across space and time through networked media. Sitting at their laptop or workstation, students can access distant experts and archives, communicate with peers, and participate in mentoring relationships and virtual communities-of practice. This interface provides the models for learning that now underlie most tools, applications, and media in K-12 education.
- Emerging *multi-user virtual environment (MUVE)* interfaces offer students an engaging "Alice in Wonderland" experience in which their digital emissaries in a graphical virtual context actively engage in experiences with the avatars of other participants and with computerized agents. MUVEs provide rich environments in which

participants interact with digital objects and tools, such as historical photographs or virtual microscopes. Moreover, this interface facilitates novel forms of communication among avatars, using media such as text chat and virtual gestures. This type of "mediated immersion" (pervasive experiences within a digitally enhanced context), intermediate in complexity between the real world and paint-by-numbers exercises in K-12 classrooms, allows instructional designers to construct shared simulated experiences otherwise impossible in school settings. Researchers are exploring the affordances of such models for learning in K-12 education.

- *Augmented reality (AR)* interfaces enable "ubiquitous computing" models. Students carrying mobile wireless devices through real world contexts engage with virtual information superimposed on physical landscapes (such as a tree describing its botanical characteristics or an historic photograph offering a contrast with the present scene). This type of mediated immersion infuses digital resources throughout the real world, augmenting students' experiences and interactions. Researchers are starting to study how these models for learning aid students' engagement and understanding.

MUVEs empower creating contexts inaccessible in the real world, while AR enables the infusion of virtual contexts within physical locations.

In both MUVEs and AR, knowledge is grounded in a setting and distributed across a community, rather than isolated within individuals. Contrary to conventional K-12 instruction where knowledge is decontextualized and explicit, in MUVEs and AR the learning is situated and tacit: Problem finding is central to problem solving. This parallels the nature of 21st century work, as well as the learning styles and strengths of today's digital-age students. These immersive interfaces for collaboration and simulation can aid students in learning collective problem resolution via mediated interaction as a key cluster of 21st century understandings and performances.

Power of Situated Learning

Situated learning requires authentic contexts, activities, and assessment coupled with guidance from expert modeling, mentoring, and "legitimate peripheral participation". As an example of legitimate peripheral participation, graduate students work within the laboratories of expert researchers, who model the practice of scholarship. These students interact with experts in research as well as with other members of the research team who understand the complex processes of scholarship to varying degrees. While in these laboratories, students gradually move from novice researchers to more advanced roles, with the skills and expectations for them evolving.

Potentially quite powerful, situated learning is much less used for instruction than because classrooms are by design isolated from the real world to encourage reflection and to provide custodial care. However, as discussed below, emerging media such as multi-user virtual environments (MUVE) and augmented realities (AR) can draw on the power of situated learning even in school settings by enabling immersive, collaborative simulations with problems and contexts similar to the real world. In particular, these emerging interactive media provide the capability to create problem-solving communities in which participants can master 21st century understandings and performances such as collective problem resolution via mediated interaction.

Situated learning is important in part because of the crucial issue of transfer. Transfer is defined as the application of knowledge learned in one situation to another situation and is demonstrated if instruction on a learning task leads to improved performance on a transfer task, typically a skilled performance in a real-world setting. One of the major criticisms of instruction today is the low rate of transfer generated by conventional instruction. Even students who excel in schooling or training settings often are unable to apply what they have learned to similar real-world contexts. Situated learning addresses this challenge by making the setting in which learning takes place similar to the real-world context for performance in work or personal life. Learning in well-designed digital contexts can lead to the replication in the real world of behaviors successful in simulated environments.

Moreover, the evolution of an individual's or group's identity is an important type of learning for which simulated experiences situated in virtual environments or augmented realities are well suited. Reflecting on and refining an individual identity is often a significant issue for students of all ages, and learning to evolve group and organizational identity is a crucial skill in enabling innovation and in adapting to shifting contexts. The social sciences see both the self and the organization as often fragmented, with complementary parts, rather than centralized and unitary. Identity "play" through trying on various representations of the self and the group in virtual environments provides a means for different sides of a person or team to find common ground and the opportunity for synthesis and evolution.

Immersion is important in this process of identity exploration because virtual identity is unconstrained by physical attributes such as gender, race, and disabilities. Virtual environments based on games such as Lineage and simulations such as Whyville (Neulight et al, in press) illustrate how participants take advantage of fluidity in the identities they present. Simulations in virtual environments and augmented realities increase the value of these explorations by providing realistic feedback on how the real world responds to various patterns of individual and group behavior.

But what is so special about the situated learning now enabled in classrooms by emerging media? After all, outside of school contexts students have opportunities for situated learning without using technology. One attribute that makes mediated immersion different and powerful is the ability to access information resources and psychosocial community distributed across distance and time, broadening and deepening experience. A second important attribute is the ability to create interactions and activities in mediated experience not possible in the real world, such as teleporting within a virtual environment, enabling a distant person to see a real-time image of your local environment, or interacting with a (simulated) chemical spill in a busy public setting. Both of these attributes are actualized in the MUVE and AR interfaces.

Immersive Presence and Enhanced Learning

Immersion is the subjective impression that one is participating in a comprehensive, realistic experience. Immersion in a mediated, simulated experience (such as a virtual environment or an augmented reality) involves the willing suspension of disbelief. As an example, when watching a Harry Potter movie on an IMAX screen, the plot and characters coupled with visual and auditory input produce a sense of psychological immersion: the audience does not focus on the sensations of sitting in a theatre seat but instead on being present in a wizarding "world," observing a fascinating series of events. The example is weak, however, because the experience is passive, as opposed to the stronger immersion induced when participants shape an experience rather than just observe it. The design of mediated-immersion simulated learning experiences depends on actional, symbolic, and sensory factors. Inducing actional immersion involves empowering the participant in an experience to initiate actions that have novel, intriguing consequences. For example, when a baby is learning to walk, the degree of concentration this activity creates in the child is extraordinary. Discovering new capabilities to shape one's environment is highly motivating and sharply focuses attention.

Inducing a participant's symbolic immersion involves triggering powerful semantic associations via the content of an experience. As an illustration, reading a horror novel at midnight in a strange house builds a mounting sense of terror, even though one's physical context is unchanging and rationally safe. Invoking intellectual, emotional, and normative archetypes deepens the experience by imposing an overlay of associative mental models. Beyond actional and symbolic immersion, advances in interface technology are now creating virtual environments and augmented realities that induce a psychological sense of sensory and physical immersion. Sensory immersion is relatively easy to foster in augmented realities, which are set in physical environments. Psychological immersion is achievable in MUVEs by design strategies that combine actional, symbolic, and sensory factors in manipulating an avatar to further the suspension of disbelief that the participant represented by the avatar is "inside" a virtual environment: the equivalent of diving rather than riding in a glass-bottomed boat.

The River City curriculum: A Case Study

In the River City MUVE, a participant takes on the identity of an avatar, a virtual persona in the world and communicates with other participants' avatars via text chat and virtual gestures. In this graphical virtual context, participants also interact with digital artifacts, such as viewing pictures or manipulating tools (e.g., an online microscope), as well as with computer-based agents.

The River City curriculum is a middle school science unit designed around national content standards and assessments in biology, ecology, epidemiology, and scientific inquiry. In the River City MUVE curriculum, students work in teams of three to collaboratively solve the problem of why the residents of River City are falling ill. Students travel back in time—into a series of virtual worlds—to the period in history that scientists were just discovering bacteria.

Avatars

Talking to Computer-Based Agents

The curriculum is historically accurate and contains pictures from the Smithsonian Institute that help to portray accurate picture of what the time period was like. The River City virtual "world" is an industrial 18th century city with a river running through it. Different forms of terrain influence water runoff in the various neighborhoods (wealthy area, middle class area and tenements). The city has a hospital, hotel, and university. The students populate the city, along with computer-based agents and digital artifacts that can include audio or video clips (such as audio clues of sick residents coughing or mosquitoes buzzing). Content in the right-hand interface-window shifts based on what the participant encounters or activates.

Inquiry and River City

Students learn to become scientists by engaging in the inquiry practices of scientists. The National Research Council defines science inquiry as a multifaceted activity that involves students actively making observations, posing questions, planning and conducting experiments, and communicating results. In River City, students engage in all aspects of inquiry as defined by the NRC.

Engaging in inquiry also involves students learning how to collect data and test their hypotheses and use the tools of scientists, such as an online microscope. For example, they can use the virtual microscope to take water samples from one of the water sampling stations in the city. Multiple sources of data collection include:

- Conversations with the residents of River City (students click on residents and choose from drop down menu of conversation options)
- Tacit Clues
    - Appearance of river, trees

- Weather (changes in seasons influence the illnesses)
- Sounds: mosquito buzzing, coughing, water flowing

- Hospital Admissions chart (students can click on and read the chart that lists symptoms and demographic info of patients)

Environmental Health meter (students can click on this tool and take readings of a locations "health")

Clues associated with Pictures (students can click on pictures from Smithsonian Institute Collection and read clues)

Sampling stations using online microscopes:

- Water Purity
- Mosquito nte

Table 1. How River City Objectives Map onto Inquiry.

Making Observations	Throughout the curriculum students are asked to make observations and draw inferences about what they see and hear as they move around the world.
Posing Questions	Students not only ask questions of the residents of River City and elicit information that often offers a clue about the problems. They also record their own questions and reflect on them as they gather data and make observations and inferences.
Planning Experiments	Students are guided through a generalized process of the scientific method, where they learn how to turn their questions into hypothesis and design a procedure.
Conducting Experiments	Students conduct their experiment in River City. They visit a 'control world' (controlled part of their experiment and gather data) then they visit the 'experimental world' (where their independent variable has been changed and collect the same data). They then compare the data gathered in the two worlds and write up their results using graphs and charts. (This is explained in more detail below).
Communicating Results	Students then write up their results in a report to the Mayor of River City. They also participate in a research conference where they present and share their findings with their classmates.

Advancing Through the Curriculum

As students move through the curriculum, they advance through four different worlds chronologically that represent different seasons in River

City: October 1878, January 1879, April 1879, and July 1879. This allows participants to collect data on change over time in River City. After collecting data across these 4 seasons, students have produced enough observations and inferences to develop a hypothesis and to design their experiment. They spend two class periods designing their experiment in face-to-face groups. The curriculum walks them through turning the problem about the illness into a researchable question, then identifying independent and dependent variables. They then develop a hypothesis and write up a procedure. Next, after designing their procedure, they go back into River City two more times to test their experiment. They first visit the control world, Fall 1879 (controlled portion of their experiment), and then the following class they visit the experimental world (changing their independent variable and contrasting data from that world to the control world).

The experimental world is identical to the control world except for the one variable that students want to change in their experiment (their independent variable). The MUVE is based on an underlying simulation that allows one aspect of the world to change. For example, if students think the illness they identified is spreading because of the mosquitoes breeding by the bog, they can choose to drain the bog. Thus, when they enter the experimental world the bog is no longer there—it has been drained. Students must then gather the same data they gathered the day before in the control world in order to see how draining the bog affects the illness. Students collect data in both the control and experimental worlds by visiting the same places and talking to the same people. They then analyze data from their experiment by comparing their findings in each world. They write up their findings, draw conclusions, and make recommendations for stopping the illness from spreading.

Essentially, students use their 21st century knowledge and skills to identify a problem and then develop and test a hypothesis based on one of the three disease strands infecting the city (i.e., insect-born, air-born, and water-born). The three disease strands are embedded in the environment as mentioned above, with historically accurate social and environmental content. After testing their hypotheses, students analyze their data and then write up their research in the form of a report to the mayor of River City. The report, based on the concept of a lab report, describes their experiment, research findings, conclusions, and recommendations for how the mayor can stop the spread of illness in River City. We have found that these reports to be accurate representations of students' inquiry learning (Ketelhut, Dede, Clarke, Nelson, & Bowman, in press). Teams of students then present their research and findings to the entire class. The purpose of this final sharing day is to see how each teams' research was a small piece of the larger picture and to connect it to the real practice of scientists.

Students participate in the curriculum along a trajectory from novice (scientist-in-training) to expert (research scientist), as they learn to develop questions, generate hypotheses, collect and analyze data, and make conclusions and recommendations. Over time, they actively disentangle multi-causal problems embedded within a complex environment. We have developed both psychometric and performance-based summative assessments of student learning and have embedded formative diagnostic evaluations of student progress in the virtual world. We also are studying whether using datamining analytics on the extensive logfiles we collect of students' utterances and actions in the MUVE may yield novel insights about learning and teaching. This extended example illustrates how situated, immersive, collaborative simulations based on MUVEs can aid students in learning 21st century understandings and performances, such as collective problem resolution via mediated interaction, while in classroom settings.

Learning 21st Century Performances in the Alien Contact! Augmented Reality In the past year, via funding from the U.S. Department of Education, researchers at the Harvard Graduate School of Education have developed an augmented reality simulation designed to teach math and science literacy skills to middle school students, with help from colleagues at the University of Wisconsin at Madison and the Teacher Education Program at MIT (*http://isites.harvard.edu/icb/icb.do?keyword=harp*). This immersive collaborative simuilation is played on a Dell Axim X51 handheld computer and uses Global Positioning System (GPS) technology.

As the students move around a physical location, such as their school playground or sports fields, a map on their handheld displays digital objects and virtual people who exist in an augmented reality world superimposed on real space. This capability parallels the new means of information gathering, communication, and expression made possible by emerging interactive media (such as Web-enabled, GPS-equipped cell phones with text messaging, video, and camera features).

In the Alien Contact! curriculum to teach math and literacy, middle school students are presented with the following scenario: Aliens have landed on Earth and seem to be preparing for a number of possible actions, including peaceful contact, invasion, plundering, or simply returning to their home planet. Working in teams of four, the students must explore an AR world located immediately outside of their school, interviewing virtual characters, collecting digital items, and solving mathematics and literacy puzzles to determine why the aliens have landed.

Each team has four roles: Chemist, Linguist, Computer Expert, and FBI Agent. Depending upon his or her role, each student will see different pieces of evidence. In order to successfully navigate the augmented reality environment and solve various puzzles, the students must share information and collaborate within and among the teams. As students collect this data, they will discover different possibilities for why the aliens may have landed; students are asked to form and defend a hypothesis based upon the data collected. At the end of the unit, the students orally present their findings as a team to the class and support these with data collected in the field. In addition, each student writes a persuasive essay detailing why they think the aliens have landed.

Implications

Its rationale draws on changes in the global and U.S. economies; the impacts of advanced ICT on work, citizenship and everyday life; and shifts in the outcomes society needs from educational systems. A contextualized conceptual framework for 21st century understandings and performances is proposed that includes an appeal to deemphasize aspects of the 20th century legacy curriculum. A process is modeled for selecting an interrelated set of neglected 21st century understandings and performances, analyzing their relative importance as educational outcomes, and developing innovative, technology-based pedagogies and curricula to aid students in learning these. While complex, this type of design-based educational research is central to preparing both students and the United States for a prosperous, stable, attractive future.

The vision of the William and Ida Friday Institute for Educational Innovation at North Carolina State University (*http://www.fi.ncsu.edu/index.html*) is "to transform education to meet the demands of the 21st century global knowledge society." Its goals are:

- To research, develop and disseminate K-20 educational solutions that meet 21st century demands.

- To generate and propagate effective technologies for teaching and learning.
- To strengthen educational capabilities of rural and underserved communities in North Carolina and beyond.

One may ask how attaining sophisticated 21st century understandings and performances relates to the third goal of equity for underserved educational populations. Our research in MUVEs and AR is establishing that even the bottom third of students who struggle with remedial curricula can learn sophisticated 21st century understandings and performances when taught using 21st century pedagogies and 21st century learning technologies. In contrast, "dumbing down" an already inadequate school curriculum and intensively implementing instructional approaches that have already failed with these pupils is a guarantee of continuing to throw away huge amounts of human talent at a time when our nation desperately needs this intellectual capacity and social justice demands that we seek alternative, more effective educational strategies.

References

Dede, C., Korte, S., Nelson, R., Valdez, G., & Ward, D. (2005). *Transforming education for the 21st Century: An economic imperative.* Chicago, IL: Learning Point Associates.

Karoly, L. A. (2004). *The 21st century at work: Forces shaping the future workforce and workplace in the United States.* Santa Monica, CA: RAND Corporation.

National Research Council. (2001). *Knowing what students know: The science and design of educational assessment.* Washington, DC: National Academy Press.

Wenger, E. (1998). *Communities of practice: learning, meaning, and identity.* Cambridge University Press, New York.

6

Project-Based Learning Approach

Project-Based Learning (PBL) is a student-driven, teacher-facilitated approach to learning. Learners pursue knowledge by asking questions that have piqued their natural curiosity. The genesis of a project is an inquiry. Students develop a question and are guided through research under the teacher's supervision. Discoveries are illustrated by creating a project to share with a select audience. Organizers support systematization of the processes that will be implemented throughout the research and project phases of PBL. Student choice is a key element of this approach. Teachers oversee each step of the process and approve each choice before the student embarks in a direction. Children with similar inquiries may elect to work cooperatively, thereby nurturing twenty-first-century collaboration and communication skills and honoring students' individual learning styles or preferences. PBL is not a supplementary activity to support learning. It is the basis of the curriculum. Most projects include reading, writing, and mathematics by nature. Many inquiries are science-based or originate from current social problems. The outcome of PBL is greater understanding of a topic, deeper learning, higher-level reading, and increased motivation to learn. PBL is a key strategy for creating independent thinkers and learners. Children solve real-world problems by designing their own inquiries, planning their learning, organizing their research, and implementing a multitude of learning strategies. Students flourish under this child-driven, motivating approach to learning and gain valuable skills that will build a strong foundation for their future in our global economy.

History of Project-Based Learning

For over 100 years, educators such as John Dewey have reported on the benefits of experiential, hands-on, student-directed learning. Most teachers, knowing the value of engaging, challenging projects for students, have planned field trips, laboratory investigations, and interdisciplinary activities that enrich and extend the curriculum. ''Doing projects'' is a long-standing tradition in American education.

The roots of PBL lie in this tradition. But the emergence of a method of teaching and learning called Project Based Learning is the result of two important developments over the last 25 years. First, there has been a revolution in learning theory. Research in neurosci-ence and psychology has extended cognitive and behavioral models of learning—which support traditional direct instruction—to show that knowledge, thinking, doing, and the contexts for learning are inextricably tied. We now know that learning is partly a social activity; it takes place within the context of culture, community, and past experiences. This is apparent in research on problem-based learning in the medical field, an important forerunner of PBL.

Research shows that learners not only respond by feeding back information, but they also actively use what they know to explore, negotiate, interpret, and create. They *construct* solutions, thus shifting the emphasis toward the process of learning. In addition, cognitive research has revealed much more about the nature of problem solving. Education has benefited from this research, as teachers have learned how to effectively scaffold content and activities to amplify and extend the skills and capabilities of students. Second, the world has changed. Nearly all teachers understand how the industrial culture has shaped the organization and methods of schools in the 19th and 20th centuries, and they recognize that schools must now adapttoa new century.It isclear that children need both knowledge*and* skills to succeed. This need is driven not only by workforce demands for high-performance employees who can plan, collaborate, and communicate, but also by the need to help all young people learn civic responsibility and master their new roles as global citizens.

In a sense, the need for education to adapt to a changing world is the primary reason that PBL is increasingly popular. PBL is an attempt to create new instructional practices that reflect the environment in which children now live and learn. And, as the world continues to change, so does our definition of PBL. The most important recent shift in education has been the increased emphasis on standards, clear outcomes, and accountability. Thus, one purpose of this edition of the BIE Project Based Learning Handbook is to incorporate the latest thinking on standards and assessment—to outline a planning process for *standards-focused* projects. But this process will continue to evolve. Remember that PBL is a field that you, as a practitioner, will help create by your actions and leadership in the classroom.

Defining Standards-Focused PBL

There is no one accepted definition of PBL. However, BIE defines standards-focused PBL as *a systematic teaching method that engages students in learning knowledge and skills through an extended inquiry process structured around complex, authentic questions and carefully designed products and tasks.* This definition encompasses a spectrum ranging from brief projects of one to two weeks based on a single subject inone classroom to yearlong, interdisciplinary projects that involve community participation and adults outside the school. More important than the definition itself are the attributes of effective projects. You willfind that theBIE planning modelis based on a number of criteria that distinguish carefully planned projects from other extended activities in the classroom. Outstanding projects:

- Recognize students' inherent *drive to learn,* their capability to do important work, and their need to be taken seriously by putting them at the center of the learning process.
- Engage students in the central concepts and principles of a discipline. The project work is *central* rather than peripheral to the curriculum.
- Highlight provocative issues or questions that lead students to *in-depth exploration of authentic and important topics.*
- Require the use of essential *tools and skills,* including technology, for learning, self-management, and project management.
- Specify *products* that solve problems, explain dilemmas, or present information generated through investigation, research, or reasoning.
- Include *multiple products* that permit frequent feedback and consistent opportunities for students to learn from experience.
- Use *performance-based assessments* that communicate high expectations, present rigorous challenges, and require a range of skills and knowledge.

- Encourage *collaboration* in some form, either through small groups, student-led presentations, or whole-class evaluations of project results.

The BIE model for PBL also addresses a singular need in the field of PBL: to create *standards focused* projects that fit well with the era of accountability and performance. Often, projects have been used as fun or change-of-pace events completed after students have been pushed through homework assignments, lectures, and tests. In standards-based PBL, students are pulled through the curriculum by a Driving Question or authentic problem that creates a need to know the material. The Driving Question is tied to content standards in the curriculum, and assessment is explicitly designed to evaluate the students' knowledge of the content.

Similarly, Project Based Learning is sometimes equated with inquiry-based or experiential learning. Though PBL shares some overlapping characteristics with these two terms, standards-focused PBL is designed to acknowledge the importance of standards and evaluation of student learning. In an era of accountability, with testing and performance uppermost in the minds of parents and educators, it is imperative that all instructional methods incorporate high standards, rigorous challenges, and valid assessment methods.

The Benefits of PBL

As a field, PBL is still in the developmental stage. For example, there is not sufficient research or empirical data to state that PBL is a proven alternative to other forms of instruction. Based on evidence gathered over the past ten years, PBL appears to be an equivalent or slightly better model for producing gains in academic achievement, although results vary with the quality of the project and the level of student engagement. Also, PBL is not appropriate as a method for teaching certain basic skills such as readingor computation; however, it does provide an environment for the application of those skills.

More important, evidence shows that PBL enhances the quality of learning and leads to higher-level cognitive development through students' engagement with complex, novel problems. It is also clear that PBL teaches students complex processes and procedures such as planning and communicating. Accomplishing these goals, however, requires time for both teachers and students to master the behaviors and strategies necessary for successful PBL. In addition to research, convincing reports have come from teachers that PBL is a rigorous, relevant, and engaging instructional model that supports authentic inquiry and autonomous learning for students. Along with encouraging academic proficiency and meeting the traditional goals of education, PBL has important benefits for today's students. Teachers report that PBL:

- Overcomes the dichotomy between knowledge and thinking, helping students to both "know" and "do."
- Supports students in learning and practicing skills in problem solving, communication, and self-management.
- Encourages the development of habits of mind associated with lifelong learning, civic responsibility, and personal or career success.
- Integrates curriculum areas, thematic instruction, and community issues.
- Assesses performance on content and skills using criteria similar to those in the work world, thus encouraging accountability, goal setting, and improved performance.
- Creates positive communication and collaborative relationships among diverse groups of students.
- Meets the needs of learners with varying skill levels and learning styles.
- Engages and motivates bored or indifferent students.

As with any teaching method, PBL can be used effectively or ineffectively. At its best, PBL can help you as a teacher create a high-performing class room in which youand your students form a powerful learning community focused on achievement, self-mastery, and contribution to the community. It allows you to focus on central ideas and salient issues in your curriculum, create engaging and challenging activities in the classroom, and support self-directed learning among your students.

PBL in Classroom

Planning for a project must take into account what is possible in your classroom. The scope ofa project will be affectedbythe bell schedule, the time of year, standardized testing, and the other myriad factors that impact your work. Perhaps the first question that usually arises is: do I have time to do this project? To answer that question, it is helpful *not* to think of PBL as taking time away from the regular curriculum. Instead, consider a standards-focused project as a central method of teaching and learning that replaces conventional instruction for a portion of your course. Standards-focused projects teach students the same essential information you might teach them through lecture and discussion. PBL teachers also find that they do considerably less "busy work" activities in the classroom. And, though projects take time to plan, teachers have more time to work with students once a project is under way.

Coverage Versus "Uncoverage"

It is true that projects do not lend themselves to covering a laundry list of topics, as too often happens in the classroom. But in the case of good education, less is more. If you are pressed for time and need to include many topics in your instruction during a year, you may want to think about the concept of "uncoverage." This means making a deliberate decision about topics that you want to teach in depth versus topics that can be simply "covered." What parts of your curriculum can be easily and successfully handled through lectures or textbook assignments? What parts require more depth? Identify those topics that reflect the most important ideas and concepts in your curricu-lum—and incorporate those topics into projects. Those are the topics with which you want students to grapple. The remaining topics you can deal with through direct instruction.

Students Capability

Two questions regarding students immediately arise when you are thinking about a project. How much will they be involved? And, are they capable of a project, both behaviorally and academically? Student autonomy is one of the hallmarks of PBL. Still, most teachers introduce student autonomy in stages, depending upon students' age and experience. Before planning your project, think about how much you want your students to be involved in its design and how much autonomy they will have in carrying out project activities. You may want to select the project topic, particularly for the first project in your classroom. With students who are eager and prepared, you may wish to have them select the project topic and define the learning outcomes. Your role becomes one of coach and facilitator, helping students shape the project so that it meets content standards and allows for a variety of assessments.

Are your students ready and capable? That question can be answered based only on your experience and knowledge. The Handbook will offer you ideas on how to scaffold lessons for students in a way that prepares them for the academic knowledge, as well as for the skills, that may be required for them to succeed in the project. Often, teachers do not introduce projects until the midfall or later, giving them time to assess students and prepare them for project work. If students have not had experience with projects, it's worth remembering that they will need training in such skills as collaboration, research, project management, and oral presentations. Plus, you may have to manage them closely until they have mastered self-management skills.

Skills

Once teachers feel comfortable with PBL, they usually find teaching with projects to be more fulfilling and enjoyable. PBL is a way of working with students as they discover more about themselves and the world, and that brings job satisfaction. However, in addition to strong instructional and organizational skills, PBL requires that teachers facilitate and manage the*process* of learning. Rather than rely on the model of the child as an empty vessel to be filled, PBL teachers must create tasks and conditions under which student thinking can be revealed—a cocreative process that involves inquiry, dialogue, and skill building as the project proceeds. Though most teachers recognize that active learning is vital, not all of us react in the same way to an open-ended process. Projects are sometimes described as chaoticormessy (thoughinawell-structured project, it only appears to be disorderly—it's really just the ambiguous problem-solving process that isunder way). Prior to a project is a good time to reflect on your teaching style and skills. How will you operate in a PBL environment? Are you comfortable with children moving around a classroom or with the ambiguity that characterizes a more open-ended learning process?

It may help to ask yourself this question: do you prefer to be a leaderora manager? Leaders facilitate problem solvingin agroup and help the group find their own solutions. Managers control the process and look for prescribed outcomes. In reality, good teachers go back and forth between the two roles. But if you are hesitant to release control over your students, you may want to avoid projects or start small until you feel comfortable and skilled in project leadership. As a leader, your job is to help each student produce a superior product by facilitating learning. As students gather data and progress in their problem solving, they will encounter obstacles and opportunities. At the heart of successful PBL is your ability to support and direct students (or conversely, your ability to let them struggle with a problem or information as they search out answers and solutions). This requires interpersonal and communication skills, as well as the ability to define the agenda for the class and pusha project through to a successful conclusion. It also includes being sensitive to the fact that students finish work at different rates, with different abilities, aptitudes, and learning styles.

PBL and School Curriculum

PBL works extremely well in schools that have extended blocks of time instead of 50-minute periods. Similarly, when schools are formed around small learning communities such as academies or houses, PBL is a natural tool for teaching and learning. But if your school does not have these reforms in place, it isstill possibletocreate excellent projects for students.

You will also find that good projects in classrooms encourage changes in the culture and structure of schools. Schools are under increasing pressuretoraise standards, improve climate, and personalize education. PBL can contribute significantly to this process by encouraging teacher collaboration, motivating students to achieve, using the tools and language of project management and organizational change, and helping to incorporate school-wide learning outcomes into the curriculum. In particular, PBL fits well with efforts to create a high-performance school culture that values both rigor and relevance. In addition, projects are a great way to involve parents and community members in the educational process, a result that often leads to more support for the school and a better understanding of the needs of students. A question often asked by teachers in low-performing schools is: can Project Based Learning work in my school? It can. For students with basic skills issues, it may be necessary to include more direct instruction during a project, design shorter projects, or tie projects closely to fewer and more specific standards. But PBL offers all students the opportunity to investigate authentic topics of interest to them, thus engaging them in the learning process in ways that traditional instruction does not.

Research on PBL

Standardized testing is one measure of achievement. Each state has its own standard measure of academic competency. Each standardized test only measures the specific content knowledge it is designed to test. In measuring basic academic subject proficiency, standardized testing shows that students engaged in PBL outscore their traditionally educated peers. However, standardized testing does not measure critical twenty-first-century skills that are integral for student success.

In one British study, over the course of three years, students were taught using traditional math programs at one school and PBL at another school. Three times as many PBL students achieved the highest possible grade on the national exam than the students at a traditional school. Students at the PBL school were equally able to answer procedural questions that used formulas, but they were superior in answering applied and conceptual problems. This researcher concluded that students acquired a different kind of knowledge from using a PBL approach. In another study, elementary students in three Dubuque, Iowa schools thatused PBLraised their IOWA Test of Basic Skills scores from "well below average" to the district average in two schools and to "well above the district average" in another school. Moreover, in three years, reading gains "ranged from 15% in one school to over 90% in the other two schools while the district average remained the same".

At an inner city, racially diverse school in Boston that implemented a PBL program called Expeditionary Learning, eighth graders exhibited the second highest scores in the district on the Stanford 9 Open Ended Reading Assessment. Similar findings in Maine concluded that a middle school using a PBL approach showed significant increases in all achievement areas on the Maine Educational Assessment Battery after only one year using the approach.

The gains made by this school were three to ten times higher than the state average. Authentic projects require different measures of success, however. In PBL, students solve real-world problems. For example, in one study, students were asked to apply the concepts of geometry to architecture and submit designs for a new playhouse for a community center. Upon evaluating these designs, 84 percent of the submissions were judged to be accurate enough to build. This is an impressive measure of achievement. Moreover, students were able to revise their designs after consulting resources, which demonstrates a high level of motivation that is uncommon in traditional learning settings. Furthermore, these students demonstrated a solid grasp of the concepts and were able to perform well on traditional tests.

Learning to be Self-Reliant

There are several phases within PBL. Each phase must be completed in a timely manner. Thorough and careful planning is essential to the flow of the project and the success of the student. In the beginning, children use organizers to isolate an inquiry question. They then brainstorm what their procedure will be for research and identify the materials that they will need to do their research. Next, students select a way to display what they have learned in the form of a project. A target audience with whom to share their project is selected, ranging from their peers, to the principal, to their parents. The audience must be authentic and appropriate. For example, if students are working on a science inquiry on the topic of energy, they may choose to research how to harness hydropower to make a machine. A group may elect to make a working catapult. The culmination of the project might be a contest to see how far they can catapult a ball or an egg, with the class as the audience. Accountability to an audience coupled with a due date keeps students on track.

Learning responsibility, independence, and discipline are three outcomes of PBL. The organizational blueprint that students have designed for themselves guides them and allows them to stay focused and on-task. As children become more proficient in the PBL approach, they learn to self-monitor their progress through daily agenda setting. At the end of each work session, students report on whether they have met their goals for the day. Students must use their work time effectively and stay focused and on-task to succeed. Goal setting helps students learn to manage their own time. It is important for the teacher to confer with students regularly to ensure that students are on track and developing their ideas and skills fully. These skills are critical for future success in both school and life.

Students learn accountability with PBL through the daily goal setting, as well as through expectations of their peers. When students work collaboratively, there is an expectation that each child will contribute to the project equally. The group dynamic creates an interdependent team in which students must each do their part, and as a result, a natural consequence exists for those students who do not demonstrate accountability—others may no longer want to be paired with students who do not do their fair share. Therefore, peer pressure contributes to the accomplishment of ongoing group tasks throughout the learning process and the culmination of a successful final product. Students are conscientious because they must complete their project in the allotted time. They can be incredibly resourceful when time is of the essence. Accountability to peers often has greater consequences and provides more motivation for students than if they were only responsible to the teacher. Children do not want to let their friends down.

Social Learning Enhances Collaboration Skills

PBL promotes social learning as children practice and become proficient with the twenty-first-century skills of communication, negotiation, and collaboration. As children work on these projects, they must brainstorm ideas and act as good listeners to their group members. Teaching students active listening skills enhances collaborative ability as well as creativity. Students learn the fundamental skills of productive communication, respect for others, and teamwork while generating ideas together. Negotiating how to collectively solve a problem is also part of PBL.

At the end of the project, students do a self-evaluation. They evaluate not only their learning, but also the success of their social interactions. They reflect on their communication skills, if they felt they listened well to other students' ideas, and if they believed their own opinions were heard. Consistent employment and practice of these skills will strengthen them over time and lead to proficiency and mastery. These skills are critical to future success in the structures of our global economy.

Intrinsic Motivation

The element of choice is crucial for students' success. Differentiation allows students to develop their own interests and pursue deeper learning. It also allows students to soar and learn at their own levels. Students use resources that are appropriate for their individual reading levels and compatible with their technology knowledge. One exciting feature provided by this intrinsic motivation is that students will often reach higher and attempt to read more challenging material to glean the information they seek. It is not unrealistic to suspect that students who are highly motivated will improve their reading abilities as they strive to understand and learn during PBL. Doppelt, contends that students' "motivation to learn their discipline and their willingness to work on their projects [for] longer hours indicate that they behave... like high achievers". In another study, attendance was found to be higher in PBL schools. These behaviors have positive effects on learning.

The active learning process of PBL takes students' various learning styles and preferences into account. Students use a range of tools and resources to conduct their research. They also choose individual ways to demonstrate their learning in their final product. A child who prefers to be reflective may journal his learning in a diary format to share with peers. Others can read the diary and then write responses. A student who thinks in more of an analytic, mathematical way may elect to create a timeline of events or graph findings to present to his or her audience. Students also may select their preferred learning environment. Students may choose to work in a quiet library or a bustling hallway, lying down in the carpet area or sequestered in the cubby area. Children learn so much about themselves when they are empowered to make their own learning decisions. Children will reflect on these choices to ensure they are making the best decisions possible. The opportunity to make mistakes is part of the learning process. When we implement PBL, we allow children to discover who they are as learners. They become able to make better choices, whether relating to process, environment, or outcome, which enables them to become more independent and responsible for their own learning.

Scaffolded instruction ensures success. *Scaffolded instruction* refers to the supports provided to students to assist them in making cognitive growth just beyond their reach. Students are involved in a discovery process when they first learn the structures of PBL, and they require much support and monitoring. Scaffolded instruction occurs in PBL when teachers use organizers that aid students in bridging the gaps that exists in knowledge and skill, and it makes the tasks manageable and achievable. As with most supports, scaffolds are temporary, and as the learner gains fluency in the skill, the supports are removed, leading to a self-confident and capable learner.

PBL in Action

PBL is an approach to instruction that teaches curriculum concepts through a project. The project is guided by an inquiry question that drives the research and allows students to apply their acquired knowledge. For example, as part of a middle school interdisciplinary study on Greece, students were instructed to choose a particular aspect of Greek life that interested them. Students chose one particular topic area, such as performing arts, visual arts, science, military, daily life, government, and so forth. After students selected a topic, they designed an independent inquiry. Each student researched independently and wrote an individual paper, and then some students worked in groups for the projects. Using their knowledge of Gardner's multiple intelligences, students created a three-minute presentation as part of a living museum on Greek life. Presentations included dramatic performances of the Battle of Marathon, debates on a Greek myth performed in character as Greek gods and goddesses in an Athenian courtroom, Greek dance, PowerPoint presentations, art, and more.

One student chose daily life as her topic. She designed an inquiry based on the oracle at Delphi. She and her teacher crafted an inquiry question together, gathered resources, and conferred regularly throughout her research and planning phases. The teacher took extensive notes of their conferences. These anecdotal records informed the teacher's instruction in guiding and keeping the student on track. They also served as a reference tool for a comprehensive final evaluation. Upon completing her research on the oracle at Delphi, the student wrote her paper. She then had to apply her knowledge through a project. For her presentation at the museum, she dressed up as the Pythia. When people visited her, she used the first-person point of view to first tell them about herself and then to tell her audience's fortune in true oracle fashion, cryptic and in riddles. The depth of her knowledge was evident in her performance. At the end of the project, the teacher graded the student's proposal, research notes, work habits, presentation, and paper. The student completed a self-evaluation, as well as a project reflection. Responses about the process were overwhelmingly positive from both the students and teachers.

Creativity within Parameters

In the twenty-first century, students use computers in very advanced ways, but we must remember that they are still children and need guidance to use technology safely and effectively. Technology as a means, not an end, enables students to experiment with different technologies for all aspects of PBL. An authentic use of technology is highly engaging to students, because it taps into their fluency with computers. Students participate in research using the Internet. During this phase of PBL, students learn how to navigate the Internet judiciously, as well as to discriminate between reliable and unreliable sources. It is important to set parameters to ensure that students can explore safely.

Students can use a multitude of applications, including Web 2.0, for their projects. Students may use a wiki to share knowledge or blog with other students to trou-bleshoot during the process segment of their projects. In the presentation phase, students may use various technologies to display their learning. Their audience may receive a podcast, a video, a photo story, a comic, and so forth. These uses of technology provide instruction to the student by demonstrating innovative usage of various applications. These applications also help students realize appropriate ways to use technology. When students share their work or challenges, a brainstorming session often helps them build on each other's ideas for future possibilities. This exercise promotes serious creativity and out-of-the-box thinking.

Real-World Connections

Research supports PBL as a tool to engage students in real-world tasks. Real-world tasks run the gamut in terms of necessary skills. It is important to remember that even though a project may be based in one cur-ricular area, it crosses over into all areas of traditional academic studies. Evidence exists that through PBL, students become better researchers, problem solvers, and higher-order thinkers. Research supports that students using PBL perform better on both standardized assessments and project tests than students intraditional direct instruction programs, and that they learn not only real-world application of skills, but also analytic thinking. In Boaler's study of students using a project-based approach in mathematics, students were better able to see the application of their learning and less likely to view math as a set of isolated skills. Additionally, children instinctively reach further when they are highly motivated and interested in their inquiry topic. Motivation is sustained through meaningful, real-world problems and projects. Real-world projects deepen learning for students. After returning from a field trip to Washington, DC, where middle school students visited various monuments, students selected a social justice issue that they felt deserved a monument. One student selected child labor laws. The student researched the topic and then designed a three-dimensional playground, with each play area representing a different aspect of the issue, to commemorate the laws.

The assistant principal in this case observed PBL in action and was amazed by the level of engagement. Students with strengths in academics were not the only ones who were successful. As the assistant principal carefully watched a special education student, he noted that the child was both determined and focused as he contributed to his project alongside his group members. This special needs student had an aptitude for construction on which the group capitalized in devising their project. Similarly, in the real world, people use their individual strengths and talents in their jobs.

Success from the Beginning

In PBL, children are constructing knowledge and building on their background knowledge. Children retain moreinformation when they learn bydoing. Dewey proposed that learning by doing has great benefit in shaping students' learning. High-quality experiences, as well as continuity of experiences, are paramount. PBL is an effective approach and is in line with Dewey's philosophies, to which many educators have ascribed for enriched learning.

The PBL approach has been implemented with success as early as preschool using the Reggio Emilia approach. Reggio Emiglia is a project-based learning approach that began in northern Italy. It is a child-centered approach where the children are encouraged to pursue their natural curiosity. The discover through experiences that are carefully documented. Teachers guide students and are resources to students throughout their studies. Students learn through collaboration and employ critical thinking skills as they engage in projects. In particular, preschool students are encouraged to explore, investigate, and experience. This is the jumping-off point to developing students' love of learning and nurturing their natural curiosity. The beginning of PBL occurs when students learn in a social environment, work hand-in-hand with their teachers to discover ideas through careful scaffolding, document their journey of learning, and finally present their learning through projects. Beginning this approach early leads to greater success, because it hones the essential skills necessary for the twenty-first century. The earlier we begin implementing this approach, the more competent children will be with the processes of PBL and implementation of skills. Research also supports that PBL is a highly engaging and motivating approach that draws more involvement, interest, and investment in learning from students. PBL raises students self-esteem by beginning the cycle of success.

Students develop twenty-first-century skills through PBL that will aid them in becoming productive members of a global society. Many of these skills are not measureable through standardized tests. We must shift our thinking about assessment when teaching twenty-first-century skills. With PBL, assessment is authentic. We measure a child's performance via rubrics, but a critical aspect of this model includes self-evaluation and reflection. Children learn from their processes. They reflect on how well they worked in a collaborative group and how well they contributed, negotiated, listened, and welcomed other group members' ideas. Students also self-evaluate their own projects, efforts, motivations, interests, and productivity levels. Students become critical friends by giving constructive feedback to each other, which helps them become aware of their own strengths and improve on their interactions with each other.

In the future, children must enter a workforce in which they will be judged on their performance. They will be evaluated not only on their outcomes, but also on their collaborative, negotiating, planning, and organizational skills. By implementing PBL, we are preparing our students to meet the twenty-first century with preparedness and a repertoire of skills they can use successfully. Moreover, PBL projects are often impressive, grand undertakings created and presented with ultimate pride and care.

As the assistant principal circulated around the room that day, he inquired of each student what they were doing, learning, researching, or making. Each student was on-task, thoroughly involved in a collaborative project, and able to explain to the assistant principal what they were engaged in at the moment, as well as what they had done and their next steps. Students articulated how they collaborated and problem-solved with their groups, and how they worked collectively to foster creativity and enhance their projects. When the assistant principal left the classroom that day, and for many months after that, the teacher was only more assured that PBL was the best approach for her students. A didactic approach kept students passive, but the engagement and enjoyment of students during PBL only heightened the teacher's conviction that she was imparting critical twenty-first-century skills to her pupils. What sealed the deal was the students' quick adaptation to the process and excitement about their learning. A big cheer rises from every student in the class when they hear that a new project will be beginning soon.

References

Boaler, J. (1999). Mathematics for the moment, or the millennium? *Education Week* 17(29): 30–34.

Dewey, J. (1938). *Experience and education.* New York: Simon and Schuster.

Doppelt, Y. (2003). Implementing and assessment of PBL in a flexible environment. *International Journal of Technology and Design Education* 13:255–72.

Gardner, H. (2006). *Multiple intelligences*. New York: Basic.

Geier, R., P. C. Blumenfeld, R. W. Marx, J. S. Krajcik, E. Soloway, and J. Clay-Chambers. (2008). Standardized test outcomes for students engaged in inquiry-based curricula in the context of urban reform. *Journal of Research in Science Teaching* 45(8): 922–39.

Gultekin, M. (2005). The effect of project based learning on learning outcomes in the 5th grade social studies course in primary education. *Educational Sciences: Theory and Practice* 5(2): 548–56.

7

Professionalism in Teaching

Contemporary educational reform – including both marketisation and centralisation, but also a new emphasis on the involvement of a wider range of stakeholders – has resulted in a period of significant change for teachers. It has also raised new questions: for example, how should we understand the role of the teacher? Who has a right to be involved in decisions about education? Consequently, and perhaps more than ever in recent times, we need to reflect on the appropriateness of existing notions of teacher professionalism to the context in which teachers work and to the goal of social justice.

Devolution and competition, alongside increasing central prescription and performativity demands, have become global trends in education policy over the past twenty years, even though the particular balance of policies has varied from place to place and, indeed, from government to government within particular countries. Yet, particularly in those countries that embarked early on these reforms, both market-based policies and so-called 'Third Way' alternatives are already demonstrating their limitations, especially in relation to social justice.

In England, the New Labour government has recently admitted that its own research demonstrates this failure: it shows that, although educational standards have risen overall during its term of office, the relative performance of children from poorer socio-economic backgrounds has not improved. This is despite the fact that some of New Labour's policies had been expected to counter the social inequities that had arisen from the policies of their Conservative predecessors. This news did not come as a complete surprise to me; as early as 1997 Peter Mortimore and I had warned that research indicated how the sort of school improvement policies then being advocated by New Labour might well have this effect, unless much stronger measures of positive discrimination were introduced. In the same publication, we deplored the way in which many politicians blamed teachers for all the ills of society and failed to recognise the strength of their commitment to educational improvement. We also argued that it was unrealistic to expect teachers alone to overcome the effects of social disadvantage on education.

Yet, there is a real sense in which recent reforms have been a response to perceived failures on the part of teachers. This view is certainly reflected in the 'official' account of reforms in England offered by Michael Barber, the key architect of New Labour's policies. He argues that there have been four phases of reform since the 1960s, as follows:

- *Uninformed professionalism* - the period prior to the 1980s, often regarded as the golden age of teacher autonomy but when, according to Barber, teachers lacked appropriate knowledge, skills and attitudes for a modern society
- *Uninformed prescription* - the period following the election of Margaret Thatcher's Conservative government in 1979 and, in particular, its imposition of a National Curriculum in 1988 for political rather than educational reasons
- *Informed prescription* - the period following the election of Tony Blair's New Labour government in 1997, bringing with it (in Barber's view) 'evidence-based' policies such as the Literacy and Numeracy Strategies and Standards-based teacher training
- *Informed professionalism* - a new phase, just beginning, when teachers will have appropriate knowledge, skills and attitudes so that the government can grant them a greater degree of licensed autonomy to manage their own affairs.

As Dainton rightly points out, Barber provides a crude analysis that is historically inaccurate. She also wryly comments that '"delivering" someone else's thoughts, ideas, strategies and lesson plans hardly counts as "informed professionalism"'.

In response, however, I shall suggest that, while New Labour's managerialist reforms have so far failed to create the conditions for 'informed professionalism', let alone the positive equity outcomes that their advocates predicted, they have contained some 'progressive moments'. These will need to be held onto as we seek to develop a form of professionalism that transcends both traditional professionalism and the attacks on that tradition implicit in recent reforms.

Nature of Professionalism

Sociological discourse about professionalism and the state can go some way in helping us to understand the contemporary condition of teachers as professionals.

The nature of professionalism was initially subjected to concerted attention by sociologists in the 1950s. The main approach at this point focused on establishing the features that an occupation should have in order to be termed a profession. A typical list included such items as:

- the use of skills based on theoretical knowledge
- education and training in those skills certified by examination
- a code of professional conduct oriented towards the 'public good'
- a powerful professional organisation

These lists reflected the nature of established professions such as medicine and law, while occupations that did not entirely meet such criteria were given the title 'quasi-' or 'semi-professions'. Moving to 'full' professional status was seen as part of an aspiring occupation's 'professional project' and this has applied to the strategy of teachers in many countries.

In contrast, more recent sociological perspectives on professionalism have rejected such normative notions of what it means to be a professional. Instead, they see professionalism as a shifting phenomenon – a profession, they suggest, is whatever people think it is at any particular time. Rather than asking whether the teaching profession lives up to some supposed ideal, such an approach encourages us to explore the characteristics of teaching as an occupation in the present.

In practice, of course, in most countries the characteristics of a profession have been increasingly determined by the state, which became the major stakeholder in defining professionalism in the twentieth century. Most professionals are employed, or at least regulated, by governments, with professional status typically dependent on the sort of bargain an occupation has struck with the state – what is sometimes called its 'professional mandate'. The nature of teachers' professional mandate has become a key policy issue for governments in many countries, sometimes as part of a broader attempt to redefine professionalism, especially in the public sector, and sometimes as a specific aspect of education reform.

Teacher Autonomy

The teaching profession in England, and indeed Northern Ireland, has never enjoyed the 'licensed autonomy' that occupations such as medicine and law have traditionally had, whereby they have been permitted by the state to regulate their own affairs. Nevertheless, from the 1950s until the mid-1970s, it experienced a considerable degree of de facto autonomy – that 'golden age' of teacher control. Parents were expected to trust teachers to know what was best for their children. Accordingly, the teacher's role included the freedom to decide not only how to teach but also what to teach. In this, they had a particular responsibility for curriculum development and innovation. Even though effectively the state paid most teachers' salaries, it did not intervene actively in the content of either teacher training or the work of teachers in schools.

From the mid-1970s, however, there were some dramatic changes in policy and, linked to these, attempts to change the nature of teacher professionalism. Due to economic downturn across the industrialised west, there was growing criticism of the 'swollen state' of post-war social democracy, not only for cost reasons but also because the welfare state had failed to deliver its original promise. This became coupled with an intellectual critique of public sector management on the part of neo-liberals and public choice theorists. The outcome was a call for public sector providers to be subjected to greater accountability – both through market-based competition and increased surveillance by the state. Particularly under Thatcherism and similar regimes elsewhere, there were swingeing attacks on public sector professions, including teachers, who were accused of abusing their autonomy to the detriment of pupils and society.

A key strand of policy, as in other countries, has been to re-position public sector schools as competitors in the marketplace, encouraging them to behave more like those in the private sector. Parents have been offered greater choice over the school that their children attend, which is often coupled with a shift to per capita funding and, in some cases, experimental voucher systems. Budgets and managerial power are handed down to schools in the expectation that they can then respond more effectively to the preferences of parents as consumers. While these developments are probably less advanced in Northern Ireland than elsewhere in the United Kingdom, local management of schools and similar arrangements are already in place. When the Transfer Test is abolished the Department of Education has pledged to put in place a new system based on informed parental and pupil choice in the context of a more differentiated system.

However, while contemporary governments have been enthusiastic about making schools more receptive to parents' wishes, they are generally unwilling to relinquish control over the outcomes that schools should achieve. Thus, we have the apparent paradox of the 'free market and the strong state'. While devolution appears to offer organisations greater autonomy, the state retains overall strategic control by setting the outputs that providers need to achieve (Neave, 1988: 11). This is operationalised through the range of targets and performance indicators, and associated league tables that have grown up around 'marketised' systems. Although justified in terms of providing information for the 'consumer' and greater public accountability, these indicators also enable government to scrutinise and direct providers. Arguably, they indirectly influence the priorities of parents – who in turn reinforce the pressure on schools to achieve government-determined outcomes.

These developments have obvious implications for teachers and teacher professionalism. Standardised criteria now feed into the framework of targets and indicators that schools and individual teachers must work to, and the new assessment regimes provide a wealth of performance data for their managers at all levels of the system. Although performance indicators severely delimit and direct what and how schools manage their resources, the stakes that are involved have still necessitated the growth of managerialism and the development of a distinct managerial tier within schools. One consequence of this is likely to be increased fragmentation of the profession.

New Labour Revisionism

In England, the Conservative government's 1988 Education Reform Act has often been seen as the epitome of a policy combining market forces and state control. Similar levels of prescription in relation to the curriculum were introduced in Northern Ireland a year later. Importantly, however, policy under the Conservatives by no means represented the height of these trends in England. Despite the proclaimed 'Third Way' approach of New Labour after 1997, in practice its education reforms have built on the 'new right settlement' and even gone beyond it – combining devolution, diversity, choice and even privatisation, on the one hand, and centralised regulation, monitoring and even pedagogical prescription, on the other.

As part of this, under New Labour, we have begun to see developments that reinforce and 'concretise' changes in the conceptualisation of teacher professionalism. There seems to have been a progressive move away from a concern with up-skilling teachers as individuals or even seeing responsibility for educational improvement as lying largely in the hands of the teaching profession, however it is regulated. Instead, there has been a growing focus on education as a collective endeavour, encompassing a much wider range of stakeholders than merely the state and teachers themselves.

This approach was effectively summarised in the 1998 Green Paper, *Teachers: meeting the challenge of change*, which noted that 'The time has long gone when isolated, unaccountable professionals made curriculum and pedagogical decisions alone, without reference to the outside world'.

It went on to list what, in the government's view, a modern teaching profession needed:

- to have high expectations of themselves and of all pupils;
- *to accept accountability;*
- to take personal and collective responsibility for improving their skills and subject knowledge;
- *to seek to base decisions on evidence of what works in schools in the UK and internationally;*
- *to work in partnership with other staff in schools;*
- *to welcome the contribution that parents, business and others outside a school can make to its success; and*
- to anticipate change and promote innovation.

In this respect, New Labour's agenda for education may provide a useful 'case study', or 'ideal type' of where professionalism in education is heading – and I want to look briefly at a few examples of the policies that have emerged from it.Certainly, there has been a reinforcement by New Labour of the need for the state to take a much more assertive role in specifying what teachers are expected to achieve, rather than leaving it to professional judgement alone. There is a real enthusiasm for intervening in the detail of educational processes, with advice on all aspects of the day-to-day running of schools and teaching itself. Furlong highlights the 2,000 model lesson plans that teachers can now download from the Department for Education and Skills (DfES) website – something that would have been unthinkable in England not many years ago and is reminiscent of traditional English criticisms of highly centralised systems such as those of France.

Literacy and Numeracy Strategies

This approach of intervening in the detailed processes of teaching, specifying how to teach in addition to what to teach, supposedly based on evidence of 'what works', is particularly evident in New Labour's National Strategies for Literacy and Numeracy. Although the levels of prescription we have seen in England have not been introduced in Northern Ireland, the Department of Education has produced the *Strategy for the Promotion of Literacy and Numeracy in Primary and Secondary Schools.* This has brought a drive for greater coherence and consistency across schools and some degree of additional target setting.

In one sense, the Strategies are just one element of a long process of curriculum reform stretching back to the introduction of the National Curriculum. But they are also qualitatively different, both in their immediate impact on teachers' work, and through the pace of change they have ushered in. Delivery has been standardised through prescribed content and a well-defined sequence and structure to lessons, coupled with the promotion of particular teaching approaches – for example, the Literacy and Numeracy Hours. Increased funding for research on 'what works', professional development courses for teachers, books and the production of classroom materials supported this effort to standardise provision.

In turn, the Strategies have included ambitious targets and a significant programme of pupil assessments to monitor achievement and the extent to which all pupils were reaching a given level in their literacy and numeracy. In this, the levers of monitoring and target setting have been such that they have enabled the centre to steer schools and teachers much more closely than before. More recently, steering at a distance has entailed a combination of target setting and incorporating schools themselves by requiring them to engage in a process of self-evaluation. As the broader Primary and Secondary Strategies – into which the literacy and numeracy strategies have been absorbed – also embrace a national approach to the improvement of behaviour and attendance, they arguably extend the scope of this central direction ever further.

Complementary Changes to Teacher Education

Another area of reform has been teacher education, which has seen changes to both its structure and content. In England, training is now largely school-based, even on programmes led by universities. It is a more practically-based form of preparation, with an emphasis on training rather than education and, in particular, the achievement of practical competences that are set centrally.

The highly diverse array of teacher training courses provided by universities and colleges in England was first brought under centrally mandated requirements in 1984. Accreditation was now dependent on meeting officially defined criteria, including the number of weeks to be spent in school and the number of hours to be spent on English and mathematics in primary training. Control was tightened from the late 1980s with a series of government circulars setting out competences that had to be met by students before qualifying to teach.

The work some of us did for the Department of Education in Northern Ireland in the 1990s was critical of this approach and we expressed the view that 'the atomisation of professional knowledge, judgement and skill into discrete competences inevitably fails to capture the essence of professional competence'. And, indeed, in some cases, such an approach led to an unduly bureaucratic model of student teacher development that, at its worst, was focused much more upon ticking boxes of statements of competence than upon the real issues related to teaching and learning.

Another development, which was taken up by the incoming New Labour government in 1997, effectively turned the competences into what was an ultimately unworkable eighty-five page 'national curriculum' for teacher training. This specified in very great detail the content that had to be covered by trainee teachers in English, mathematics, science and ICT. As Furlong et al point out, although the curriculum was designed to constrain teacher educators rather than the trainees themselves, it could be argued that the 'hidden curriculum' of this approach provided '...appropriate socialisation into a profession in which official prescription of teaching approaches (encroaches) on autonomous professional judgements'.

New Labour has now abandoned this national curriculum to focus on the stipulation of standards to be achieved by all trainees. The resulting standards do respond to criticisms of earlier versions by recognising the importance of reflexive practice and, overall, represent a somewhat more manageable and holistic set. But it took almost a decade for the English authorities to recognise what we always argued in Northern Ireland – that individual competences that were not thoroughly and consistently underpinned by clear professional values would fail to deliver the sorts of professionals needed in the twenty-first century.

The English standards are currently undergoing a further process of revision as the Training and Development Agency for Schools (TDA) develops a framework to cover teachers' whole career rather than just the initial training. But there are still different sets of standards for different groups of teachers, some which the TDA finds it difficult to define clearly, e.g. Advanced Skills Teachers and Excellent Teachers. As my colleague, Sara Bubb, who is working closely with the GTCNI on the development of its own scheme, has put it:

> It's such a shame the TDA hasn't taken this golden opportunity to draft just one well thought through set of standards for the whole of the teaching profession, like the new 27 Northern Ireland competences...These recognise that each standard is a continuum to be met to different degrees depending on a teacher's role, experience and context. Doesn't that make more sense?

The TDA review has also specifically addressed the issue of teachers' research skills. This represents a move towards recognising teaching as a research-based profession. As their draft standards currently stand, however, the only teachers for whom the use of research to inform teaching is stipulated are those with Advanced Skills and Excellent Teacher status.

Looking more generally at Continuing Professional Development, in England there are now much broader opportunities opening-up for extended professional development through, for example, the TDA's Postgraduate Development Programme. But, as with the draft teacher standards, these opportunities are currently available only to a small proportion of the workforce. At the same time, other courses for teachers have become increasingly centrally-defined and focused on short-term practical training closely tied to government Strategies – for example, additional phonics training to support the Literacy Strategy. In this sense, CPD opportunities are now largely focused on the needs of the school and its pupils rather than the individual teacher. The GTCNI is currently working to establish a 'mixed economy' model that addresses individual as well as school-based and systemic needs. Nevertheless, and particularly so in England, this shift reflects what is a broader significant development for the future of teacher professionalism – the emphasis on education as a collective endeavour and the role of other stakeholders in raising standards in school.

Workforce Remodelling in Schools

An important aspect of New Labour policy in England has been its school workforce remodelling agenda and the 2003 National Agreement on Raising Standards and Tackling Workload. A key element of this concerns the use of teaching assistants. While most sections of the support staff workforce in English schools have grown in recent years, the number of teaching assistants has risen dramatically. Between 1997 and 2005 the number almost trebled – from 35,500 to just under 100,000. By comparison, the number of full time equivalent (FTE) 'regular' teachers in the maintained sector rose by just 4,000 to reach around 430,000 last year.

The growth in teaching assistant numbers in England has been accompanied by marked changes in the nature of their responsibilities. This has involved a shift in focus from purely 'care and housekeeping' towards greater involvement in the actual process of learning – including, for example, assisting with the assessment of pupils' learning. This expansion of the number and role of teaching assistants is not an entirely new idea in England. The 1967 Plowden Report and 1975 Bullock Report urged that more profitable use be made of welfare assistants and ancillary help. By the 1990s, concerns about teacher supply and teacher workload again highlighted the potential for making greater use of support staff. It was the literacy and numeracy Strategies, however, that were the main driver for the first real expansion of teaching assistants and a widespread movement into learning support and even teaching-type roles in mainstream classrooms.

While the remodelling agenda has seen administrative roles reallocated from teachers to support staff, it has also seen a 'reaffirmation' of the new role of teaching assistants. In particular, in 2004 the government established the Higher Level Teaching Assistant training and assessment programme, whereby teaching assistants can pursue Higher Level Teaching Assistant status. The government has taken the same approach to the training of teaching assistants as it has with teachers – setting out standards that must be evidenced. In this case there are thirty-one such standards to meet, many of which are not dissimilar to those for teachers.

The government has played an active role, then, in blurring the distinction between teachers and teaching assistants. Many of the teacher unions have accepted this, albeit with varying degrees of enthusiasm, as a means of helping teachers to focus on teaching rather than administration or behaviour control. The largest teachers' union – the National Union of Teachers – however, refused to support the workload agreement. The union presented this in terms of the potential for the dilution of the professionalism of the teacher function and declining standards where staff without a teaching qualification were left in charge of whole classes – which 'Higher Level' teaching assistants are indeed permitted to do. By contrast, the government argued that the agreement was part of a process in which different professional and professionalising groups recognise their complementary roles in improving education in the interests of all.

A recent review of teachers' pay and conditions in Northern Ireland found strong opposition from both management and unions to the introduction and employment of Higher Level Teaching Assistants. This was partly because there is no general shortage of teachers and partly because their use is seen as reducing the standard of teaching provision.

Children's Agenda

Linked to workforce remodelling in schools is an even broader 'Children's Agenda'. Legislation based on the *Every Child Matters* Green Paper has sought to ensure multi-agency work in the interests of children and involve children and young people themselves in decision making. To support this policy, Local Authorities are being encouraged to bring together education and social services departments into powerful education and children's services departments and to establish 'Children's Trusts' to co-ordinate these services with other statutory and voluntary agencies. As part of this development, an 'extended schools' programme seeks to establish wider services in all primary and secondary schools – including study support and family learning opportunities and swift referral to a wider range of specialised support services, if not on-site services in childcare, youth justice, health and social care. This is something that has been tried successfully in Scotland and is often seen as vital if the effects of social disadvantage on educational achievement are to be minimised.

In Northern Ireland the government will shortly publish its strategy for children and young people. Its consultation document incorporates many of these themes, emphasising the need for organisations at all levels and in all sectors to work together to support a 'whole child' needs-centred model. Draft actions for the Department of Education include exploration of the extent to which schools could be resourced to become multi-agency centres with out-of-hours usage. These kinds of developments will obviously bring far-reaching changes to the way in which different welfare services are configured, but also to the way both teaching and support staff work with other professionals.

Parents and Business

At the same time, particularly in England we have seen a greater emphasis on the voice of parents and business in relation to what happens in schools. Local Authorities and Ofsted have both sought to give more attention to parents' interests. Ofsted, for example, will now be able to respond to concerns raised by parents themselves about their children's schools. Meanwhile, businesses and other stakeholders have been increasingly encouraged to become involved in the education sector by part-funding and running anything from a local initiative to national programmes and individual schools. Specialist schools with sponsors now constitute the majority of secondary schools in England and all secondary schools are now being encouraged to take this path. Similar thinking underlies the Academies programme and controversial proposals for Trust schools.

Responses to Recent Reforms

Faced with the sort of reforms outlined above, there must be a strong temptation on the part of the teaching unions, and indeed the General Teaching Councils, to adopt defensive, exclusory positions associated with traditional models of professionalism. This is in some ways understandable – particularly in the face of government reforms that have undermined key elements of teachers' autonomy and bargaining position. However, we would argue that it is also likely to prove untenable and we need anyway to consider what might be a more genuinely progressive strategy.

Of course, these tensions are not just being played out through the unions. Those of us within the education research community have ourselves raised a range of deep-seated concerns about recent education policy in terms of its implications for teachers. In particular, the process of marketisation and centralisation, growing performativity and the shift to standards-based teacher training have all been seen by some of my colleagues as an unacceptable attack on teacher autonomy and teacher creativity, transforming teachers from professionals to technicians. For Sachs, writing in the Australian context but referring to cross-national trends in policy, the modern professional in the eyes of governments is increasingly one who works efficiently and effectively in meeting the standardised criteria set for the accomplishment of students and teachers as well as contributing to the school's formal accountability processes. As Furlong similarly argues, this is a form of professionalism which accepts that decisions about what to teach, how to teach and how to assess children are made at school and national level rather than by individual teachers themselves. As he continues, this brings with it a move away from seeing the individual teacher as an essential actor. As a sociologist influenced by the contemporary approaches to the study of professionalism that outlined earlier, we would argue anyway that what we are seeing in interventions such as New Labour's in England is not necessarily an example of de-professionalisation in some absolute sense, but an attempt at *re-professionalisation* – that is, the construction of a different type of professionalism, considered by those like Michael Barber to be more appropriate to the times and to New Labour's political project.

If this is the case, there may be possibilities for pursuing other strategies of re-professionalisation. It may be that new 'prospective' identities could be constructed as an alternative both to an outmoded traditional professionalism and New Labour's version. It is surely not necessary to move from academic critique of recent reforms to an argument that teachers' professional judgement, whether individual or collective, should not be challenged. Indeed, to this extent, the questioning of traditional modes of professionalism by New Labour and similar governments elsewhere trades upon legitimate concerns about who has the right to make decisions about public education in a democracy.

Hence, we are not entirely persuaded by the alternative solutions that academic commentators have typically offered so far. While these sometimes include calls for the 'democratisation' of the profession, they do not amount to the sort of 'democratic professionalism' that we would advocate. For example, although Leaton-Gray's conception of a more engaged professionalism properly entails fuller engagement of teachers with their professional associations, it ultimately looks rather too much like a traditional understanding of professionalism – with an emphasis on teachers exerting greater influence over policy and extending their autonomy as an end in itself. This is perhaps not the best way to win friends and influence people. As Lawton argued many years ago, there are different levels of decision making in education and the further one gets from the individual encounter in the classroom, the more other stakeholders need to be involved. But even in the classroom, the active role of other adults and, indeed, students themselves is increasingly recognised as important in the development of appropriate learning environments. The capacity to collaborate with others, rather than merely instructing them, must surely be an important competence on the part of contemporary professional teachers. In England, the expanding role of teaching assistants is a case in point. Similarly, both the English and Northern Ireland education departments are looking more closely at school councils and other mechanisms for pupil involvement in decision making in schools.

With regard to teacher education, we have never taken the view that the government-defined standards cannot encapsulate the requirements of a forward-looking professionalism. And even the officially specified competences and standards have now begun to modify the narrow technicist model of professionalism, initially in Northern Ireland but subsequently in England. Furthermore, the developments around the children's agenda broadly defined will require a move away from purely cognitive targets for education and are likely to require some rebalancing of the standards and inclusion agendas. These are positive changes that should be welcomed and capitalised upon by teachers as extending their influence, but in partnership with others.

In the parallel example of nursing and related professions, Gough pointedly suggests that, in an era of patient empowerment, 'enabling people around us to change is dependent on transforming ourselves first'. Advocates of a new style of professionalism within these occupations have seen the managerial reforms associated with markets and consumerism as offering possibilities for partnership, collaboration and reflective practice more suited to contemporary conceptions of citizenship and democracy than are traditional modes of professionalism within the health service. Thus Gough argues that empowering patients involves unpicking 'old style professionalism' and demands a new emphasis on 'how the patient can be best served through new ways of working – not shoring up old professional demarcations and engaging in endless turf wars'.

Established between 2000 and 2002, the General Teaching Councils each place raising the status of teaching and maintaining and promoting the highest standards of professional practice at the heart of their remit. At the time, the establishment of the Councils was seen by some as the turning point at which teaching had become a bone fide profession in terms of the traditional characteristics of a profession that I referred to earlier. This was especially so when they went on to develop codes of professional conduct. This aspect of the Councils is also reflected in the current membership of their governing councils – with the exclusion from membership of other sections of the school workforce and, certainly in England, the limited influence of other stakeholders.

Having achieved, at least in some respects, the century-long occupational project of making teaching a profession in the traditional sense, it hardly seems fair to suggest that further change may be necessary. But we do need to consider whether, if the respective Councils are to maximise the positive influence of teachers in the changing context I have described, this is the model that serves them best. The dilemma about which way to go in response to recent developments is already evident in debates within England, and I would be surprised if similar issues did not arise in Northern Ireland. Take, for example, some reflections on the part of the Chief Executive of the GTC for England, Carol Adams, regarding the children's agenda. As Carol notes, this agenda – and similar developments in Northern Ireland – raises a number of considerations for the teaching profession and its representative bodies. On the one hand, could pupils, parents and the wider community become confused about the unique role and contribution of the teacher? Could a child's right to learn be threatened by the new multi-disciplinary agenda? While Carol herself welcomes many aspects of the new agenda, she argues that we need 'to hold fast to the simple premise that a school is a centre of learning' and thereby be clear about the role of the teacher.

On the other hand, this does not necessarily require a defensive, exclusionary and inward looking stance on the part of teachers. Indeed, if the key question is how can teachers maximise children's opportunities to learn, that can only be achieved by working ever more closely with the other stakeholders. Bringing about the conditions in which all young people can realistically, in the GTCE's own words, 'access the best possible standards of learning and achievement' will necessitate much closer working with other professional groups and with progressive social movements, as well as changing teachers' conventional ways of working where necessary to support the positive aspects of the new agenda. What we must achieve is surely a balance between defining the teacher's proper role and staking out the territory too rigidly. In this respect, it is good to see that the GTCE has recently questioned why the TDA and the Children's Workforce Development Council (CWDC) are consulting simultaneously on distinct sets of induction standards rather than working in tandem.

Towards a Democratic Professionalism

However, it is notable that the GTCE's concern here is to facilitate inter-professional working between distinct groups within the children's workforce. But the sociological critique of professionalism as elitism could also apply to inter-professional agreements.

In a democratic society, the professions also need to be open to the concerns of other stakeholders. For myself, I have no problems about the government's demand that other stakeholders should have a role in education decision making, though I do have a problem about its limited conception of who those other stakeholders might be and about how it goes about seeking involvement from them. In my view, genuine stakeholder involvement should be welcomed by the professions and the democratisation of professionalism should be adopted as an alternative to both the traditional professional project and the managerialist professional project currently promulgated by governments. A democratic professionalism would seek to demystify professional work and build alliances between teachers and other members of the school workforce, such as teaching assistants, and external stakeholders, including students, parents and members of the wider community. For many of these groups, and particularly marginalised sub-sets of them, decisions will have traditionally been made on their behalf either by professions or the state.

If teachers are to make a real contribution to the equity agenda as well as the standards agenda, they must work actively with others committed to teaching for a just society. A democratic professionalism thus encourages the development of collaborative cultures in the broadest sense, rather than exclusive ones. It certainly suggests that the teacher has a responsibility that extends beyond the single classroom – including contributing to the school, other students and the wider educational system, as well as to the collective responsibilities of teachers themselves to a broader social agenda. Indeed, under democratic professionalism, this broader agenda becomes part and parcel of the professional agenda rather than being counterposed to it.

Sachs' notion of an 'activist identity' for teachers goes some way towards recognising this. Her activist professional works collectively towards strategic ends, operates on the basis of developing networks and alliances between bureaucracies, unions, professional associations and community organisations. These alliances are not static, but form and are reformed around different issues and concerns. Activist professionals take responsibility for their own on-going professional learning, and work within multiple communities of practice.

Democratic professionalism and this associated 'activist' identity require not merely stronger professional bodies and associations but ones that are themselves prepared to work in an open and meaningful way with a much more varied range of stakeholders. In England this is not proving easy, not least because recent policies have undermined both the morale of, and public trust in the teaching workforce. This, in turn, has limited the extent to which teachers can engage authoritatively with other stakeholders. In Northern Ireland, however it may seem to you, the relative standing of teachers is such that you are starting from a position of greater strength and confidence as you confront the need to work with others to help shape the progressive opportunities that are provided by policies like those relating to the children's agenda.

References

Adams, A. & Tulasiewicz, W. (1995) *The Crisis in Teacher Education: a European concern?* London: Falmer Press

Davies, C. (1995) *Gender and the Professional Predicament in Nursing* Buckingham: Open University Press

DES [Department of Education and Science] (1984) *Initial Teacher Training: Approval of Courses Circular 3/84* London: DES.

Lawton, D. (1980) *The Politics of the School Curriculum* London: Routledge & Keegan Paul.

8

Learning Networks and Connective Knowledge

In pre-modern societies, children grew up in a world whose norms and behaviour system was inherited from their elders. Parents got the children involved in their everyday work, into the life of the family and the community, and all the ceremonies. Socialization, work, living conditions and relationships – *informal learning* according to present day terminology - were uniform within the framework of family, relatives, village and church.

In modern industrial societies, specialized institutions took over the tasks of teaching and educating. The school system became multifunctional and performed a range of duties, such as childminding and nurturing, ensuring equal opportunities and mobility, transmitting knowledge, providing a moral upbringing, a general education and satisfying the demands of the labour market.

After a while, with the general introduction of compulsory education and the accessibility of higher education, carrying out the mass of heterogeneous tasks became impossible, and the contradictions that ensued led to a growing number of critical phenomena. There were several answers to the crisis. Pedagogical reformers tried to model, in a school form, the organic unity of the pre-modern world, and its most famous representatives chose child-centeredness, activity centeredness and independence as their slogans. These experiments all aimed to create islands within which the distances arising from the modern alienated world could be eliminated.

Radical critics of the school system imagined its renewal taking place outside the institution of school. In his book on the worldwide crisis of education Philip H. Coombs, dreamed of revealing its ills with the help of scientifically based systems analysis, and of solving the crisis with comprehensive, institutional reforms initiated from the top. The ideologists of de-schooling, on the contrary, question the very right of schools to exist. They regard school as a bureaucratic, factory-like institution, an education "kolhoz", the scene of social taming. Their most famous representative, Ivan Illich, outlines the re-socialization of teaching and education, where individuals bypass the formal school system by learning in a self-organising way, from life, contemporary groups and from their elders with the help of critical reflection. A system of informal and accidental activities and the exchange of abilities take the place of bureaucratic, industrialized teaching, organised from the top. This model defines public education as a service centre and suggests that a "free choice of partner" in education can be realized with the help of a great communication network.

Thus, already in Illich's time, the notion appeared that networking was able to create completely new tools for knowledge production and knowledge exchange. The "de-schoolers" based their vision of re-socialization, of open, self-organising, networking public education on this idea. However, at the time, their reform proposals – open educational institution systems for every generation, organically integrating everyday operators into studying, learning based on cooperation and dialogue, making use of different sources of knowledge, integrating the experience of older and peer groups – remained utopias. Their ideas concerning the realization of the "educational web" - for example establishing a database for learning, making public individual ability-portfolios (*e-portfolios*), organising a network for contemporary groups to pool their expertise, or a reference service of those individuals and institutions who are potential participants in teaching - lacked the necessary highly developed, widely accessible technological infrastructure, and the market pressure of the IT industry did not yet exist.

The situation changed radically when networking technology – at least in the developed countries of the Northern Hemisphere and in Australia – reached the critical level of accessibility and prevalence. There was widespread demand for informal learning and with the slogan of lifelong learning, the political will emerged. These facts caused significant changes in the nature of the criticism against schools: Illich's utopia of re-socialized learning and socialization within networks suddenly became a real possibility.

Web 1.0, eLearning 1.0

As the use of the Internet spread, it became possible to acquire and store digitised versions of many different kinds of learning content (texts, pictures, audio and video). Although it was possible to access a wide range of information with by this means (known as web 1.0), it was not yet truly interactive. Contents could be placed on the homepages and databases, but it was not easy to create one's own content and share it with others. The typical Internet user browsed the web pages and downloaded content, but did not actively participate in the content-creation process.

Parallel to web 1.0 becoming more widespread, *learning management systems, (LMSs)* based on the internet became popular as well: these systems organised the databases, communication tools, task solutions, administration – in other words the whole learning process – into units. Online courses, which copied traditional educational patterns, appeared on the World Wide Web in the form of replica modules and lessons. Standardized, time limited, linear courses were created, with tutors and formalized, automatically verifiable tasks. This form of education, eLearning 1.0, is actually the technologically supported variant of traditional knowledge distribution, the virtual extension of textbooks and classroom teaching. Even in this environment, learning remained a passive process, managed from above or outside. The formalized, centralized, bureaucratic world of education of industrialized societies was extended into a digital environment.

Web 2.0 and eLearning 2.0

The situation changed completely when the phenomenon called *web 2.0* started to spread. "Digital natives" of web 2.0 not only searched for information on the web, but also became content providers themselves. The areas and tools of interactivity have become practically unlimited. Personal and institutional information is freely available on the World Wide Web and the technology exists to allow individuals to harness collective knowledge and entertainment portals for their own purposes. Students can create and exchange content in a cooperative way, within networks of their contemporaries. Blogs, forums, chats, wikis, newsgroups, and networks of friends and acquaintances provide an immense communal information production and exchange framework. The belief of hitherto criminalised file-sharers – that information is not for hiding but for passing on to others – became widespread. Increasingly sophisticated tools, from refined search engines through Wikipedia to well-maintained debate- and knowledge portals, are available. By this means it has become possible to construct personally reflected knowledge adapted to one's individual needs from information represented in cyberspace. These characteristics form the didactic basis of eLearning 2.0.

In the field of eLearning 2.0, knowledge chosen, organised, distributed and controlled by the authorities has been replaced by personal information management based on immediate needs. Consequently, the importance of official intermediaries and institutions is decreasing. Within networks of contemporaries, cooperation, learner-centeredness and the ideal of self-organised learning become a real possibility. The boundary between learning and teaching becomes less distinct. For the "download generation", the Internet is not a medium for learning; it is the platform and the centre of personal study. In the milieu of eLearning 2.0, the opportunity exists to reconstruct an organic learning environment.

Which developments have generated these changes?

- High-speed broadband Internet (access) has become accessible to large numbers of people, significantly increasing the rate of data acquisition.
- Information has become ubiquitous and can be reached with mobile tools.
- As *open source software* has spread, so content management is very cheap and simple making possible the creation of personalized *e-portfolios*.
- A wide range of new, free tools is at our disposal: blogs, wikis, file exchange programs, forums and tools that make collaborative content development possible.
- Freely usable content has appeared (open courseware, open content, CCL – Creative Commons Licence).
- New software supporting social networks is spreading rapidly.

The changeable, uncertain employment situation and the rapid technological changes that school curricula cannot follow have brought about the political challenge of "*lifelong learning*". As an alternative to formal education, company retraining and private courses try to compensate for the shortcomings of the education system. In many cases, companies prefer independently organised, online training and the exchange of expertise outside working hours.

It has become a political requirement that students be given the opportunity to participate in web 2.0-based, eLearning 2.0-based education in addition to the traditional, basic school training. As adults, they will only be able to keep up with the challenge of global knowledge exchange and be able to use interactive networks if they become familiar with these tools and opportunities at an early stage. Thus, one of the tasks of formal school training is to develop, in addition to the basic ones, skills that ensure that students feel at home in the 2.0 interactive knowledge-management environment. The most important competences should be searching for and evaluating information and making connections between different fields of knowledge, ideas and concepts. The real didactic question is how, according to their individual needs, students can be brought to the point where they can contextualize and connect information originating from different sources, using the exchange of thought (by way of a network-enabled discourse) and aided by other web 2.0 tools.

The phenomena of web 2.0 pose a new challenge to the traditional school system. If it does not want the gulf between this generation's culture and school to deepen even more dramatically, education must inevitably incorporate the elements of eLearning 2.0 into its repository of tools.

The Apple Education portal demonstrates the cultural differences between the new generation that uses web 2.0 (digital native users) and the teachers who were socialized in the paradigm of industrial society (digital immigrant teachers) as follows:

- Digital Native Learners
- Prefer receiving information quickly from
- multiple multimedia sources.
- Prefer parallel processing and multitasking.
- Prefer processing pictures, sounds and video before text.
- Prefer random access to hyper linked multimedia information.
- Prefer to interact/network simultaneously with many others. Prefer to learn "just-in-time."
- Prefer instant gratification and instant rewards.

- Prefer learning that is relevant, instantly useful and fun.
- Digital Immigrant Teachers
- Prefer slow and controlled release of information from limited sources. Prefer singular processing and single or limited tasking.
- Prefer to provide text before pictures, sounds and video.
- Prefer to provide information linearly, logically and sequentially. Prefer students to work independently rather than network and interact. Prefer to teach "just-in-case" (it's in the exam).
- Prefer deferred gratification and deferred rewards.
- Prefer to teach to the curriculum guide and standardized tests.

Network Theories and eLearning

According to Castells, the basic paradigm of the information age is networking and the space of flows which "reigns above the historically constructed space of places [...] In other words, flows become the units of work, decisions and *output-control,* instead of organisations" (quoted by Nyíri 2006). These prophetic words convey the most important feature of the organisation of learning in the information age. An ever greater part of the processes of learning and socialisation can be moved from the "institutions of stone" to decentralized, self-organising networks supported by information technology – the "space of flows". Learning in this de-institutionalised space is not about an organisation centrally defining the input and expecting that every learner reach the output result within a certain unit of time on a pre-defined, uniform route. In this learning paradigm, the guiding principle is considered to be the common definition of outcomes. However, the roads leading there are not common – they are individual routes developed from flows within networks connecting personal knowledge with knowledge from external sources.

It supports the basic, decentralized, "de-schooled" learning-organisational principles of eLearning 2.0. Barabási and Buchanan pointed out that many networks were scale free. "Scale free distribution means that many network elements have very few neighbours. At the same time, the number of elements with many neighbours is not zero." Distribution according to power functions characterises these networks. "Power functions mathematically define the fact that in real networks, the majority of points have only a few ties, and these numerous little points coexist with a few large central points that have an unusually large number of ties". In his book, Péter Csermely endeavours to prove that weak ties are what make networks strong. "A tie between two elements of the network is weak if taking away or adding the tie does not influence in a statistically sensitive way the average of the network's typical characteristics (usually one of the group-defining characteristics of the network). Weak ties stabilize networks". Jones and his co-authors examined the role of weak ties in network learning. They interpreted learning as a network process, which includes the ties between the students and their tutors, and the ties between the students and other sources of knowledge. Within this process, all ties are equal and none of them are privileged.

Imagine a centralized learning network, in which the professor, or the compulsory, very formalized syllabus or department represents the central, strong tie, while the interconnections between the students (the exchange of knowledge amongst student), and the connections between students and other information sources are insignificant. The network has few weak ties. If the central element is damaged (the professor becomes ill, the department is closed down, or there is a shortage of the required textbook, which is the unique source of knowledge), the network collapses. This is because the various weak ties that make the networks strong are missing. Scale free learning networks, supported by information technologies, are a lot less vulnerable to this kind of disturbance. In such a network, knowledge sharing amongst students is much better developed. Students store a vast amount of the curriculum in their own *electronic portfolios*. Learning blogs, wikis, forums, social networks (independently created contents) offer additional resources. Students can also be connected to experts, students and lecturers from other institutions and older people. They can intensively use the syllabus-archives created by students from other institutions. Assistant lecturers participate in the network and preserve the knowledge of their professors in their own e-portfolios. Learning becomes collective knowledge management based on many weak ties, and not on the central role of the professor or the formalized syllabus. Apart from a few strong ties, (since the strategic guidance of the professor may still remain important), the network is made up of very varied, heterogeneous weak ties. The network becomes strong: if the professor falls out of the system, the stored knowledge elements and the weak ties that can be mobilized do not allow the network to collapse or weaken.

Perelman, who produced a radical criticism of the school system in the early 1990's, created the concept of hyper learning (HL) to denote this type of network learning:

> "HL is not a single device or process, but a universe of new technologies that both possesses and enhances intelligence. The "hyper" in hyper learning refers not merely to the extraordinary speed and scope of new information technology, but to an unprecedented degree of connectedness of knowledge, experience, media, and brains - both human and non-human. The "learning" in HL refers most literally to the transformation of knowledge and behaviour through experience."

Perelman says that the ubiquitous, intelligent tools of information technology motivate us to participate actively in learning. Broadband information transmission makes it possible for everyone to call upon knowledge everywhere, at any time. Not only do advanced search-engines make navigation on the sea of information possible and effective, but they also efficiently aid understanding and contextualisation. This is all the more true because those tools, based on artificial intelligence, are becoming increasingly effective in the assistance they provide. In the future, the gauge of individual knowledge and the guarantee of success on the labour market may be the informally acquired competence visible on one's electronic-portfolio, and not an official diploma.

Connectivism: Learning Theory of the Future

The basic level of learning theories based on network theory is concerned with the organisation of individual knowledge – the cerebral system connecting knowledge elements, in fact, the neuro-psychology of individual knowledge organisation. For an individual's knowledge organisation, strong ties are represented by knowledge elements that have been connected into a formal system. To these are weak information ties, which are more accidental and associated with a set of heterogeneous, weakly embedded aspects. The greater the number of weak pieces of information that surround the knowledge with strong ties, the more willing we are to accept them as valid. The strong tie itself may be strong enough for us to consider the information as valid, but such a condition is a lot more vulnerable. If the source of information which is considered universally valid becomes, for some reason, discredited, that immediately causes all information originating from that source to become invalid. If, however, this connection is surrounded by versatile, secondary, weak information, then it ensures stability even in the case of damage. Siemens writes the following about this:

> "How does knowledge flow within a network? Which factors have an impact on the process? If we tentatively ascribe life-like properties to our learning networks, we can partly answer this question. Any living organism seeks two primary functions: replication and preservation. Nodes within our networks follow similar aspirations. Established beliefs and learning often ensure that new information is routed through (i.e., contextualized) the existing network. New information is evaluated and coded reflective of the existing meme of the learning network."

Using the tendencies of the network as a basis, Georg Siemens founded a learning theory of the information age called connectivism. In this theory, Siemens surpasses the traditional theories such as behaviourism, cognitivism and constructivism. (Even this last one - which stresses the socially motivated nature of learning - focuses on individual learning techniques and the processes of inner mental activity, and does not take into consideration the way learning takes place in organisations and network structures.)

Connectivism considers learning as a process in which the role of informal information exchange, organised into networks and supported with electronic tools, becomes more and more significant. Learning becomes a continuous, lifelong system of network activities, embedded into other activities. The motivation for gaining and contextualising information becomes stronger if searching and evaluation becomes a cooperative, network activity. Students can significantly improve the efficiency of their learning if they take part in a network, or virtual community dealing with the given subject. Thus the collective knowledge once again becomes a source of individual knowledge ("cycle of knowledge development"). As the number of cooperative activities increases, personal social networks become the scene of informal exchange of expertise, and "communities of practice" develop. Besides the questions of "how" and "what" to learn, we now have the question of "where to learn".

Siemens makes it clear that in networks, contextualising information and determining validity may both become collective processes. So-called feed-aggregators help the collecting and feeding back of information into one's own knowledge network. Instead of consuming information that has been embedded in connections by institutions, learning may become an active creation of knowledge.

Network Learning

The learning-organisational, knowledge-creating theories of eLearning 2.0, hyper learning and connectivism express the hope that networking supported by advanced technology can put an end to the modern division between institutional learning and personal knowledge and become a tool of reintegration.

There is a desire to decrease the alienation of the world of traditional school with the help of the information flow taking place in the social networks of the virtual world and in cooperative, creative areas of learning. We talk about network communities, organic and open learning environments, the intertwining of everyday activities and learning, the gradual disappearance of the border between spontaneous and institutional learning, the intermingling of childhood and adulthood. Although this desire was just a utopia in the age of the early, radical school criticisms, or when the first network learning theories appeared today, in the globalised environment of the information society, creating new forms of embeddedness in the virtual space of social networks has become common practice. The spread of new forms of learning also implies various potential conflicts. There are numerous signs that the new forms of informal network learning can only be fitted into the narrow, bureaucratically controlled framework of traditional institutions that are limited in time and resources, with great difficulty. The pedagogical debate concerning this issue often goes in the wrong direction, because the discussion is between two incompatible conceptual worlds. An important educational-sociological, network-research and pedagogical question of the coming period will be how the institutions of the official school system will accept this phenomenon, to what extent they will integrate or reject it, and what types of conflicts, compromises and solutions this process will develop.

In traditional societies, socialisation did not take place in separate institutions, but rather took place in the family and within small communities. In modern societies, specialized institutions have taken over the roles of teaching, educating and child minding. Mass-education could only be organised in a standardized, industrial way. Pedagogical reformers wanted to change this alienated socialization into socialization based on independence that could be provided in child-centred schools. The radical critics of the school system wanted to de-school the whole of society, saying that spontaneous activities and the network of knowledge exchange could replace formal school.

With the spreading of information technology, the utopia of network learning may become a reality, at least technically. A vast amount of spontaneous knowledge exchange is taking place on the interactive World Wide Web. It is on the basis of this that the theories of eLearning 2.0 and connectivism declare that network participation and access to information and to software that interprets and contextualizes information makes a completely new, cooperative, self-organising form of learning possible. This process questions the role of traditional educational institutions today. While the forms of eLearning 1.0 only meant the mechanical transposition of traditional linear learning to a virtual medium, the mode of operation of eLearning 2.0, (organised into networks, self-organising, embedded into activities) may be the starting point and driving force of a learning-organisational process that takes advantage of the opportunities offered by the information society.

References

Castells, Manuel (1996): *Information Age: Economy, Society and Culture,* Volume I: The Rise of the Network Society.Blackwell, Oxford.

Coombs, Philip H. (1968): *The World Educational Crisis: A Systems Analysis*.Oxford University Press, Oxford.

Downes, Stephen (2006): *Learning networks and connective knowledge*.http://it.coe.uga.edu/itforum/paper92/paper92.html, accessed 17 November 2006.

Field, John (2006): *Lifelong Learning and the New Educational Orde*r.Trentham Books, London.

Papert, S (1993): T*he Children's Machine: Rethinking School in the Age of the Computer*. Basic Books, New York.

Perelman, Lewis J. (1992): *School's out. A radical new formula for the revitalization of America's educational system*. Aron Books, New York.

9

ICT and Learning in the Knowledge Society

Modern civilization is characterized by the growing pace of change. The economy now undergoes a radical transformation within a single generation. Because of the enormous difficulty in understanding, appreciating and even surviving change, we talk about the impact of these changes as future shock. On the other hand, these fundamental shifts do not appear suddenly, as bolts from the blue: they are always a part of a longer historical evolution, in which technological development plays a part. It is not out of place to cite Alvin Toffler who coined the term *future shock* about forty years ago:

> In dealing with the future, at least for the purpose at hand, it is more important to be imaginative and insightful than to be one hundred percent "right". Theories do not have to be "right" to be enormously useful. Even error has its uses. The maps of the world drawn by medieval cartographers were so hopelessly inaccurate, so filled with factual error, that they elicit condescending smile today... Yet the great explorers could never have discovered the New World without them.

We believe that ICT will be a key factor in future positive change - provided they are in the possession of people who use them creatively and for the common good.

Mindcraft Economy

The economy has classically been divided into agricultural, manufacturing and service sectors. Today, these sectors have been joined by a fourth category: the booming *knowledge sector* consisting of *knowledge workers.* In an increasingly 'smart' automated environment, mental work is moving from crunching and tossing data to creating information and knowledge, and then communicating, exchanging and sharing it with fellow-workers. In short, as it was already noted more than decade ago, *mindcraft* is replacing *handicraft*. The ubiquitous computer and its related ICT devices have become critical tools for much of the world economy.

At the same time, *knowledge work* has become, not just another sector but a cross-sectional drive, a main carrier, and a cutting edge for contemporary economic activities. Observers talk about the emerging *mindcraft economy* of the 21st century, an economy that presupposes continuous learning within elaborate systems that combine human agents and intelligent ICT-based machines.

Globalization and ICT

One of the major trends in the global economy is the movement of material industries from developed to developing countries. This process involves information industries as well. While this change is positive in many ways, the distribution of wealth is unequal and much of the world continues to suffer from severe problems of poverty, hunger and illiteracy. At the same time, more countries have a chance to take leading roles in the new information or knowledge society, which generally assumes a multi-centrist and multi-cultural worldview. ICT can help educators achieve this kind of society by creating opportunities for:

- greater individual success, without widening the gap between the poorest and the richest;
- supporting models of sustainable development; and
- more countries to build and use information space, rather than having a few countries and mass media monopolies dominate dissemination of information and culture.

The world's most serious problems - the growing demand for food, shelter, health, employment, and quality of life - cannot be solved without highly efficient new technologies. With the advantages of being nature-protecting, non-polluting, less energy consuming, and more human-friendly, ICT applications are becoming indispensable parts of contemporary culture, spreading across the globe through general and vocational education.

Technology —A Double-edged Sword

ICT already influence the social and political life of all nations. However, their influence is not always for the better. The use of message-forming and transmitting technologies in some cases impedes justice and concentrates power by reducing reciprocity in communication. Emergence of huge media conglomerates is vivid evidence of this.

Even more impressive lessons, both warning and encouraging, can be drawn from the recent history of the fall of great totalitarian states. One might suggest that the fall of the Soviet communist empire had already begun when Joseph Stalin died in 1953. Not coincidentally, the change to a more liberal regime coincided with the proliferation of TV broadcasting and the introduction of home tape-recorders in the USSR. The impact of those types of ICT was equally significant but different in its directions and consequences. Television, owned by the state, became, and for the next forty odd years remained, another tool for *vertical* brainwashing and manipulation of public consciousness, exercised by the totalitarian regime.

The same historical period was marked by a rising tide of underground dissemination of the written word (and, if caught, severely punished). Forbidden manuscripts of prose, poetry, political philosophy, social critique, and reports on violations of human rights were duplicated on mechanical typewriters that produced four carbon copies at a time. Photostat copying was too complicated and demanded special skills to be used widely. In the early 1970s, the old fashioned photostat copier was supplanted by the electrochemical xerox copier, which was extremely fast and easy to operate, but kept under strict police surveillance in governmental offices and inaccessible to private persons. Fax machines followed a decade later, giving additional impetus to the already visible process of decay and disintegration of the totalitarian stronghold. Toward the end of the 1980s, communication barriers (censorship, radio jamming, and all that) went tumbling down along with the Berlin Wall.

Future generations of historians may be tempted to interpret ICT as the main leverage for all these cataclysms. Needless to say, it would be an obvious exaggeration. History paves its way through time by much more complicated trajectories. In fact, Mikhail Gorbachev ascended to power and launched his famous *Perestroika* (re-building) before such novelties as the Internet, and even phone-fax, had become common commodities in the

USSR. Nonetheless, it would not be too strong an exaggeration to say that the personal computer (with printer and modem to connect the Internet), neglected by short-sighted Soviet authorities, hammered the last nail into the coffin of communist ideological and political rule in Russia and Eastern Europe.

Similarly, we believe that the worldwide proliferation of ICT will help offset cultural imperialism, ideological totalitarianism, and information monopoly. The Internet and desktop publishing will play a crucial role in democratizing the dissemination and use of information. In addition, ICT create new options for the preservation and revival of indigenous cultural traditions and spiritual values. Even a teacher with a class of students, can design a set of fonts for their native language, make a multilingual dictionary, record folk songs and dances, make pictures of handicrafts, and put everything together as an Internet page. We hope that linguistic barriers such as the historically and politically imposed dominance of a few languages may be weakened by the worldwide availability of ICT and its thoughtful application for educational purposes.

Finally, ICT also change age and gender distribution and opportunities in the work place. Women and young people can learn to use ICT and work in ICT environments as well as men.

Individual Needs and Expectations of Society

Life in the new knowledge society demands more independent and responsible behaviour and much less routine execution of orders. To prosper, and sometimes even to survive, people now need to be able to make responsible decisions in new and unexpected situations. Most of all, they need to continue to learn throughout life. Individuals seek to use ICT for personal growth, creativity and joy, consumption and wealth. They also need to be able to analyze mass media information critically and to use it productively.

These individual needs require knowledge and skills to search for information, to analyze, synthesize, evaluate, channel, and present it to others, and to exercise judgment in order to predict, plan, and control fast changing events. The skills noted above are indispensable to ICT-supported and non-ICT learning environments. However, more and more industrial, professional, and business occupations call for knowledge-based and skilful intellectual work. A worker's ability to use ICT fluently is necessary in more and more occupations. Former skills have become obsolete. The abilities to make pen-and-paper arithmetic calculations, for example, or to write in calligraphy, are now viewed as specialized abilities (though both are still useful in the education of students).

At the same time, it is now vital for every child, adolescent, and adult to have at least a general notion of their technological surroundings at home and at school, on the street, in the office and work place. To be sure, any new technology brings dangers and temptations. A recent example of such risks is encouraging a *grasshopper mentality,* as seen in much of the Internet surfing across content, and the pollution of the Internet environment.

Now, what can we as educators do in carrying out our mission, and how can ICT be used to enrich learning opportunities in our schools?

It is essential to develop a vision of the future. This is true, not only because the world is becoming a knowledge society, relying heavily on new knowledge, skills and experiences, but also because we live in a technologically dominated socio-economic milieu that is based on short-term consumer-driven goals of production, and only secondarily on holistic, long-term concern for sustainable development. With our minds fixed narrowly on the technology that supports a comfortable life - even school life! - we may forget, or even act in conflict with, humane and democratic values.

Radical Changes Needed in School

In the 21st century, the ever-increasing needs of individuals and society are placing a heavy burden on established educational institutions. At the same time, traditional structures and modes of teaching appear less and less responsive to the challenges of our turbulent times. There is a clarion call for innovation and transformation among educators everywhere, especially in the elementary school, the most crucial stage in the development of a human being. Furthermore, the internal problems of schooling are inseparable fromexternal changes on a global scale, and must be seen in the context of contemporary world problems. These, in turn, will not be solved unless approached and treated educationally, as well as economically, politically, and socio-culturally.

Students who enter school are communicative, curious, creative, and capable of learning many things. They have proved this already by mastering a mother tongue, physical motion, complicated games, and many other life skills. However, we believe that the traditional school of the 20th century, which is still very much with us, diminishes these abilities over the period of learning. We need a new kind of school for the 21st century.

Educational Trends

From a consideration of societal perspectives, we turn now to an examination of educational trends over recent centuries.

Ancient Legacy and Modern Trends

Trinity of Education

There is a venerable tradition, extending at least from Jan Amos Comenius in the 17th century to Max Scheller in the 20th century of subdividing general education into three domains. This approach stemmed from the old tripartite notion of the human creature consisting of:

- a body that needs food and shelter, physical comfort, and fleshly pleasures, as well as other material goods and man-made things, available only in an artificial environment;
- a soul, suffering from solitude and searching for another soul, longing for sympathy and understanding, willing to give love and be loved in joyful communion with the universe; and
- a spirit, striving to orient itself towards the Initial Cause (Prime Mover, Life Source, Perennial Wisdom, Ultimate Tuth, and Final Goals) of human existence, transcending all temporal and spatial boundaries.

The corresponding educational (i.e. cultural) domains have been designated by various words. In summarizing (very roughly) their essential meanings, we might call them:

- *Labour-technological education*, aimed at mastering arts and crafts, logic and mathematics, engineering, natural, social and behavioural sciences, and other activities enabling individuals to fulfill their needs and desires by efficiently processing, governing, and controlling matter, energy, and information in a world of objects and objective phenomena.
- *Communitive (interpersonal) education*, aimed at learning the ways and means of subjective-emotional relations and interactions between human beings (and, to a degree, non-humans). This can be done through ethical and aesthetic teaching, caring for those in need, playing games, dancing, singing, and story-telling; ritual and myth, folk-lore and philosophy, poetry and theatre, music and fine arts; discussing and

solving problems of civic life, thus actively participating in public endeavours of social concern.

- *Transpersonal education*, aimed at the catechization and initiations of neophytes into the creed, mysteries, and sacraments of a particular religious confession or ideology; helping individuals to pose a question of their relations to the Absolute; or just endowing a person with a sense of belonging to something infinitely greater and more potent.

Diversions and Estrangement

The so much talked about education-and-culture crisis often labeled as the *Conflict of Two Cultures,* or the *Snow-Leavis controversy* has resulted, to a large extent, from the historical schism between the educational domains described in the preceding section. In the 17th century, Western Europe hailed the advancement of scientific learning and technological inventions, based on newly discovered mechanical laws of motion. Water-, and later steam- and electric-driven machines, self-acting and labour-saving, relieved man of gaining his daily bread by the sweat of his brow, and promised to turn his life into an earthly paradise. Believers in science and engineering did not foresee that the humanization of the machine would have the paradoxical effect of mechanizing humanity.

Rationalism Backfired

Since the mid-19th century, we have witnessed the dominance of the rational and technological aspects of culture over the spiritual and cultural. Ironically, the rational domain has itself begun to suffer from the severing of its vital connections with the spiritual and cultural domains. The system of mass education - one of the really miraculous inventions of that era, along with medicine - itself falls victim to the triumphant march of Reason.

Religion, philosophy and art, once so nourishing to humane values, have been made arid and sterile, incapable of counterbalancing and complementing rational and intellectual development. Meanwhile, the latter has encountered increasingly loud callings to fight against the proliferation of advanced technologies and even to penalize efforts to make new ones. This kind of debate has had led nowhere.

The 20th century witnessed, on the one hand, the highest degree of techno-scientific refinement such as, for instance, magnetic resonance imaging, among numerous examples. On the other hand, the 20th century also saw the creation of the most sophisticated devices to exterminate millions of defenceless people by, for instance, self-guided ballistic missiles with nuclear warheads. Examples here are numerous as well. Rationality, devoid of humane values, runs the risk of stagnating, or running wild, to our own destruction.

From Schism to Convergence

We need to envisage measures and take modest, practical steps toward restoring a lost balance and creative interconnectedness, which might be achieved by making each domain more perceptive and responsive to the true nature, needs, and aspirations of each. Perhaps the best advocate of such a convergence in the 20th century was the Russian philosopher Nikolai Berdyaev. Here are a few key points, extracted from his works, *Spirit and Machine* and *Man and Cosmos. Technics*:

> The role of technology is two-fold. It has both positive and negative meaning.
>
> Technicalization dehumanizes man's life, while being in itself a product of the human spirit. But the relationship between spirit and technics is more complicated than it is usually thought of. Technology can be a force capable not only to de-spiritualize, but spiritualize as well. When obeying only the law of its own, technology would lead to the technicalized world wars and to an exorbitant etatisme, the absolute Supremacy of the State. The state gets omnipotent, even more totalitarian - and not under totalitarian political regimes only; it doesn't want to recognize any limits to its authority and does treat the man as his own means and tool.

Berdyaev's views suggest a healthy ground upon which educators of the labour, communitive, and transpersonal domains might collaborate productively. A hopeful future lies, not in the further adaptation of human personality to the machine, but in the re-adaptation of the machine to the human personality for truly noble, humane purposes. Just as the autonomous nervous system liberates the mind for its higher functions, so the new technology can bring about a similar release of creative energy. To achieve this end, we must go beyond technicalities and tackle the more profound issues of education.

Liberal and Vocational Education

A False Dichotomy

The rift between academic schooling and master-apprenticeship training goes back to the classical age of ancient Greece, when the liberal arts curriculum was originally designed as vocational education for politics. The first goal of such instruction was apprenticeship in the skills of rhetoric, in preparation for a career in political argumentation. At that time, the ability to do or to make something, and the ability to talk about doing or making it, were literally one and the same thing. However, with the vast expansion of academic institutions since the early 19th century, rhetoric came to be seen as a means, not an end of teaching. As a result, rhetorical methods of academic vocationalism have been misapplied to a range of non-political crafts and skills which, to be learned effectively, need doing to be mastered.

We believe that rhetoric, as a fully-fledged ICT-supported subject matter, could provide a collaborative community of practice built in the classroom. There, students, through assisted participation in rhetorical activity, could undertake what is now often called *cognitive,* or *semiotic apprenticeship.* That is, they could individually reconstruct the resources of culture as tools for creative and responsible social living in the classroom, the school, and the wider community.

A long time ago, distinguished voices were pointing towards this false dichotomy of technical and liberal education. Alfred North Whitehead entitled his 1917 Presidential address to the Mathematical Association of England *Technical Education and Its Relation to Science and Literature.* He wrote:

> There can be no adequate technical education, which is not liberal, and no liberal education, which is not technical: that is, no education which does not impart both technique and intellectual vision. [...] Geometry and mechanics, followed by workshop practice, gain that reality without which mathematics is verbiage.

ICT demonstrate that technical-vocational and liberal education can be taught together; they need not suffer from an impenetrable barrier between them. In vocational-technical education, essential knowledge and skills are transmitted, not by means of lecturing from a position of authority, but through a working interaction between master and apprentices. For a long time, vocational learning was looked upon as unquestionably inferior to academic instruction. Today, however, educators are reconsidering vocational learning as a useful basis for schooling.

Smarter People for Smarter Machines

We can sum up our argument so far by offering three points:

1. The post-industrial mindcraft economy and global society depend on smart machines AND a smart workforce, using high-end technologies with even greater competence.
2. Training and skill enhancement are part of a lifelong learning process.
3. Adolescent schooling, techno-vocational education, and actual work need to be interrelated. These truths apply to technologically advanced societies and to developing countries alike. Indeed, nations moving from ancient to modern agrarian economies must be even more prepared for the accelerating pace of change, because their youth will have even more to learn and master over their working life span. Befriending ICT in the initial stages of education will help young people come to terms with what lies ahead.

The Only True Education

Our aims as educators must go beyond specialized training of craftsmen or factory workers. The only true education is one where all arts, crafts, sciences, and technologies are linked and facilitate mutual cognitive development, productive creativity, and personal growth. The *new literacy,* a term used more than a decade ago (Anderson 1993) to embrace the changed literacy demands resulting from the new technologies in schools, and ICT offer educators, perhaps for the first time, an opportunity to create such an ambitious scheme.

The question is how can we create both the educational framework and the technologies to carry on a project of such proportions?

Continuous Educational Development

We need to build a continuing mechanism for the uninterrupted development of new curricula and new modular courses in an increasing variety of different learning environments. Furthermore, this needs to be extended from earliest childhood education through to adult education. Deep questioning is taking place regarding general schooling in our society:

- What should a student be required to know and do to succeed in the 21st century?
- What should a teacher be required to know and to do to help students acquire the desired knowledge and abilities?

- What role can ICT play in helping both teachers and students perform these new tasks?

New Learning Activities

Memorizing is not enough. The old pedagogy was justly criticized for presenting content in lecture format, as a series of abstract notions and formal rule-following to be memorized and reproduced by a student orally or in written or behavioural form. In many schools, little has changed. Much teaching is still conducted on this basis, while insufficient attention is paid to learning strategies (the tools and procedures a person uses to learn). A small percentage of students (those usually called bright or gifted, who are capable of building their own learning strategies) learn best under these conditions. However, most young people — and we would add, adults, too - need concrete, visualized, experiential, self-initiated, hands-on, and real-world learning opportunities. Yet many of these students are typically pushed aside and labeled *weak, poor* or *lagging behind.*

There is a movement in many countries, and within different education systems, to allow more variability and flexibility in the initiatives of individual teachers and local educational communities. Changes are needed in the status and functional role of teachers. Contemporary teachers do not have to pretend that they know everything in order to formulate problems and ways to solve them. At the same time, teachers are taking on the increasingly important roles of advisor and learning facilitator. The new focus is on the process of learning and providing environments and tools that encourage everyone to become successful and responsible learners.

Three Rs for the 21st century

The new kinds of activities to be learned and new learning activities lead inevitably to a drastic revision of the idea of literacy, considered for many centuries the main goal of primary education.

The traditional notion of literacy (including so-called numeracy) was based on the Three Rs (Reading, wRting, and aRthmetic), together with accurate handwriting (preferably calligraphic), and memorizing certain excerpts from textbooks and classical poetry by heart.

Now, we see an urgent need for a *new literacy* that is ICT-based and can be presented in three components corresponding to the traditional Three Rs:

- [Reading] - finding information by searching in written sources, observing, collecting, and recording;
- [Writing] - communicating in hypermedia involving all types of information and all media; and
- [Arithmetic] - designing objects and actions.

To sum up, we must reshape drastically both educational content and learning procedures. The new literacy shuns memorization of facts and rules. It stresses the ability to find facts and imagine unprecedented options. A capacity to understand and invent rules, posing problems to oneself, planning and designing one's own activities, come to the forefront. The goal of this kind of education is not a narrow technical fluency, but personal development alongside the core competencies for high-level thinking and acting.

Calling for New Dimensions of Teaching

Modern society needs educated citizens who can make decisions and implement them in a rapidly changing world. Individuals, organizational structures such as corporations and governments, and educational institutions, should be prepared for life-long learning. Information processing and communication are becoming major activities in daily life, and effective citizens and leaders of the 21st century will be required to understand and fluently use the latest sophisticated tools to manage an enormous amount of data, information, and messages. *Future shock* means there is an urgent necessity to solve unexpected or ill-defined problems. Therefore, lifelong learning will be the normal state for a modern individual.

One of the major changes in education can be described as a general shift from teaching to learning. This does not mean that the teacher is becoming any less important. Rather, the teacher's role is increasingly to assist students to become good learners. At the same time, teachers must help create stronger relationships between the subjects of study and concrete reality, putting them in a more relevant context for students. In many cases, this implies an integration of disciplines and cooperation among teachers of different subject areas.

Global Awareness and Cooperation

Educators all over the world have been working for decades to reform their local school systems according to their specific conditions, aspirations, and traditions. These educators are becoming aware that their local endeavours need the support of the global educational community to succeed.

Global awareness is greatly encouraged by the progress of modern information and communication technologies. ICT offer a wide array of materials for building new schooling systems that allow long-distance exchange and interaction between geographically spread groups of teachers and their students. These materials are flexible and responsive to the changing needs of learners of all ages.

Meeting this challenge, in turn, requires collaboration across national, cultural and institutional boundaries, and among individuals and groups who have been isolated. Electronic mail, bulletin board systems, teleconferences, and virtual communities on the World Wide Web (WWW) allow reciprocal communication among individuals and groups with common interests. Education researchers can team up with classroom practitioners to form research collaborations. Working together, regardless of where they live, scientists, teachers, and students are already finding once unimaginable freedom to investigate and understand powerful ideas that may have a global impact. A UNESCO-IBE document puts it this way:

Current trends such as worldwide economy, the information technology revolution, the crisis in traditional ideological paradigms, massive migration, the growing concern with global problems such as the environment, drugs and AIDS, have modified not only traditional social relationships, but also culture's role in the development process. Two apparently contradictory trends dominate modern society, or, more correctly many societies that are now in transit: standardization of cultural patterns and the search for basic reference points for cultural identity. The tensions, the imbalances and, in many cases, open conflicts have worsened to such point that some analysts estimate that future conflicts will take on cultural character...

Education, both formal and informal, is at the centre of this renewal of methods for cultural dialogue.

Information Processing

It commences with a discussion of various societal perspectives - the accelerating pace of global change, globalization and ICT, and so on - concluding that radical changes in schools are needed. Next, we touch on key educational trends and suggest that a new literacy is required for the 21st century, calling for a different kind of teaching.

Technologies and Tools

As a wise man noted centuries ago, neither a bare hand nor an intellect alone can get jobs done. We need tools. And ever since the dawn of human history, people have been inventing and using tools - stone axes and hammers, potter's wheels and furnaces, levers, and pulleys - to process food and materials and to harness the energy needed for their physical survival and well being. Similarly, people have used tools for information processing and communication exchange. The invention of language made our far-off ancestors capable of processing and controlling their own thoughts, feelings, and behaviour. Words can be considered as the tools of our mental activities, and the first and foremost of the latter is the activity of learning.

Until recent centuries, these activities have been manifested almost entirely through the organic functions of our minds and body (i.e. speech), and slightly supported externally by rather primitive tools and techniques (e.g. writing stylus and pen, or abacus). Then the printing press appeared. During the 19th and 20th centuries, new tools for storing and transmitting information appeared. Today, computer-centred ICT are extending and amplifying our capacity for computational operations, logical reasoning, heuristic search, and grasping of coherence and hidden interconnectedness in chaotic signals and disparate data. That is, a computer is never autonomous but, rather, connected to a growing number of electronic digital devices, aggregations and networks for data and information acquisition, storage, processing, distribution and multimedia delivery. All these entities are subsumed under the generic name of ICT.

Educational Technology of Mind

We turn now to the educational technology of the mind, or an analysis of what is involved in learning. In most learning activities, the following phases can be recognised:

(a) Accepting and analyzing a problem.

(b) Making sure we have no ready-made solutions for it.

(c) Deciding to launch a project, setting the main goals and objectives, weighing our mental and material resources.

(d) Discovering that we are not equipped enough to cope with it successfully.

(e) Seeing what additional specific knowledge, skills, or experience we must obtain to arrive at a solution.

(f) Going through a corresponding process of research learning, training, drill and practice.

(g) Designing a set of possible solutions (generating options, comparing alternatives, evaluating), and then choosing the one that seems most suitable.

(h) Imagining what will happen if the chosen design is implemented. What changes will it make to our immediate surroundings and broader physical and socio-cultural environment? What consequences and side effects might it cause? How could we prevent, avoid, or repair them? Re-assessing the overall approach to tackling the problem.

(i) Reflecting upon what we have done: repeating mentally the road taken and actions made; describing the essentials; scheming about if, and how we could use our newly acquired knowledge, skills, and experience to address other problems in the future. This pattern of learning activity phases, which we might call the basic educational technology of mind, can be developed and supported with various software, hardware, and courseware technologies of computer simulation, email networks, interactive multimedia, and other advanced uses of ICT

Learning as Information Processing

Generally speaking, information is the content of all messages we receive from other people and the world at large, as well as those we originate ourselves and send back in exchange.

Information manifests itself wherever and whenever we find or create any patterns. A pattern is such a distribution of events in a time or space continuum that we can recognize and nominate, then compare to some other pattern and, finally, discern the former from, or identify with the latter. One may draw a parallel between the notion of pattern and the notions of order, organization, and form, as opposed to anything disordered, chaotic and formless; in this perspective, information can be understood literally as *putting into form.*

Human information processing - be it purely organic or instrumentally supported and extended by the most sophisticated machines - encompasses collecting, storing, retrieving, sorting out, assembling and disassembling, re-working, and transmitting patterns used in thinking and communication, as well as inventing, designing, constructing, and manufacturing any tangible object. Any learning begins with seeking for, finding, and testing patterns - coherent clusters of information - favourable to our survival, comfort, and unfolding of our hidden potential. Even infants strive to explore their immediate surroundings by trial and error; they imitate adults' actions (e.g. smiling) and see whether something is edible, pleasant, amicable, hostile, or good as a tool to reach something desirable. The information gathered, interpreted, and evaluated during such explorative and imitative-reconstructive behaviour is stored in children's memory as mental models for their future purposeful actions, both physical and intellectual, including all kinds of consecutive learning endeavours.

ICT make natural tools in education because of the simple and fundamental fact that learning is largely based on dealing with information. Listening, talking, reading, writing, reassuring, evaluating, synthesizing and analyzing, solving mathematical problems, and memorizing verses and state capitals, are all examples of off-computer information processing. Even more importantly ICT can be used for other types of information processing, previously marginal in the traditional school, but now becoming more and more essential, like project planning, or the search for new information outside school textbooks, as well as in the processes of so-called creative writing (drawing, constructing). In many other school activities (such as sport, for example), different kinds of interaction between students and teachers can gain from using ICT. The human dimensions of ICT manifest themselves in providing powerful means to open dialogue, fruitful interaction, and synergy between a teacher and a student or, rather, between Master and Apprentice, as well as among apprentices themselves -whether in close contact or by long-distance.

Historically, information processing and communication have been major school activities. These occurred mainly between the teacher and student with the very modest external support of pencil, paper, and chalkboard. Now, the extensive use of computers, with versatile sensors, peripherals and extensions, allow teachers a whole new degree of sophistication and flexibility.

References

Anderson, J. (1993). *The New Literacy and Technology.* Keynote address to the International Reading Association Convention, San Antonio, Texas, April 1993.

Bederson, B., Shneiderman, B. (2003). *The Craft of Information Visualization: Readings and Reflections.* Morgan Kaufmann Publ., San Francisco.

Bonta, P. (1990). *Building on Intuitions: Music Composition in a Logo Environment.* In Idit Harel (Ed.). 1990. *Constructionist Learning.* MIT Media Laboratory, Cambridge, MA.

UNESCO. (2002). *Information and Communication Technologies in Teacher Education: A Planning Guide* (Ed. P. Resta). UNESCO, Paris.

UNESCO-IBE. (1995). *Teacher Training and Multiculturalism: National Studies.* IBE, Geneva.

Vygotsky, L.S. (1978). *Mind in Society: The development of higher psychological processes.* Harvard University Press, Cambridge, MA.

10

Digital Tools for Teaching and Learning

A computer and its peripherals are often likened to an organism able to interact purposefully with its surrounding realities, which are perceived and modified through various receptors and effectors. This view helps to explain the principles of industrial robots, guided missiles, and similar automata, but the metaphor leaves out many other important applications of ICT.

One could also describe these complex hardware and software systems as sets of smart tools or, rather, as teams of highly disciplined, indefatigable, semi-self-governing artificial agents ready to execute strictly defined tasks. By wisely commanding, controlling, and managing the work of those tools or agents, we can increase:

I. the sensitivity of our senses, which enable us to perceive events and communicate with other humans and machines over long distances;

II. the amount of data, information, and symbolic expressions that can be processed and logically analyzed in a split second;

III. the efficiency, accuracy and precision of our manipulations of both symbolic and material objects of the most diverse kind; and

IV. our capacity to make sound decisions based upon intuitive judgments and tacit knowledge.

Still another way to understand ICT is to imagine them as extensions of human organs and systems, including perceptive, reacting, thinking ones. These extensions operate mostly in the created (artificial or virtual) reality,, presented mostly by visual images. So we can use digital tools to clarify our inner picture of the outside world, as well as to enhance our ability to manage space and time while operating personal computer - a machine that works in permanent contact with a human. Co-ordination between the human body, our senses, and the personal computer is a critical issue in the effectiveness of using ICT. This coordination is similar to that required by other artifacts designed and targeted to human needs: tools for handicraft, furniture, eyeglasses, and many other material objects.

Information Basics

Information Objects

Technology can provide our eyes with a static image (or picture) or a dynamic (changing) video image. It can also present us with an audio (always dynamic) sound. And both can be combined in video recording and playback. These are the basic types of information objects.

Humans can also structure information objects. For example, we invented languages and characters for their communication. Texts (sequences of characters) are formed information objects. There is also the possibility of making complex objects from simpler ones by means of links. A link is an imaginary connection, association, or arrow going from an element of one object (for example, a word, or a piece of an image) to another. The complex object constituted by such linked objects is called a hyper-object. ICT provide us with tools to transfer immediately from one object to another, or between hyper-objects.

Information Space

As humans, we store a huge amount of collected information outside the human brain, in libraries and archives, and in other types of storage, and increasingly in ICT digital devices. These might include an individual, personal information space (like a personal library). Similarly, groups and organizations build their own information spaces. Thanks to the Internet, most of these information spaces are now parts of single global information space, in theory accessible to everyone.

Digital Transformation

Signals and images in the physical world are either continuous or analogue. To be stored, transmitted, and processed by modern ICT, they must be transformed into digital, or discrete, signals. The simplest example of discretization is measurement. When you measure length, weight, or time, you transform an analogue value into a digital one: the result is a finite sequence of digits. In the following graphs, temperature is presented as a continuous curve. It is approximated by measurements in fixed moments, one an hour with an accuracy of one degree.

Storing Information, Memory and Compression

When we store information (in a computer memory or in another way), we measure the needed memory size using specific units. To store the simplest piece of information, a '0' or '1', we need 1 bit. One byte equals 8 bits, and can store up to 256 different symbols - for example, the English alphabet (in upper and lower case), plus digits, and punctuation marks. Therefore, when we say that the memory size of a computer is 6 gigabyte, this means that the memory can store approximately 6,000,000,000 symbols. Bits are abbreviated as b, bytes as B.

In some cases, information can be compressed to occupy less space, and then de-compressed (decoded) to restore it close to, or often identical to, the original. Compression requires less memory volume for storage, and allows quicker transmission time.

Here are some figures on the size of information objects given in orders of magnitude:

1 page of text occupies 1-10KB

1 picture of the screen of a modern computer of a good quality occupies about 1-10MB

1 minute of digitized sound of good quality occupies approximately 10MB (or, if compressed, with a minor loss of quality, it takes about 100KB)

1 minute of digitized video of good quality occupies approximately 100MB (or, if compressed, with a minor loss of quality, it takes about 1MB).

Transmitting Information

Information is transmitted between people in different continents or inside the human brain in the form of signals. The signals are dynamic changes, or waves. Two major types of waves around us are: sound waves in solid, liquid or gaseous media; and electromagnetic waves transmitted in a vacuum (in any mediuma transparent for them), or channelled in a wire or optical fibre. The most important kind of waves is constituted by periodic changes (oscillations) in a medium. These periodic changes are transformed, distorted, reshaped or modulated, to transmit a signal. The frequency of the changes is measured in Hertz (abbreviated as Hz). One change per second is 1 Hz. In the case of sound, the frequencies that can be perceived by humans are in the range of 20 Hz to 20 KHz. In the case of electromagnetic waves, the frequencies used to transmit information are:

Visible light between 430THz (Red) and 750 THz (Violet)

Radio (RF) in the range 100 KHz to 10 GHz (including frequencies for AM, FM, TV, cellular, and satellite transmission)

Microwave between 10 GHz and 1 THz

Infrared (IR) about 10 THz - visible light (Red)

Ultraviolet is visible light (Violet) - 100 THz

X-Ray is 100 THz

Visible light is limited by the physiology of the human eye. The limits indicated for visible light are not conventional but *natural* – starting with red and going to violet. Other borders are more a question of terminology.

In the process of information transmission, when modulating a wave of a given frequency, we actually occupy, not a single frequency for transmission, but a band of frequencies. With a wider band, we can transmit more information. In simple cases of wireless transmission, we cannot use the same band in the same geographic area for two simultaneously transmitted signals. Instead, we use higher and higher frequencies for transmission. For wired transmission signals in the RF range, we use in metal (copper) wires, while for visible light we use special plastic optical fibres.

Hardware Components of ICT

In this section, the focus is on what is termed *hardware* – the components of ICT like the computer itself, storage media, and input and output devices.

Computers

The computer is a universal information processor. In theory, any kind of information processing can be done on any computer but, in reality, this is not true. A specific task for a specific computer may require too much time, or the computer's memory may be too small. Computers process information in the form of electric signals. In other existing technologies, simple information processing can be done also in the form of air or liquid streams.

There are attempts to produce computers that use light processing, or biochemical mechanisms similar to that of living organisms, but these approaches are at a premature stage.

CPU

Information processing is done by computer hardware. The most important components of computers are (electronic) semiconductors, similar to the components of radio or TV, but much more sophisticated. The number of electronic elements inside these components can be counted in millions. These elements are joined together to form integrated circuits (IC), commonly referred to as *microchips,* or simply *chips.* The core device in any computer, called the *central processing unit* or *CPU,* does all information processing. Today the CPU occupies a metal box in which you can see dozens of integrated circuits, wires, and cables connecting them. (Yesterday's computers were much bigger and occupied a full room, or even a whole building.) The main IC in the CPU is the processor itself, which does most of the active task of processing, including adding numbers, comparing strings of symbols, sending information to memory, retrieving it from memory and, very importantly, reacting to signals from the outside. The work a computer depends not only on its constitution as an electronic device, but also on the information stored in it or that it receives while in operation. This information can be considered as instructions that tell the computer what to do, and is called *software.*

Information is stored, transmitted, and processed in the form of strings of zeros and ones. The input of information into a computer usually involves the transformation of images or sounds into digital and discrete strings. The output involves the reverse transformation. These components of hardware and software responsible for these transformations and making them perceptible to the human senses, are called *interfaces.* Computer information is stored in special types of IC, called *storage* or *memory chips.* A computer's speed is an important factor in its performance. It is measured in MHz, which refers to the number of changes inside a computer that can take place in one second.

Monitor

An important component of any modern computer used by a human being (and for this reason called a *personal computer),* is the *screen or monitor.*

Monitors not only display information but can also support direct interaction. For example, if you need to make a technical drawing of a particular detail with a computer, you move your hand equipped with one of many input devices, to create a line or activate a detail on the screen. The whole system of using physical movements to manipulate information and present this manipulation in intuitive screen images is called *graphical user interface* or GUI.

Connections

The CPU is connected with other ICT devices via communication channels. The most common communication channel is a cable plugged into a computer at one end, and to another device at the other end. The cables and sockets can cause problems, including incompatibility of sockets in the case of connecting your computer to a local telephone line abroad. A popular alternative to cables is wireless (radio-frequency or infra-red) connection. To simplify the graphic presentations, we do not include cables in the pictures, and say more about these connectors in the sections that follow.

Computer Sizes

Computers that are placed on the desk of a clerk, student, or teacher are called *desktop computers.* Sometimes, however, the computer itself is placed under the desk with the monitor and keyboard on top. These computers usually weigh several kilograms, with the monitor usually being the much heavier component. Other computers are portable or mobile. Their weight and size permit them to be carried comfortably. Computers of a size and weight of a large notebook, which is easy to carry, are called *notebooks* (formerly, *laptops).* Today's notebooks weigh as little as 1-4 kg. Computers the size of one's palm, and weighing less than 1 kg, are called *palm computers, handhelds,* or *palms.* All such computers are called *personal computers,* or *PCs,* because they are intended for individual usage.

CPUs today are very small. We can say that for most school applications the size of a typical CPU is not a limitation. On the other hand, in some classroom situations, the size of the whole computer matters. If we place a monitor on a student's desk, it must be large enough to be comfortably visible, yet small enough to leave space for student work.

Energy for Computers

Electricity is needed to run a computer and its related devices. The power consumption for a desktop computer is typically 100-500 watts. In many countries, this resource is widely available, but in others it is still a problem. For them, alternative power sources such as solar batteries, wind generators, and accumulators (rechargeable batteries), as well as UPS (Uninterruptible Power Supply), should be considered in the planning of ICT implementation. Solar batteries, for example, cost a few dollars and can supply a palm computer with energy, provided they are exposed to sunlight a couple of hours a day.

Portable computers can use the same power line as desktop computers. However, it is much more convenient to have a portable computer that can function, for a while at least, with rechargeable batteries. These can support the computer for a few hours, and then need to be recharged from a power source. In the best cases, recharging takes much less time than the computer needed to use up its power, and recharging can occur while the computer is in use. A bad aspect about accumulators, apart from their weight and considerable cost, is that, if used intensively, they last only a few months. Even in the best cases, a rechargeable batteries' life is much shorter than the life of the computer itself.

In many cases, the modern processors that have appeared over the last few years require more energy to run than the older ones. Roughly speaking, every action of the CPU needs a minimal amount of energy to be used. If the processor works faster, the same amount of energy is used in a shorter time. As the computer runs, this energy dissipates in the outside environment in the form of heat, and so computers come equipped with special cooling mechanisms like fans.

Peripherals

For the best utilization of ICT in education, a teacher needs a wide range of devices connectable to a computer, and these are referred to as *peripherals.* The major categories of peripherals are devices for:

- *Input*: alphanumeric keyboard, musical keyboard, microphone, tape-recorder, tablet and stylus, scanner, digital photo camera, video camera, sensors, and probes.
- *Output*: monitor, printer, projector, headphones, speakers.
- *Control*: motors, lights for robotics construction kit, and sensors.
- *Communication*: modems, communication lines, satellite and local network equipment, and wireless networks.

Having a wide range of peripherals for educational and general use is more important in a school than the number of computers. We consider these categories of peripherals in a little more detail in the sections that follow.

Different components of a computer as well as peripheral devices need to be connected via channels for information flow. In most computers today, cables do this, but wireless connection is increasingly possible as well, which then requires, of course, that the device has its own source of energy (usually, power line or batteries).

Storage

Information is stored in *integrated memory circuits* or *memory chips* in the computer's CPU. However, there are other ways to store information. These other means differ in capacity (the amount of information they can store) and access speed (how fast the information can be retrieved). Stored information can be retrieved and, in some cases, changed. Read-only memory (ROM) means that the user cannot change any retrieved information. In the opposite case, we talk about *rewritable memory,* stored on a computer's hard drive or on portable discs. The cost of storing information is constantly and rapidly decreasing.

The key storage devices currently are flash cards, magnetic tapes and discs, and optical discs.

Flash Cards

Additional memory chips - so-called *flash cards* – can be easily inserted into and removed from the body of current computers. They do not require batteries to keep information stored. The capacity of one card today is in the range of 10MB to 1GB and access is fast enough for most applications. Flash cards are widely used in digital and other applications. They are rapidly replacing discs. Some versions of ROM cards are used in game consoles (where they are also called *cartridges).*

Magnetic tapes

Magnetic tapes, similar to those used in tape-recorders, can be used for storing digital information as well. To read or write information on a tape, a special device similar to a tape-recorder is used, called a tape drive. The drive can be external to a computer or placed inside the CPU box. The capacity of a tape can be up to 10 GB and even more. Access speed, however, is slow, which can be critical for certain applications, though this is less important for most school uses. Magnetic tapes are rewritable.

Magnetic Discs

The idea of disc storage can be traced back to gramophone recordings at the beginning of the 20th century.

Information on those discs was per-manently stored in the form of small mechanical (geometrical) changes in the surface of the disc. Some of today's versions of disc storage use a magnetic principle similar to tapes, and these discs are rewritable. Discs with the capacity of about 1MB are also called *diskettes;* you can insert them into a drive (disk-drive), or remove them. It may take up to a minute for a computer to read from or write to a diskette. Newer discs have a capacity of up to 1GB.

Optical Discs

Information can also be stored on a disc as an optical trace. This principle is exploited in *compact discs* (CD), widely used now for storing music. The capacity of a CD-ROM is approximately 1GB. Access speed may not be fast enough for some applications involving sound or moving pictures. To address this problem, observe the different speeds marked on CD-drives: 2x, 6x,... 48x... A newer form of CD-ROM is called *digital versatile disc* or DVD, which looks similar to a CD but can store 10GB or more information. Rewritable CDs and rewritable DVDs have appeared in recent years.

Human Movement as Input

The most common way to input information into computers is by human hand through a variety of devices: keyboards, the mouse, graphical tablets, and touch screens.

Keyboards

The most important input device for computers currently is the keyboard, which serves mostly for text input, and, to a large extent, imitates the keyboards of typewriters. The computer has many advantages over a typewriter, even apart from its more sophisticated software and other applications. The first of these is how easy it makes it to change, delete or insert any word or phrase. The next is the ability to copy any text fragment and to move it as a solid object anywhere within a text, or to another text, usually referred to as *cut-and-paste.* Touch-typing (not looking to the keyboard and using 10 fingers) is a useful skill in the educational context today. Students can learn touch-typing faster than handwriting; they can type faster than they can write; and the results are more attractive and much easier to edit and revise.

Extensive work with the keyboard, however, sometimes causes muscular tension and requires special precautions, which students and teachers rarely take. Newer ergonomic keyboards are becoming more prevalent, as is the use of alternative methods of writing such as script and speech recognition. Different arrangements of characters on the keyboard could make typing more effective. A radically new tool, called the *Twiddler,* is an ergonomic handheld, touch-type keypad designed for chord keying, which means that like a piano you press one or more keys at a time. Each key combination generates a unique character or command. Because of resistance to change, widespread adoption of these tools does not look probable.

ICT: New Tools for Education

Keyboards of notebooks are usually built into the *book.* Keyboards are not usually built into palm computers. Sometimes a keyboard is represented by a screen image on which you type by touching keys with the tip of a special pen. Sometimes, lightweight unfolding keyboards are used for palm text input.

Musical Keyboards

Musical keyboards look like a traditional piano or modern rock-group synthesizer keyboard, only smaller. Attached to a computer, this peripheral can be used far beyond the imitation of a piano. The standardization of digitized sounds of most instruments in MIDI (Musical Instrument Digital Interface) allows students to play and even to compose musical pieces performed by different instruments or an orchestra, and immediately hear a performance of the piece by those same instruments. Notes input with a musical keyboard can then be edited with a mouse. The avenues for students' musical self-expression are in this way dramatically enlarged.

Mouse and its Alternatives

To manipulate screen objects, you need to *point, choose, grab,* and *open* them. In today's computers, these operations are usually done with a special instrument, which indicates an object on the screen and moves it as a solid body. This instrument is called a *mouse,* a handheld, traditionally grey, plastic body that you move on the table-top, which is usually covered by a small mat called a *mousepad,* designed to improve the movement of the mouse. As you move the mouse, a small object (an arrow, for example), called a *cursor,* moves on the screen, mimicking the mouse's movements on the table. The mouse has buttons that help you to extract, pick up, and manipulate objects. You move the cursor to an object and click a button; the object now is attached to the cursor and can be moved. If you click another button, the object *opens up.* These actions are part of GUI or the graphical user interface.

There are other devices to transform movements on screen into information manipulation inside the computer similar to the mouse. They all act similarly, but the physical movements of a human hand working with them can be quite different:

A handheld mouse, not lying on the table, can have a small gyroscope inside, and is useful when you show something to others on a big screen.

A *trackpad* is a small panel (about 3 by 4 cm) over which you move your index finger to control the cursor.

A *trackball* is a ball about the size of an egg embedded into a panel, which you can rotate.

A *joystick* is a small lever (as in a car transmission gearshift) used mostly in computer games.

There are also very small joysticks inside some keyboards called *trackpoints,* which you can push and deflect with your finger. These are also used as the mouse part of the Twiddler mentioned above, where the trackpoint is controlled with the thumb.

Wireless mice that have no moving parts are more reliable and have become more popular. Among them there are handheld mice that you do not place on a table but move in 3D space.

Graphical Tablets

Another type of input is to draw or write with a pen. The difference between a computer pen or stylus and an ordinary one is that the computer pen moves over a special surface called a *graphical tablet,* and the trace of the move can be represented on screen. The computer can also measure levels of pressure. With appropriate software, a computer can imitate almost all existing drawing techniques and create some exciting new ones. The computer is very useful for technical drawing - now, mostly part of computer-aided design or CAD.

Handwriting

The most effective way to start written communication for children (and adults) is to have them type on a computer. But handwriting is still a popular and useful skill. Consequently, handwriting recognition, which immediately transfers handwriting into block letters on the screen (and text in computer memory), is a valuable supplement to keyboarding, and sometimes a major input technique (for example, in certain kinds of environmental observations). With palm computers, you can write text that can be recognized by the computer using a special stylus. Handwriting and drawing by hand on a large whiteboard can be done with a computer also. In this case, you write or draw on the board with a special marker that is traced by an infrared or ultrasonic detector.

Touch Screens

The devices discussed above are intuitive enough but nevertheless separated from the objects on a computer screen. Another promising type of device combines seeing with touching, allowing you, for example, to outline an object on the screen with your finger and then move it to a different position with the same finger. This is already achieved with touch screens. A finger cannot indicate a very small object on a screen. However, this limitation can be relaxed by using a *stylus* on the screen (a kind of pen or pencil designed for this kind of interaction). Touch screens can work well and are more intuitive for small children, but are not widely used. One reason for this is their cost, which is higher than an ordinary screen and mouse. Nevertheless, they are the most popular devices in most information kiosks and in palm computers.

Visual Input

In the mid 19th century, photography was invented as a means of fixing and storing visual information in an external medium using a chemical process. In the 1930s, devices were introduced that transform visual information into electronic form for immediate transmission via electromagnetic waves: TV technology. In the 1950s, simultaneously with computer technology, methods to record and play back analogue TV and still images appeared: the videotape. At the end of the 20th century, digital photography and digital TV became an integral part of computer-based ICT.

Cameras

Cameras store or transmit visual images. The photographic camera stores a still image on photographic film for further chemical development. Instead of putting an image onto a film, a *digital camera* places it in the computer's memory, or in the memory of the camera for transmission to a computer for storage or direct printing afterwards. An interesting application of digital cameras is the projection of a small image (such as a bug, for instance) onto a large screen. Nowadays, digital cameras can store video images also.

Scanners

Scanners look very like copying machines, but are smaller and usually work more slowly. Instead of producing a paper copy of an image, a scanner transmits an image in digital form to a connected computer. Scanners can be used to transform information from a paper source - a text, an image from a book, a drawing, or a photograph - into a digital image. Additional devices can be used for scanning 35mm slides. There are also handheld pen-size scanners that you can move over a line of text or a bar code for input or storage inside the scanner. Special 3D (three dimensional) scanners can produce scanned images viewable from different angles.

Optical Character Recognition

A special situation occurs when an image is a text (or text combined with graphics) in printed or handwritten form. In this case, the image of the text can be transformed (converted) into a computer text file that can be processed as one does other texts in the computer (e.g. insert a phrase; change a shorter name to a longer one, and so on). This process of transformation from picture to text uses sophisticated software called *Optical Character Recognition* (OCR).

Aural Input

As with visual information, non-electronic, that is mechanical technologies, were developed first to store sounds. Then, electronic technologies were developed to transmit sounds (telephone, radio), followed by electronic media and tools to store sounds (tape-recorders).

Microphones

Microphones transform sounds into electric signals for storage or transmission. There are different types of microphones and different ways to work with them:

- A microphone can be fixed in a stand in front of a speaker who is standing or sitting.
- Speakers can hold a microphone in their hand.
- A lightweight microphone can be attached to a speaker's clothes.

Information converted by a microphone into electrical signals can be transmitted via a wired or wireless channel to other devices.

Sound Recording

Sound can be recorded with a usual tape-recorder. To process sounds with a computer, you need to convert them into digital form. A microphone can also be plugged into a computer directly. In this case, the computer serves as a recorder. Digital recorders to store sound in digital form using flash cards are becoming increasingly popular. Modern computers can easily store hours of speech. Music recordings, processed and compressed by computer (in MP3 format, for example), occupy very little memory. The spread of this process, on CDs and through the Internet, is changing the recording industry and affecting mass culture.

Speech Recognition

During the last few years, software has been developed that allows a computer to transform human speech into a text file similar to the conversion of handwriting as discussed above. This transformation can be done with a level of quality that makes it adequate for educational applications, and is useful, for instance, in learning English.

Sensors for Input

Measurements of the environment like temperature, humidity, acceleration, or magnetic field, can be input to a computer-linked device called a *sensor*. A sensor generates an electrical signal that is then usually transmitted to a computer via an interface.

More sophisticated sensors can measure such parameters, store, and display them, even if a sensor is not connected to a computer. This can be done by individual sensors or by what is called a *data logger,* a special device or small box to collect and store data. The content of measurements can then be transferred to a computer. Very promising in school education is the growing number of sensors - from those that measure acid rain and heavy metal oxides ratio in potable water to the Global Positioning System (GPS), which allows anyone to find geographic coordinates and related information on the earth's surface.

Output

Output refers to information that a computer sends to a human user, or, sometimes, to other technical devices.

Visual Output

The most immediate computer output is a visual image on the monitor screen.

In most computer applications, the image on the screen is discrete, and consists of millions of picture elements called *pixels.* The colour and brightness of each element appears as a combination of three colours called *RGB* for red (R), green (G), and blue (B), with varying brightness for each colour. In reality, for every particular screen, each of these three basic colours consists of the entire spectrum of light waves. The brightness (intensity) of the three basic colours is coded by a symbol from a finite range. The symbol and the range of old computers were just one byte (8 bits). Today, colours are usually presented by 3-byte coding (24-bits) representing millions of colours) or 4-byte coding (32-bits) representing billions of colours. The latest technology appears to be able to capture all possible variations in colour. In normal light conditions, the human eye can recognize differences in brightness (contrast) in the range of 1:10,000 or even more. Existing output screens can provide differences in brightness up to 1:1,000. In many cases - in most school conditions, for example - ambient light reduces the contrast radically, and so teachers need to adjust conditions of vision and the absolute brightness of screens. The optimal brightness of screens lies in the range of 50-400 Lux.

Resolution (the number of pixels in rows and columns) is usually named by acronyms such as SVGA (800x600) and XGA (1024x768). The ratio of the two factors is 4:3. The resolution is limited by characteristics of the screen, but mainly by a computer's power to *refresh* images quickly, which is needed to make visualization of the processes adequate and the computer-human interface smooth. XGA is the most widespread resolution in use today but higher resolutions called SXGA and UXGA are coming.

TV screens similar to, or the same as, computer screens used today, offer a slightly different way of presenting information - partly digital, partly analogue. Generally, today's TVs produce less detailed images than good computers, though the newest TV standards have images of the same quality as good computer images. This improved definition is called *HDTV (high definition TV).* The move to HDTV is accompanied by a trend to change the aspect ratio (the fraction of screen width to its height) from 3:4 to 9:16, which is the ratio usually seen on cinema screens.

Theoretically, the limits of a visual image are the limits of human perception, which means that the screen can provide all the colour and brightness variations in the smallest details in the visible field (and even pay attention to two-eye stereoscopic vision). In reality, existing screen images are somewhat more limited: they have less detail than the human eye can grasp. The human retina has about 300 million cells whereas the best screens today have about 10 million pixels. Eventually, there is a natural limit to the improvement in quality that the human eye can perceive, which will occur when the computer screen is large enough to cover the prime area of clear vision and, at the same time, the smaller pixel-like details are no longer seen separately.

Of course, further improvement can help in some applications. For example, a graphic designer can look at a large screen containing a larger image, and then move in closer to look at a detail. That kind of situation can be covered by the standard zoom options of software systems.

In some countries and regions, there has been concern over monitor safety. This problem has two aspects. The first is image quality. Older monitors (especially bad quality TV sets that are sometimes used as monitors) have a blinking, non-stable image, and can cause considerable eye tension. The second issue is the radiation (mainly radio frequency) that the monitor emits. National and *de facto* international safety standards have been established. Presently, monitors are as safe as possible, especially in combination with other proper conditions such as attention to ambient light. One of the key parameters of image quality is refreshment rate, which by most standards, should not be less than 85 Hz. In many newer computer models, it is about 100 Hz.

The classical display technology is the cathode ray tube (CRT), used in most TVs as well as in most monitors. This device is limited by its large depth-dimension and weight. A safer and more comfortable alternative is the LCD (liquid crystal display) monitor, which takes up much less space on a desk, and is important for many classroom applications. They are more expensive than CRT monitors today, but the prices for a whole computer system are not dramatically different.

Projectors

Computer images can be projected onto a screen. The beginning of projection traces back to the centuries-old *Laterna Magica* and Shadow Theatre. Projection flourished in the cinema era. Pre-electronic projectors used transparent film with an image to be projected. The 35mm film can be used in a roll as in dia-projectors (almost non-existent today), or cut into slides for use in slide projectors. Today, all slides (or screens - information objects to be projected) can be made on computer or be input to a computer and presented on computer screen. Special software used for projection of screen images, constructing, and organizing them is called *presentation software.* One of the popular software products here is Microsoft's PowerPoint.

Electronic technology has made it possible to project computer-generated images as well as images from a camera and from a VCR (video cassette recorder). The projected images, different from a computer monitor or TV screen, can be of any size. The only limitation here is that the brightness of the image is reduced proportionally to the area (or squared linear size) of the image. If the ambient light in a room is stronger than the projector's light, differences in colour and brightness of different parts of the image on the screen are not seen clearly enough or, in some cases, at all. The projection device is usually called a *multimedia projector* or *LCD-projector* (indicating, not in all cases correctly, the technology used), or beamer.

Projector technology has developed affordable solutions that are available now in many schools. A computer presentation or video image can be brought to any classroom using a portable screen (weighing less than 2 kg), a portable projector (less than 2 kg), and a computer (less than 2 kg). In fact, each of the items can weigh less than a kilogram.

One of the important trends for monitors and projectors is standardization of the digital interface between computer and the device. The *DVI (Digital Video Interface)* standard describes the digital interaction between monitor and computer.

Stereovision

The ability to see with two eyes is important for human perception in some cases. For example, stereovision is useful to estimate distance along with other instruments like accommodation, head movements, and relative size of objects. Accordingly, it is possible to improve perception on a computer by creating a stereoscopic output. This can be done with separate screens for each eye, or by showing on the screen alternating pictures for each of the eyes. Closing screens for eyes alternately can solve the problem of showing to each eye what is needed. The closing can be implemented, for example, by glasses in which the lenses are made out of liquid crystal and become transparent and opaque alternately.

Printers and Plotters

A printer transforms screen images into images on paper, so-called *hard copy.* A natural consequence of this is a need for paper and ink. The problem of cost here can be serious for schools in particular, because it is so easy to generate printouts in large quantities.

Laser printers produce black and white images and text of good quality for all school applications at an affordable price. In fact, laser printers changed the appearance of the world of written text. Once, the quality of print correlated with the respectability of the author but this is no longer so since, at first glance, all printed papers look the same. Alternatives to laser printing are *LED (light-emitting diodes)* and *ink-jet printing.* These printers are used in schools as well, but do not provide any considerable advantage. The generation of printers before laser printers were so-called *dot-matrix printers,* which used principles similar in some respects to old typewriters with printer ribbon and mechanical impact. Dot-matrix printers are useful if a school has poor quality paper or if you need to use wider paper or long rolls of paper (for banners, for instance).

It is desirable also to have *colour printers* in schools. A little while ago, the price of colour printers and supplies was too high for most schools but, in recent times, the situation has changed and colour printing has become much more affordable. A recent invention in printers is so-called *Random Movement Printing Technology* (RMPT). Printers using this technology can be the size of a computer mouse and used in the same way: randomly moving it over a sheet of paper of any size leaves text printed on it.

A device similar to a printer in its functionality, but based on a different technology, is a *plotter* in which an image on paper appears, not as a combination of dots, but as a continuous line of ink.

Audio Output

The audio channel is under-exploited in modern ICT in comparison with the visual channel. An important aspect of aural perception is locating the sound source using bi-aural (stereo-phonic) mechanisms. Two loudspeakers of mediocre quality are the most widespread audio output for consumer computers. Headphones can be used for stereo output as well. Some are better than others in quality of sound and the level of blocking of outside noise. Headphones can provide better quality than loudspeakers of the same price. In general, headphones are more useful for schools than speakers. Headphones can be coupled with a microphone.

Control

Control applications were among the most important applications of ICT before the advent of personal computers. Among specific cases are control of industrial machinery, power plants, and missiles. By contrast, personal computers mostly control output devices like printers. However, even this situation is changing, since a personal computer can, for example, be the control centre of an *intelligent house,* where the owner instructs the computer to operate all home appliances.

Communication Channels

As noted above, computers are connected to other ICT devices by communication channels that can be wired or wireless.

In general, wired (cable) connection remains the more common type of connection. A cable connecting a computer to a peripheral can be used for three purposes:

1. to transfer energy (electrical current) to a peripheral;
2. to transfer control signals to and from a peripheral (for example, a printer can receive a command "start printing", and send a feedback

"not-ready", or "start sending the image to print", or "out of paper"); and

3. to transfer input or output information (text to be printed to a printer, or sound to be digitized from a microphone).

It is common to transfer different electrical signals through one cable in several separate wires. (Actually, the same wire can be used for many signals simultaneously as well.) For different channels of communication, different cables are used. When we connect a cable to a computer or peripheral, we use *sockets,* sometimes called *ports* or *plugs* in the computer's box.

A crucial issue in the use of cables is standardization. Travellers, for instance, know well that about a dozen power plug standards exist internationally and perhaps a hundred telephone plug standards. Fortunately, standardization in the computer world is becoming more prevalent. At the same time, manufacturers are producing more and more new sockets. Consequently, when connecting a computer to external (peripheral) devices, one must be aware of such labels as PCMCIA, USB, IEEE 1394, and DVI. An important characteristic of a channel is the speed of transmission it allows. For some applications, including school ones, it is also important to plug in or unplug a peripheral device while the computer is working. Old interfaces often required the computer to be turned off while you plugged in or unplugged a device. The newer USB interface does not require turning off the computer while connecting a new device.

After decades of experimenting, wireless connections have become more and more reliable and popular. Using these channels can be critically important for schools, because they provide much needed flexibility. A channel allows computers to be moved between classrooms while keeping the network still operating. In the classroom, it allows children to sit where they are most comfortable without having to struggle with cables. Wireless connections can still be used between keyboard and computer. Brand names like Bluetooth, Airport, as well as standards of Wi-Fi (wireless fidelity), or IEEE 802.11, are used to describe common wireless interfaces. Wireless communication, however, has its limitations since, for example, infrared connection works well in a direct-sight situation only.

Networking

Computers linked to communicate and exchange information constitute a network. The most common standard of communication via wired local area network (LAN) is IEEE 802.3 *(Ethernet* is another name). It can be wired or wireless.

Sometimes a single computer called a *server* is dedicated to information storage and exchange for a network. Other computers are *clients.* Often, computational and storage power are concentrated in the server, and client computers are made as simple as possible. Such clients are called *thin clients.* These computers have few precise mechanical works (spinning discs) and a small and cheap display that is hard to break and easy to replace. In the school context, relatively primitive computers can be useful when all that is needed is basic text processing. It may then be sufficient to have just a keyboard with simple electronics, small memory, 4 or 8 lines of LCD and interfaces. The *thin computer,* also called a *thick keyboard* or *smart keyboard,* consists of a keyboard extended by a minimal display device to see what you are typing, and has a limited memory, an interface to transfer your text to a server or a printer, a processor to manage all of these, and a power supply (usually an inexpensive accumulator battery).

Internet

The next natural step is to link or network separate computers. Two computers can be linked via modem but this process is expensive if the computers are really distant from each other. We may compare this computer linking with the courier mail of the past, where a messenger brings a letter from one point to another. The high cost of this form of communication was reduced by the modern postal service. Developers of the Internet (known also as the *Net* or the *Web)* thought similarly that having electronic post offices functioning automatically in many places would cut the costs of individual communications radically. As with ordinary mail, one can move bulk mail between two major post offices in two cities as well as deliver individual letters locally. In the computer world, this is called *email,* and it was the starting point of the Internet.

Several important features contribute to making the Internet the most democratic information medium today. Besides sending and receiving electronic mail, the Internet provides an opportunity to place an information object (however complex and possibly linked to other objects) on a computer, give it an address, and make it available to a range of users who are also connected to the Internet. Hundreds of millions of people in every country of the world now use the Internet. A popular way to communicate over the Internet is to post information (usually text or pictures) to a personal or business *homepage,* or *website.* Another Internet feature is *user-groups* who have access to *bulletin* boards - a collection of information on a specific topic that can be read and extended by members of a specific group with access. Emails move so quickly - in seconds from any sender to any receiver - that they allow for an exchange of information *online* (staying Internet-connected, sending and receiving messages).

Today the Internet is the biggest ever network channel and source of human information. Over the last decade, the Internet has grown exponentially in numbers of participants and in the amount of information available. Access to the Internet is possible, not only with the average personal computer, but also with simpler equipment called a *network computer* (a kind of thin client), which has an Internet resource and connection but without computer software and storage. A TV set with a simple device like a Nintendo-SEGA game machine can be adapted to provide access to the Internet. So can an enhanced telephone set.

Videoconferencing

The idea of combining telephones and TV communications has been tried for many years. The principal problems have not been so much technical as organizational, to do with infrastructure (allocating channels), and economic (it has been extremely expensive). In the last decade, however, computer algorithms and standards of compression, as well as channels of communication, have improved greatly. A roving video camera attached to a computer can automatically focus on a person speaking. Participants have microphones mounted on their desks and when they ask a question, the camera moves in to film them, and the image is displayed on a monitor screen. A human face and figure, slides, video, Internet, whiteboard writing and drawing can all be seen on-site or transmitted via the Internet. The result is an instant multimedia presentation.

Channels for Distant Communication

For most educational institutions today, telephone lines and modems are the usual communications media for connecting with the Internet. The speed of information transfer via telephone lines is usually below 56 Kbps (if the fre-quencies used are the same as for voice transmission). It is possible to transfer data and pictures and even low quality, live video signals via such channels. Telephone lines can also be used to transfer radiofrequency signals to make transmission much faster, which is the technology used in *digital subscriber lines* (DSL). An alternative is a radio channel via air (amateur short wave or another radiofrequency band, for example 2.4 GHz). An example is GPRS (General Packet Radio Service), a standard for wireless communications that runs at speeds up to 115 kilobits per second. Satellite communications in GHz bands are among the most rapidly growing new ICT media today. When the rate is fast enough to transfer an acceptable video-audio signal, it is usually described as a *broadband* channel (starting from 300 Kbps). Optical fibres with much higher frequencies provide broadband connectivity.

Digital Information Resources

Information Objects and Their Screen Presentations

Graphical user Interface or GUI

Early personal computers could not display graphics well. The only information objects to be displayed then were texts, arranged in lines. A profound breakthrough in the history of computing was the invention in the 1970s and its adoption in the early 1980s of what is called *graphical user interface* or GUI (Apple's LISA, Macintosh, and, then, Microsoft's Windows). The difference in perception and understanding of an information object presented as a text, a table, a formula, or a computer program, in visual form can be dramatic. The ability to deal with an information object as something real - that is, a manipulable object - makes it even more powerful. Generally GUI allows you to use your eyes for information perception and your hands for actions over information objects.

Desktop and Window Metaphor

In many computers, before dealing with any specific information object, you find the computer screen organized as a *desktop.* Several object names, called *icons,* lie on this desktop. You can move these and place them wherever you like. You can *open* an object, see its presentation (text or picture) on the screen, and work on it. Some of the objects are folders. Inside folders you find the names of other information objects - some of them are the names of other folders. Some of these are executable programs and you can start running them, usually with a graphical effect of the run seen in a *window* on the screen.

One-dimensional Editing

Texts

From the birth of the personal computer, working with texts has been the major application of ICT. Soon it initiated a new culture of writing since text on screen turned out to be much more flexible and transformable than written or typed text. The technology influenced the psychology and social context of writing, which, in turn, changed technology.

Here is an example of how technology is changing the nature of text. In traditional written language, we may write, for instance, "see p. 56" or "compare Johns and Black, 1992". In reference books structured alphabetically like encyclopedias, these references can be given also by a difference in font, as in "This work led to the teaching *of pedagogic anthropology* in the *University of Rome."* Here combinations of words in italics - *pedagogic anthropology* and *University of Rome* -refer to other sections or chapters, which can be found alphabetically, with explanations about pedagogic anthropology and University of Rome respectively. The action of looking for another page, or another volume of the same encyclopedia, or even another book at a different library, is very much simplified with computers: to find a reference or link, you simply click a button and you are immediately transferred to the desired pages, books and libraries. To create a link, you work in a text-editor in a natural and elementary way. The text containing these links is called *hypertext.* The links are sometimes called *hyperlinks.* It is more natural to call them simply *links.*

Sounds and Musical Tones

Recorded sound can be presented on screen and edited in the same way as any text.

A special type of sound is a musical tone. Here the sound can be composed, not only changed. The usual notes can be presented on the computer screen and used in a standard way. Notes can be represented in a more graphically intuitive way by height and length in combination with MIDI interfaces.

Video

Working with pre-recorded video-fragments, their cutting, sequencing in an arbitrary way, adding sound and special effects is now possible using ordinary personal computers. For children starting from an early age, this kind of video editing constitutes a powerful environment for their communicative development.

Timeline

A timeline of events can carry icons or pictograms, or other names linked to information objects representing events. In this way, a timeline is similar to time wall-charts. In these charts you can see the whole timeframe, with much more detail of events. The timeline can also be represented as moving in response to the cursor.

Two-dimensional Editing

Images on computer screens are combinations of pixels, and so the obvious way to construct or change an image is to create it pixel-by-pixel. To make this process simpler, we can use a *magnifying glass* tool. Of course, in most cases, this method takes too much time, but it can be used in special cases to make minor changes. More often we use corresponding methods of editing images by:

- changing digitized photographic pictures, or
- making and changing different types of drawings.

Pictures

In the case of photographic images, the computer extends dramatically the set of tools and operations available: resizing, cropping, lightening, darkening, sharpening, and so on. In this way, photographs can be transformed quite professionally, and then combined in sophisticated ways.

Drawings

In computer drawing, there are two major options:

- Using a brush tool or pen tool.
- Using additional software tools similar to a ruler, compass, and templates.

In the first option, software and hardware were developed to mimic traditional techniques and introduce new ones. The second option, the computer version of technical drawing, has developed enormously, especially in the field of Computer Aided Design (CAD).

Maps and Multilayer Images

One option with computer images is to have several *layers* for an image, which is helpful in an application such as editing maps.A special kind of graphical design is the production of plans and geographical maps. Today this is done mainly in so-called *Geo-Information Systems* (GIS). Maps produced with GIS are examples of *multilayer images* that can be edited in each layer separately. Good GIS has sophisticated mechanisms to represent objects like rivers, state borders, and place names on maps in order not to overlap.

Three- and Four-dimensional Editing

Computer Aided Design

Computer Aided Design or CAD has replaced traditional drawing almost completely. CAD allows you to create a 3D object on the screen that you can then turn around in space or zoom in on to see in more detail.

Like pre-computer design, CAD systems:

- have developed in different directions, for use in architectural design, fashion design, machine construction (cars, aircraft), electronic design, and other fields; and
- use libraries of ready-made templates from particular professional fields, and multi-layer construction.

So-called *Computer Aided Manufacturing* (or CAM) is computerised design of the manufacturing process. CAD/CAM is a combination of two.

Computer Animation

Sophisticated and expensive instruments as well as children's simple tool-kits can be used to create artistically impressive or scientifically precise and enlightening computer animations. More and more movie scenes are now produced in artificial settings with characters designed on a computer by means of special software.

Students' animations are usually simple and two-dimensional (flat). Adding a time dimension makes them 3D objects. Simple animations made by groups of students over several hours can be more educative for the creators and more exiting for the spectators.

Multimedia Presentations

Tools are available to make and show sequences of static (still) screens of images. Screens can contain visual representations of various information objects: pictures, drawings, diagrams, tables, as well as important lines of text, visualizations of experimental data, and mathematical models. A sequence of screens constitutes a *slide show.* Such sequences can run autonomously, without a human operator, but are much more effective in association with live human speech. This is a so-called *multimedia presentation.*

Combinations of different kinds of output and different kinds of information objects are usually called *multimedia.* This term was coined in the early 1960s to denote the new synthetic genre of *avant-garde* artistic stage performances comprising action-painting, music, declamation, pantomime, slide-projections and dynamic colour lighting effects. In the 1970s, multimedia became the trade expression applied to joint enterprises in designing, producing, promoting and marketing best-selling books bundled with hit-movies of the same plot (or vice versa), accompanied by the film's music soundtrack, T-shirts emblazoned with portraits of starring actors, and other paraphernalia. The computer industry picked up this coinage in the mid-1980s and used it to describe hardware and software configurations able to run alphanumeric, graphic and sound processing sub-routines simultaneously. Of all technologies, computers are ideally suited to mixing or combining media.

Human-computer Interaction and Communication

Virtual Reality and Cyberspace

Cyberspace and *virtual reality* (VR) are perhaps the most frequently heard, and least defined, expressions of the digital era. The term *cyberspace* was coined by the Canadian science-fiction writer William Gibson, author of *Neuromancer*, who fathered a genre of morbid cyberpunk novels. *Virtual reality* was concocted as a commercial brand name for a line of advanced graphic videogames in the early 1990s. Both coinages stuck and became household words in media and computer science. Cyberspace connotes an informational space that is generated *inside* each functioning computer and spreads *outside* toward a final confluence with other local cyberspaces in the emerging global web of interconnected computer networks. Virtual reality refers to the patterns of ongoing events in time and space that are perceived by our senses through visual, audible and tactile interfaces.

A VR is a computer world that tricks the senses or mind. A virtual glove might give you the feel of holding your hand in water or mud or honey. A VR cyber suit might make you feel as if you swam through water or mud or honey. VR grew out of cockpit simulators used to train pilots and may shape the home and office multimedia systems of the future. The idea of advanced VR systems as future substitutes for sex and drugs and classroom training is the stock and trade of modern science fiction or 'cyberpunk' writing.

Virtual reality has entered modern slang. Even contemporary anthropologists and philosophers use the term *virtual realities* (with no reference at all to digital technologies) to discuss dreams, myths, hallucinations and poetic fantasies, as well as a psychic fabric of scientific hypotheses, theoretical thinking, logical and mathematical reasoning, and other imaginative functions of the human mind. The shortest path to grasping the idea of computer-based virtual realities is to play a video game of car racing or, even better, war aircraft fighting, so popular among teenage boys. However, the use of simulated reality for learning purposes goes back at least to the 1960s, when professional flight simulators were introduced to train pilots and air craft controllers. They make an exemplary case, which we now consider.

Let us assume you are a novice sitting in the cockpit of a small plane that rests on the ground. Through the windshield you see a runway and adjacent airport facilities. On a panel below is the flight instrumentation: altimeter, air speed and horizon indicators, vertical velocity gauge, compass and other navigational equipment. The engine is already warmed up; your hands and feet are on a throttle lever and rudder pedals, and you are about to begin your maiden flight. By command from the digital instructor, you push the throttle to full and see the plane start rolling down the runway. Gathering speed you raise the elevator, and the plane takes off - you are airborne! Excited, you gain height, but all of a sudden heavy clouds appear with rain and a severe thunderstorm. The plane starts banking (horizon line is tilting), and in a panic you try to damp it by turning the ailerons, but in vain. The next moment the plane dives, goes into spin, hits the ground and explodes in a ball of fire. Luckily, except for the authentic cockpit, sensual impressions, motor responses and manipulative activity of yours, everything you have seen behind the windshield or read on instruments' dials has been computer-simulated - the runway, rolling, speed gathering, take-off, height gaining, rainy clouds, thunderstorm, banking, diving and crashing. In other words, all these events belong to the domain of virtual, not genuine reality.

Nonetheless, this was a reality you could perceive and interact with as if it was authentic and genuine. More to the point, the outcome of such interaction might be quite different had you been more knowledgeable and experienced in piloting. Now this goal is within your reach. By re-starting the simulation program, you can repeat your virtual flight over and over again. Most probably, your initial attempts will end lamentably several times in a row until you manage not only to take off but also to land the plane safely. Indeed, you must try hard to avoid previous mistakes, improving your performance in operating the controls while doing climbs, glides, turns and descents, and learning how to solve various navigational problems.

It is customary to summarize the main attributes of virtual reality in three words: *Presence, Interaction* and *Autonomy.* These attributes are especially relevant in using the most advanced (still rare today, but tomorrow undoubtedly more frequent) VR-based educational environment.

The first attribute of virtual reality, presence, is the belief in one's authentic, or genuine, existence in the simulation. This is more easily achieved by perceiving the VR environment not on a separate screen, but inside a data-helmet with goggle-like displays, one for each eye, with sensors reading a positioning of the user's eyeballs and head. As you move your eyes and head to the left, images are rapidly updated and you feel you are actually looking at objects on the left. You may also be equipped with a pair of data-gloves (and, someday, probably, a data-suit) coupled with viewpoint control enabling you to see your hands and body in the simulation (at least their graphic or symbolic representations, say a finger, a palm, or catching glove shaped as a cursor on the screen). Presence extends the friendly, business-as-usual feeling of the iconic interface to include the actor/player/learner. The sense of presence is also enhanced if a consistent way of interacting with the microworld's objects is used. If a squeezing glove can grasp objects, the user's belief in a real, stable world naturally increases.

The second attribute of virtual reality, interaction, is the ability to change features of the simulated world in a consistent, natural, and organic fashion. This is achieved by making the data structures of the world-model mutable in natural ways (e.g., by cutting holes, lifting things, or joining them together). Properties such as conservation of volume and shape, constancy of colour and of manipulation technique, support natural interaction. The three-dimensional physical world, which in fact is logically complex, seems simple and unambiguous to people with a lifetime of experience in navigating it. The third attribute of virtual reality, autonomy, means that the objects presented have inherent behaviours and can be trusted to exhibit them automatically when simulated. In other words, if the virtual universe plays its part, the user's mind is freed to do the creative work of designing and constructing her or his own learning projects. The task in question may consist of altering the universe's laws and testing the results.

A situation gets more complex when a student moves from a solitary activity in a closed virtual micro-world to a networked cyberspace on a global scale. For example, there are collaborative games that involve building complex worlds with hundreds and even thousands of players. It has been found in such situations that no amount of central planning on the part of teachers suffices. *Top-down* design of virtual worlds (such as is certainly necessary in packages like the flight simulator) may be counterproductive in collective games aimed at the development of creative capacities. We believe it is better to populate a pre-fabricated environment with users, to observe their needs, to provide them with tools as required, and then to let them build the world(s) they want. Text on a computer screen is an example of virtual reality in the broadest sense. The basic human actions in this reality comprise creating a new element (typing a character), extracting (cutting), or adding part of an object (pasting). As mentioned above, this type of environment is characterized by the term WYSIWYG. Hypertexts are created in a more sophisticated manner, using a special computer language called *HTML (Hypertext Mark-up Language)* and special editors. A modern language to describe objects of all types is called *XML.* A language to create VR 3D-objects permitting VR-actions and feedbacks is called *VRML (Virtual Reality Markup Language).* Three triggering mechanisms, supported by VRML, are:

1 Proximity - execution based on viewer position.

2 Viewpoint - execute when selecting viewpoint.

3 Touch - execute on viewer clicks.

A more advanced version of the language is X3D (eXtensible 3D).

Speech Synthesis and Analysis

How does one *teach* a computer to talk? How can a computer form an oral image of a sentence of text? How can we inform a user about anomalies or routine events occurring while operating a computer (technical errors, incoming electronic mail)? These situations involve *speech synthesis.*

The simplest solution is for the software maker to pronounce and record the sound beforehand. However, it is impossible to record all conceivable texts that a computer might have to pronounce, and equally impossible to dictate all possible sentences.

However, we may record separately the minimal acoustic atoms of speech, and then try to compile sonic images of words in the same manner as we compile their written images out of letters. But if we do this literally, atom by atom, we will get something unintelligible to the listener. This is especially true in difficult languages like English and Russian. As a compromise, we may record the soundings of every word in a language (quite a big job), some of the most frequent word-blocks, pairs or groups of words often pronounced in one phrase, words that sound differently when they appear in various parts of a sentence, depending on whether these are interrogative or imperative mood, and so on. Modern computers have sufficient storage capacity for such an undertaking. There is no doubt that in the near future word-by-word synthesized speech will have attained a sufficiently high quality to be marketable as a good substitute for sentence recording. As for *analysis* of audible speech, progress in this field requires, besides an increase in storage capacity, solving what might be called the *problem of understanding,* particularly with regard to context. A computer has to be very smart indeed to understand the subtleties of human speech.

Computers for Special Needs

A well-known phenomenon of living organisms, including humans, is compensation - the ability to substitute some if its functions and organs for lost ones.

Computers and ICT are involved in the process of compensation in many ways. Computers can improve human senses, or substitute one for another. They can do even more, and operate different devices such as home appliances. Even for persons with the most severe challenges, the computer is a helpful tool with which to communicate and control the environment. Visual disabilities can be compensated for with tactile or aural perception. Braille coding was invented long before computers, but Braille is a good example of discrete (in fact, binary) coding. It encodes any letter as a combination of dots in given positions, and so tactile reading and writing in Braille have been the form of written communication for blind people for years.

Modern ICT have improved on Braille in straightforward and important ways. There is software to translate letters, digits, punctuation marks and other symbols into Braille codes; a special printer using special paper then can print these codes and other graphical images in relief form for a blind person. It is also possible to provide online reading: on a computer extension, pins corresponding to Braille dots pop up on a template line to form Braille letters. Alternative keyboards are also available for blind people, including ones especially designed for Braille (9-keys). They include a Braille line on which the typed text is *displayed.* Keys of ordinary keyboards can be marked with Braille dot-letters as well.

Another channel of perception for blind people is aural. Besides simple recording, computers can help to transform text into audible speech. In the simplest case, a computer reads aloud a sequential text, word-by-word. More advanced *screen readers* exploit structures beyond linear text, including hypertext. There are structures of text in programming languages and other professional environments that screen readers can navigate a blind person through. For the non-blind, an aural channel can be used for input as well. In fact, full communication between user and computer can be based on verbal processes. A possible consequence of this is a decline in Braille literacy among the blind population, as there has been in other skills such as knowledge of multiplication tables since the advent of the calculator.

The hearing-impaired can also be considerably supported by ICT in two major ways. The first is the well-known amplification of incoming sonic signals. Unlike the old fashioned analogue hearing aid, digital devices can provide immensely wider customized choice and fine tuning of frequency equalization versus loudness levels to help compensate for an individual's aural deficiencies.

ICT: New Tools for Education

The second aid is a speech visualizer for persons with more serious hearing losses. Invented in the early 1940s and named *Visible Speech,* this device analyzed sound energy distribution of different speech formats, and displayed them as patterns of white, grey, and black patches on a monitor. The observer had the burden of guessing, interpreting, and deciding whether or not these images represented particular articulated syllables. Today, the digital automated system converts spoken words into a typed text shown on the screen. In this way, even totally deaf people can converse through the telephone or in other situations where they cannot hear a speaker's words. For blind-deaf persons, the output signals of such systems may be fed into a digital Braille display to provide the same opportunity.

In other areas, kinaesthetically (motor) impaired people can control their environment with the help of a computer and additional hardware. Text entry can be a major method of general communication for children (and adults) who have various types of problems including severe physical disabilities. Children with cerebral palsy, for example, are able to communicate more easily by using bigger trackballs. There is a whole spectrum of new and emerging input devices, including some controlled by human breath only. At the same time, human adaptation can be high. For example, some people can type quite effectively on a standard keyboard with only one hand.

Software Tools

Software, the name given to the coded instructions that tell computers what to do, comes in many different forms. Here we focus on software tools that are useful for schools.

Operating Systems

The software foundation of a computer system is called its operating system (OS). It is the environment with and through which other software communicates. OS with Graphical User Interface was developed by Apple and used in Macintosh computers. The most popular operating systems today are versions of the Windows system developed by Microsoft. In the 1980s, an operating system for larger computers called UNIX was created. A version of UNIX that is popular and available for no cost today, even for less powerful personal computers, is Linux.

Personal Productivity Tools

The most popular application of computers today is text writing and editing, which extends to producing hypertexts and presenting Internet pages, spreadsheets, and sending and receiving emails. These tools are often called *office applications* because they are widely used and effective in offices. The dominant product integrating various office applications is Microsoft Office: a simpler but free competitor to it is called *Openoffice.org*.

Work with information objects assumes the ability to find any object you need. This search in a collection of objects can be based on looking for objects with specific attributes. Thus, you can look for a book with a specific author, title, or publisher. A software system that supports these kinds of activities is a *database*. One can use a database to:

- search for a particular object;
- add a new object (new entry);
- change the system of fields (for example, delete the field "publisher" and add the field "most relevant school subject"), and format of screen presentation and print-out; and
- construct a new database that makes connections with existing ones and transfer information between them.

Professional Tools

In most fields of human endeavour, specific applications have been developed with specific software tools. These collections of tools are called *virtual workshops*. In fact, you can call a collection of these instruments an editor of virtual reality. They can also be referred to as *automated instruments,* or *electronic assistants* of a human editor. Thus, in certain professional fields, we have specialized mathematical text editors, sound editors, database editors, and so on.

CAD-systems, noted above, are used in different areas of design, including machine construction (for example, automotive and aircraft production), architectural design, book design, and microchip design. Naturally, specialized hardware can be required for CAD such as a more powerful CPU, monitors with higher resolution, graphical tablets, and plotters. Geo-Information Systems, also noted above, are specific tools for the design of maps and plans.

A special kind of design activity is the design of processes. Among these are:

- computer-aided manufacturing (CAM), usually based on CAD design;
- design of human activity in project planning and implementation; and
- software design (also known as computer programming), one of the most sophisticated areas of human activity today.

Numerical Data Processing and Visualization

Under *Hardware* above, we discuss data collected by peripheral sensors such as the parameters of a physical system, biological experiment, or chemical manufacturing. Other data collected might be the results of polls and elections, which can be input manually or by using a scanner for written documents, or directly, as in the case of voting, through a computer terminal, or counting people with a photo-sensor. All these kinds of data can be organized in tables or databases, and then processed to make them *smoother,* to find, for example, median values.

Simulation

If we have a mathematical description (that is, a mathematical model) of a real-life system or process, we can simulate it with a computer. *Simulations* can be time-consuming: it might take a week, for example, to develop a really good simulation of the next day's weather. In some cases, however, we can shorten the process of simulation by using more sophisticated mathematical methods and algorithms.. A system for simulating complex systems behaviour based on differential equations and graphical diagrams is called *system dynamics* and can be implemented with the help of a software environment (virtual lab) called *Stella.*

In many cases, we may have a small piece of text (for example, the name of an information object) associated with two other pieces of text. It happens that the first and the second elements of the pair are taken from given lists, and are usually presented as a table or spreadsheet like the following:

	John	***Xenia***	***Zulfia***	***Tang***
Geography	A	A	B	B
Mathematics	C	A	A	A

Here we have school subjects as one list, students' names as a second list, and marks associated with them as table entries.

The situation becomes more interesting when you introduce dependences between the cells of a table. For example, you can require that the number in a cell should be the sum of numbers of two other given cells, or even the total sum of a full column. This leads to what are called *electronic* (or, better, dynamic) *spreadsheets* – a tool of visualization and simulation used by bookkeepers, economists, and others.

Control

Control is one of the most important real-life applications of ICT. Some of the processes of control are invisible, automatic, and do not assume ongoing human involvement. Others are interactive and assume the permanent participation of a human being in the system. In both cases, visualization is important.

Information Sources and Hypermedia

As we have seen, a great deal of information can be stored in a computer. A server, for example, with the capacity of a terabyte and costing a few thousand dollars can store the text of a million books, or about one thousand hours of video. Practically all the texts ever written could be stored in computers in one modest size building. Before long, one will be able to do the same with all art galleries, photo collections, and scanned archives of important documents, major speeches, music, and popular or artistically created movies. Nor is it necessary to have all this information in one place. The sources of information can be distributed all over the world and accessible via the Internet.

Major efforts in these directions are being made in the form of electronic libraries, digital archives, libraries, and museums, and individual attempts. Some of these depositories are proprietary and closed for outsiders or require a subscription fee; but many are free to enter, open for the public, and can be used freely for educational purposes. In this context, two major problems arise: the *quality of information* and the *accessibility of information.* Neither problem is new. The first problem exists in the form of some tabloid newspapers or amateur writers. To some extent, control over quality has previously been based on moral and legal boundaries, but even more on economical and technological mechanisms. Distributing information widely was expensive: it pays generally, for it to be accurate. The second problem is clearly seen in lost scientific and technological inventions, forgotten addresses and telephone numbers, and lost birth records. To deal with this problem, people invented libraries and archives, sophisticated forms of indexation and catalogues, review journals, citation indices, telephone directories, and all types of reference books, with their associated footnotes and references.

With the dawn of the Internet Age, these problems became more severe. The Internet is full of poor information and hard-to-access or wasted information. To find needed information, you can spend hours and still not find what you want. For this reason, some say the Internet is useless, even destructive and dangerous. In overcoming these difficulties, the world ICT community has invented many mechanisms.

Hyperlinks. The encyclopedia mechanism of reference has been extended enormously. A major opportunity provided by modern ICT is the ability to gather in a single computer information contained in millions of volumes contained in other computers. By using the mouse to click on a word on the computer screen, you can immediately *call up* (possibly, in a different window) a piece of information referred to by the author of the initial text who provided the link or reference. Catalogues and reference libraries of Internet resources have been developed and placed on the Internet by institutions and individuals.

Descriptions. Books and museum collections are searchable because items there have been described and the descriptions are stored in catalogues. ICT are ideal for making catalogues but descriptions need to be added. In the past few years, major attempts have been made in this direction by establishing standards of so-called metadata.

Standards. Another dimension is standards for storing data like texts and images. There was a time when you bought a new computer and a new text editor only to find that you could not read your old files. Therefore, a strong trend is to have a system of standards that are free, open, written in understandable form, and which describe how data are stored and displayed on screen.

Reusability. Many information objects are present as parts of other objects. An immediate example is a painting in a museum collection. For obvious reasons, especially in education, we would like the opportunity to access such an individual object independently. Technically it is easy, but serious organizational and copyright problems await solution.

Search engines. Major attempts are being made to keep track of all Internet information resources. This tracking can be based on an analysis of word content. Thus, you can ask a search engine to show all references to a word, or word-phrase, over the entire Internet. More sophisticated searches can be done using more complex inquiries, for instance, containing a certain combination of words, together with a particular word, but perhaps not containing some other word.

Portals. Search engines are approximate search methods, and they do not evaluate the quality of any information found. Another approach, combined with the search engine approach, consists of evaluating and describing Internet resources by particular organizations or professional associations to ensure quality of the resources as well as quality of the search, and to gather all this information in a single location, called a *portal.*

Safety systems. The mechanisms noted above do not limit access to the Internet by any computer. At the same time, there is increasing concern among parents and teachers over the dangerous influence of the Internet on the younger generation. Pornography, hate, violence, and narcotics are often targeted specifically at young people. Concerned citizens are therefore seeking to form a barrier against this influence - an Internet safety infrastructure. Parents or a school can subscribe to a safety service, and all access to the Internet will go through this infrastructure, which does not permit the user to go to proscribed websites.

Health Problems

Today, the computer is the major component of the working environment for millions of people. While working with computers can be more or less effective, it can also be damaging to one's health. The major human organs involved here are eyes and hands. Problems with eyes are caused by concentration on screen images, which are aggravated by unclear or flickering images, by glare, and from bright reflections on the screen. The problem with hand muscles is described as *Repetitive Strain Injuries* (RSI). In these cases, proper posture, exercises, and relaxation during work are helpful. For students, these considerations are even more important.

Other negative factors are excessive heat and noise. As previously noted, modern computers need increasingly more processor power for software applications. Fans installed alongside the CPU dissipate the resulting heat, but these produce noise. Another source of noise is the disc drive. High temperature can also cause emission of gases from different components of computers like plastic. There is debate about possible health problems associated with electromagnetic radiation of different frequencies emitted by computer monitors. While there is no evidence of damage caused by the electro-magnetic fields of modern monitors, nevertheless, caution is advisable because students are increasingly using computers in schools. Repetitive strain injuries are not new. Prior to office machines, accounting clerks used to suffer severe cramp in their hands, which often led to permanent disfigurement. Pianists and other musicians suffer similar ailments from hours of practising, and sometimes promising students are so afflicted that their professional careers are disrupted. Similarly, students with an aptitude for computers may never get to reach their potential because of hours of damaging keyboarding. Video games are doing their share of damage. It is important that potential sufferers are aware that the prevention of RSI may simply require finding a comfortable and efficient posture, and maintaining a balance of movements while working.

Children are generally enthusiastic and become easily infatuated with ICT. They often keep performing an enjoyable task with great concentration until near exhaustion (e.g. making and playing their own animated cartoons for hours with few, if any, breaks). Prolonged activity without regular breaks can cause eye focusing problems (accommodation) and eye irritation.

When a student's focusing system is locked in to a particular target and viewing distance, the eyes may be unable to focus smoothly and easily on a particular object, even long after the original work is completed.

Eye irritation may occur because of poor tear flow over the eye due to reduced blinking. Blinking is often inhibited by concentration and staring at a computer screen. Desktop monitors are usually located higher in the field of view than paperwork, resulting in the upper eyelids being retracted to a greater extent. Therefore, the eye tends to experience more than the normal amount of tear evaporation, causing dryness and irritation. Younger students are not the same size as adults. Most computer workstations are arranged for adult use and, since children are smaller, computers do not fit them well. Therefore, students using a computer on a typical office desk must often crane their necks upward further than an adult. Because the most efficient viewing angle is slightly downward about 15 degrees, problems using the eyes together can occur. In addition, students may have difficulty reaching the keyboard or placing their feet on the floor, causing arm, neck, or back discomfort.

Students viewing a computer screen with a large amount of glare often do not think about changing the computer arrangement or the surroundings to achieve more comfortable viewing, and this can result in excessive eye-strain. Inadequate lighting can lead to visual headaches that often occur toward the front of the head, and toward the middle or end of the day. Other symptoms -eyestrain, tired eyes, double vision, and red or dry eyes - are more general. The lighting level for the proper use of a computer is about half as bright as that normally found in a classroom. Increased light levels can contribute to excessive glare and problems associated with adjusting the eyes to different levels of light.

Here are some recommendations for parents and teachers:

- Have students' vision checked to ensure they can see clearly and comfortably, and to detect any hidden conditions that may contribute to eyestrain.
- Limit the amount of time that students can continuously use computers. A 10-minute break every hour will minimize the development of focusing problems and eye irritation caused by improper blinking. Also consider having shorter, more frequent breaks.
- Check the height and arrangement of monitors. A student's size should determine how the monitor and keyboard are positioned. In many situations, the computer monitor will be too high in the student's field of view, the chair too low, or the desk too high. A good solution to many of these problems is an adjustable chair that can be raised for student comfort, since it is usually difficult to lower the computer monitor. A footstool may be necessary to support the feet.
- Check the lighting for glare on the computer screen. Windows or other light sources should not be directly visible when sitting in front of monitors. When this occurs, the desk or computer should be turned to prevent glare on the screen.
- Reduce the amount of lighting in the room to match the computer screen. A smaller light can be substituted for a bright overhead light, or a dimmer-switch can be installed to give flexible control of room lighting. In other cases, a three-way bulb can be turned to its lowest setting.

Different safety and ergonomic requirements for interacting with computers and other equipment like printers have been developed in different countries. One internationally respected set of requirements has been developed by TCO, the Swedish labour association.

Major Trends in ICT

In this section, we look at major trends in ICT that might determine one's choice of computer, and what is likely to lie ahead in ICT.

Sometimes we hear from decision-makers in the field that young students need less powerful computers, and that when we want to teach programming to high school students, we need powerful ones. In fact, we believe the opposite is true. Young students need big, bright, intuitive, interactive computers.

It is more important to have modern and advanced computers in primary schools than at other levels of education because they can help provide students with opportunities to create and display according to their rich inner world, enabling them to express themselves more adequately, and opening up more opportunities for learning. Friendly interfaces, high quality graphics, and sound can dramatically extend the range of ICT applications in primary school. To achieve this, all the resources of present and future personal computers are needed. Otherwise, we risk missing that sensitive period in a student's growth when both body and mind are receptive to the acquisition of perceptual traits and symbol-manipulating skills that are essential for further intellectual and creative development. This view cannot be overstated. Unfortunately, many policy-makers in education remain unaware of these facts and are still recommending obsolete computers for kindergartens.

One impressive but, of course, overly simplified way to describe and predict developments in technology was formulated by Gordon Moore in 1965 in an article for the magazine, *Electronics,* on the future development of the semiconductor industry. Moore described an exponential curve of quantitative changes of computer power measured in terms of the density of microelectronic components in one integrated circuit of CPU or memory. For the last few decades we have seen this parameter double about every 18 months in line with his predictions. This exponent affects growth in computer speed and memory size. Recently, Moore announced an update to his law, but whether growth will slow remains to be seen.

What has been happening to computer cost over this time? The answer is not quite so optimistic. New technology is generally expensive; the price of a new computer model stays high for several months, then falls for a couple of years and begins to stabilize after major consumers and producers have moved to newer technology Before ending the line, liquidation prices can appear. Then old models are replaced by new ones of almost the same (inflation-adjusted or not adjusted) price, as the previous model was two years earlier, after it had fallen from its peak. In absolute figures and not taking inflation into account, we can say that the prices of the most popular personal computers are 4-6 times lower today than they were 20 years ago.

The price of ICT is determined to a great extent by the size of the market. If a tool is in demand and easy to use, the price falls. The prices of the most popular computers are slowly going down. The specialized tools of ICT will eventually be as affordable as home appliances such as TVs or stereo systems. There are good reasons to buy recently stabilized equipment. However, it is shortsighted to buy obsolete computers for schools. Accepting donations of used computers can initially be exciting; it can also lead to complete disillusionment in the technology. Even more than in other cases, we need schools to invest their additional resources in good technology, so that teachers' time can be spent on teaching and not with time-wasting obsolete equipment.

The increasing power of computers has allowed qualitative changes in human work with computers. The first computers using Graphical User Interface were a thousand times less powerful than computers of today in memory size and processor speed. We now consider the major dimensions of changes in ICT.

Consumer Society and ICT

Investment in the development of more powerful computers is demand-driven. How is the demand generated? Of course, people are always interested in storing more information, and faster retrieval. At the same time, software companies are releasing new versions of their popular software that use the full power of the latest processors from hardware manufacturers. Software producers then help drive demand.

One of the results for this escalation is that powerful computers running memory-hungry applications are at the limits of their power. An unexpected consequence is that most computers have become noisier: more powerful processors emanate more heat, and to dissipate this heat more powerful and noisier fans are needed.

Ease and Comfort of Use

People without extensive training are frequent users of computers today. They have some skills in the special applications for their work and a vague general understanding of how a computer works. One reason for this development is the user-friendliness of computers, which means they allow you to do simple things simply. The easy-to-use Graphical User Interface (GUI), for example, permits users to rely on their intuition to operate in three-dimensional space. Like other interfaces, GUI allows mistakes (for example, in text-writing) to be easily rectified.

These improvements have allowed computers to be used by professionals from different fields. The next step is to bring some ICT to non-professionals. Today's computers are still more difficult to operate than a TV or microwave; and desktop computers are still not comfortable enough to be part of everyday life because of the space they occupy, together with heat and noise. Nevertheless, searching for information on the Internet utilizing the screen of a home TV is now possible, simple and cheap. The growing information culture and new literacy is likely to bring simpler modes of operating widespread ICT appliances, greater clarity of user manuals, and better understanding of these by lay people.

Further Visualization

Visualization has been called the *second computer revolution.* The number of pixels on a computer screen and the speed with which an image changes, as discussed above, determine the quality of the computer image. Recently (on the computer technology time-scale), computers have become capable of TV/video applications. We can now store hundred of hours of TV-quality video, show it as *seen on TV,* or without advertising, and edit it as needed in a way similar to text-editing. Of course, image quality depends also on having high quality peripheral devices: for output, computer monitors and projectors, and, for input, cameras and scanners. Here, too, we can see how computer power drives demand.

Quality of Sound

Improvement in quality of sound follows a similar path as quality of visual images. On the one hand, sound requires less memory and computational power to work with. On the other hand, manufacturers and consumers usually underestimate the value of computer sound. Sound quality is important from psychological, emotional, and ergonomic points of view. We expect higher standards of computational power to improve sound quality and to herald more applications of sound, as well as in speech synthesis and speech recognition, language and early learning.

Human Movement and other Types of Communication

Currently, a person interacts with a computer mainly in two-dimensions. The keyboard and the mouse are operated as discrete objects. The computer screen is a *desktop.* Is it possible to move to another dimension, one that allows objects to be grasped, touched, moved, and smelled? Numerous research projects are underway, some of which promise to become part of mainstream reality in the next decade. Intensive research is going on, for example, in the fields of kinaes-thetic input and output. A computer will *feel* human movements visually or via special sensors. It will also provide feedback through gloves with motors in them. Smell input (and output) is also in the experimental stage.

Computer reaction to movements - for example, changing visual images in response to a head turn or other non-verbal cues - can be achieved with the use of trackers mounted on head or fingers, or seeing human movements. A haptic device involves physical contact between the computer and the user, through technology such as a joystick or data gloves that sense the body's movements. With a haptic device, the user can feed information to the computer and receive information in the form of sensations on parts of the body. For example, in a virtual reality environment, a user could pick up a virtual tennis ball using a data glove. The computer would sense the movement and move the virtual ball on the display. At the same time, the user feels the tennis ball in his hand through tactile sensations that the computer sends through the data glove, mimicking the feel of the tennis ball in the user's hand.

That type of interaction can be implemented with an *exoskeleton* – a system of artificial bones and muscles (electric motor-based) tied to the human body to imitate reaction of the environment. In particular, force feedback (FFB) simulates weight or resistance in a virtual world. Force feedback requires a device that produces pressure on the body equivalent or scaled to that of a real object. It allows a person in cyberspace to feel the weight of virtual objects, or the resistance to motion that they create. Tactile feedback (TFB) produces sensations on the skin, typically in response to contact or other actions in a virtual world. Tactile feedback can be used to produce a symbol, as in Braille, or simply a sensation that indicates some condition such as heat. Touch and hold are not the only physical relations in the real and virtual worlds. The proximity of an object can be manifested by a sound, for example. Sound can also represent execution of a procedure like opening a door or giving a greeting.

To summarize, we see among existing and emerging extensions of the usual computer interfaces the following:

- Larger screens, including touch-screens.
- Stereoscopic images (different for different eyes).
- More use of trackers.
- More proximity.
- More sound feedback including proximity.
- Computer-generated odour.
- More accurate and sophisticated force feedback.
- Tactile feedback, specifically aspects of touch not covered by force feedback.
- Accurate simulation of the behaviours and other characteristics of soft tissues.
- Integration of data from several sources.
- Integration of the real world with virtual worlds or switching between real and virtual worlds.
- Video and audio input via head-mounted devices simulating human perception.

Computers to Go

The real limitations of computer size, weight and portability do not follow from its computational or memory power, but from the ability of humans to receive information (via video-monitor) and to send information (via keyboard). Therefore, the following general options exist:

Notebook computers are complete computers with full functionality and with all major devices of the desktop computer. A popular current version does not contain any drive for removable discs (floppy, CD or DVD), but has USB ports to which you can plug in a flash card or external drive. Notebooks can communicate with all peripheral devices via RF and IR channels, and with the outside world via radio-channels as well. To make it even smaller and cheaper, there are also *sub-notebooks* that have a less convenient keyboard, smaller and weaker display, and less functionality, in particular, usually having a less powerful OS than desktop and notebook computers. For greater savings, you can get *smart keyboards* with a very simple (for example, 8 lines of text) display, with the major function to store text input. The price can be 3-4 times less than the price of a regular computer, and so this is a popular option for schools.

Palm computers or palms have the functionality of sub-notebooks, but are even smaller with just a screen of palm-size. The screen is used also as an input device for handwriting, pointing and moving objects. Palms are really good for taking notes on the move, and for collecting data from different sources (like measurements from sensors).

Wearable Computers

The changes discussed immediately above lead next to the concept of wearable *computers.* The key devices of wearable computers are *glasses* through which computer images are displayed (in particular, these can be images of real reality). A pair of stereo glasses can be fitted with a pair of stereo speakers, and a microphone in a VR-helmet.

A further idea is *to wear* a computer that has no input-output devices in it, and is connected to the world through wireless channels only. Such a computer might receive your email, for example, but to read it you need to come to a screen with a wireless interface compatible with the computer. A wearable computer would *recognize* context - that is, it would *know* not only "what time is it now", but also "where you are" and "what is happening around you" and "how you feel".

Local Information Space

A VR-helmet is a very *local* presentation of the information space to a human. There are other means for providing comfortable access to information and instruments to work with at home, at work and study places. These include:

- Screens and speakers for output (including touch screens, for output and input).
- Wireless keyboards, mice, hand-held scanners, and speech recognition devices for input.
- Common information space for all points of access organized for sharing by many users.

For example, in a school-and-home integrated network, students could come to any computer with their keyboards, or even mobile phones, and enter their own information space incorporated into the school information space and global information space.

The Human Element

Physically, access to information is limited by a computer's communication speed, which is limited by bandwidth, and this, in turn, is limited by frequency range. However, the human factor is more critical here. Everybody seems to agree that Internet surfing can be even more harmful for children than TV-viewing. Sophisticated search engines and agents can help but most of the work to make information available and to ensure its quality must come from humans. Therefore, the Internet community and infrastructure of support of many other people are needed.

Merging of Mass Media and the Internet

As previously indicated, computers are now integrated with television. Cellular telephones give you a keyboard, a TV-screen, and an Internet connection. Increasingly, content, media, and devices are integrated in a digital format.

ICT: New Tools for Education

Computers also serve for information searching, storing, and processing (for example, to find a TV transmission via an Internet TV-portal, or to cut out commercials and store a show along with adequate text description).

More Models of Reality

Even an autonomous, non-Internet-connected computer is a powerful device for constructing your own information objects - indeed your own models of reality. Constructing static objects, books, and graphical art can require considerable computational power. Even more power is needed for computer simulation and visualization of the results of the simulation. Progress in this direction is based on increasing computational power and, even more, on developing more sophisticated tools that are comfortable for human use.

More Understanding from Computers

From the beginning of the computer era, the idea existed to delegate to the computer the most sophisticated functions of the human brain. Progress in this area has been slower than expected. Eventually, however, some of the hoped-for developments have occurred, for instance:

- Computers now play chess better than humans.
- Computers recognize oral speech and handwritten words.
- Computers recognize objects in environments and act accordingly.

Economy of ICT

Unlike matter or energy, an information object can be consumed many times with no additional cost for its reconstruction or refuelling.

Digitization prices have dropped, so that it is becoming affordable for libraries to make their unique collections digitally available. Huge libraries can be stored on a single desktop server. CDs and DVDs have become easier to copy in the technical sense. It is not hard for pirates to break copyrights. More and more music is available on the Internet, and music albums of a favourite composer can be stored on one DVD. Information tends to be free. From this perspective, there is a growing interest in the UNIX operating system. Originally developed as an advanced, heavy-weight, and hardware-demanding operational environment, but more robust, reliable and safer than Windows or Mac OS, UNIX, and especially its modern lighter version Linux, can run on smaller computers than today's versions of Windows. And Linux is free of charge, as are many applications developed for it. Other applications, like OS Lindows and applications for it are much less expensive than most commercial software.

In fact, there is a lot of free information on the Internet. Several countries have launched free electronic archives, and digitized their cultural heritage.

The idea of open and free information space is at once popular but also disturbing, not only among educators, but among software developers as well. Many software products in schools are open and allow:

- teachers and students to use data and images for their personal use;
- students to create experiments in virtual labs, and teachers to create tests; and
- students to store their work for a period of study in a unified information space open to other students and teachers, parents and other schools.

The major question is how will the creators of original information work be paid for their work. A possible answer is that information will be free, but that human service provided on demand will be compensated adequately. Questions of further development of free information resources are under consideration currently by an important international association called The World Wide Web Consortium (W3C).

References

Card, S.K., Mackinlay, J.D., and Shneiderman, B. (Eds). (1999). *Readings in Information Visualization: Using Vision to Think*. Morgan Kaufmann.

Friedhoff, R. and Benzon, W. (1989). *Visualization: The Second Computer Revolution*. Harry N. Abrams, New York.

Gardner, H. (1993). *Multiple Intelligences: The Theory in Practice*. Basic Books, New York.

Heineke, W.F. and Blasi, L. (Eds). (2001). *Methods of Evaluating Educational Technology*. Information Age Publishing, Greenwich, Connecticut.

UNESCO. (2002. *Information and Communication Technology in Education: A Curriculum for Schools and Programme of Teacher Development* (Eds J. Anderson and T. van Weert).UNESCO Paris.

11

Schools in Transition

By permeating contemporary schooling with useful digital technologies, we can make profound changes in the whole existing system of education. However, change is a process, not an event. Just buying and installing hardware and software is not sufficient to make ICT into a genuine educational technology. This task of implementing ICT in schools demands gigantic efforts, widely time-spread, and covering many diverse but interconnected fields – at the national, regional, and individual school levels. We are talking about restructuring the very foundation of schools, perhaps even greater than the one initiated by the invention of printing press. The utmost precautions must be taken not to destroy, or discard anything of value in current practice. On the other hand, we need to be aware of the really deep changes that have begun in education around the world, and which we must direct and manage with care and courage.

Teachers and Learners

Before focusing on ICT in classrooms, some background in pedagogy, and examines what is involved in teaching and learning, as well as the institutions - schools - that we have developed for teaching and learning.

Educational Events

An educational event occurs between someone who is willing to educate, namely the teacher, and another, willing to be educated, the learner. A synergy of wills is a prerequisite. Otherwise, there is no place for proper education, and we should talk about conditioning, drilling, training, moulding, pressing, or whatever else might happen between those officially labelled as *Teacher* and *Student*.

The teacher is always in search of a learner, and vice versa. When there is no learner in sight, teachers will try to awake, or invoke the will to learn in anyone they happen to meet. The teacher does this by challenging the other person's curiosity, ambition, inquisitiveness, or just playfulness with any means at hand. Anything that works is good for this purpose.

A learner is also always in search of a teacher. Where there is no teacher available, learners will recruit anyone they meet as a possible teacher. If there is no one at all, they will figure out a kind of virtual substitute teacher inside their own soul.

We discern three facets of any educational event: encounter, communication and interaction.

1. Encounters are face-to-face meetings; situations when you find yourself faced by other individuals and feel prompted to relate somehow to their presence.
2. Communication is an exchange of messages, sent and received by at least two people, expressing their feelings, thoughts and intentions to each other in the hope for reciprocity.
3. Interactions are processes where two, or more *actors* (in our case - teacher and learner) influence and affect each other's actions and behaviour while striving to reach their goals, doing some common work, or performing a joint task.

Any interaction, by definition, generates information. Not all information generated by an interaction needs to be communicated; some parts of this information may be intentionally concealed. One actor may purposely search for, uncover (at times compel), and collect the information that another actor tries to conceal.

At times it is difficult to draw a strict line between communication and interaction. For example, if during language classes (especially on rhetoric), a teacher uses verbal means to enact modes of argumentation for students, communication and interaction become one and the same. A number of authors, analyzing patterns of communication in European cultural (especially educational) traditions, have pointed out such recurrent themes as surveillance, interrogation, and the threat of punishment.

Basic Activities in Learning

Let us recollect some well-known facts about human information activities and other actions in the process of learning that will later be transferred into ICT contexts.

Communicating by Different Ways and Means

For centuries, communication between human beings has been carried out in oral and written form. Oral communication goes through the aural channel of information, more often than not supported by the visual channel (a speaker's movements and everything else that constitutes theatrical aspects of communication).

Oral communication used to be immediate until recent centuries when it became possible to have it recorded. It was an interesting moment in human history, when the recording of dynamic images of communication (as well as images of the world) was invented and developed, before the recording of dynamic sound was possible. This was the era of the Great Mute (as they used to call the cinematograph until it was coupled with recorded sound), where moving pictures on the screen were accompanied by sub-titles (and live music) only.

Communication can go in one direction as in radio and TV broadcasting, or in two directions as in oral discussions or telephone conversation.

Written communication goes through a visual channel, where text is supported by pictorial illustrations.

All these models and modes are presented in learning and teaching, and all have been, and are being, radically changed by ICT.

Object Making

Learning can involve also doing something in the physical world, particularly, making objects. This includes making messages, which, in this respect, intersects with the communication process, though the accent in the doing is made on constructing the message, not delivering it. Therefore, cases of doing in learning are represented by constructing:

- an information object (an actual or potential message),
- an information process (composing and editing),

- a mental, inner object (reasoning and imagining), and
- a material object or process.

These activities, while being in many aspects interrelated, can be efficiently supported by different uses of ICT.

Observation, Reflection, Imitation

Observation is another process involved in learning. The learner is an active participant in the game here. A further important element in the formation of a thinking human being is reflection - the process and the ability to observe yourself and your activity *from the outside.* An ancient and powerful tool for reflection is a mirror. Observing another human in order to copy, imitate, and do the same, is another important model of learning. The modern type of mirror that keeps track of disappearing images is a video-recorder.

Information Searches and Questioning

Searching for information was not a popular activity in traditional schooling but has become more and more important in modern life. Previously, if any searching was done, it was primarily in a person's memory. People were considered intelligent, knowledgeable, and wise if they could *output* quickly the needed information from memory. Even then, books (of wisdom) were occasionally used to answer a question, but the books were not considered as an everyday source of information with the exception, perhaps, of medical doctors and lawyers. Today the search and retrieval of needed information is becoming a core activity in work and learning. Asking an expert is a special case of information search.

The faculty to question was recognized long ago as a mark of the genuine philosopher and scientist; but it was also reflected in ironic sayings like "One fool can ask so many questions that a thousand wise men will never answer". As with information searches, questioning is becoming more and more important in the information age. Receiving aural and visual information in studying a school subject is a prerequisite, but it is just the first step to assimilating its content. Tue learning occurs only in an intensive conversation between teacher and student, as well as between students, as all good pedagogues since the days of Socrates have known. What a pity that this principle was forgotten, or neglected by those teachers in many 20th century-era schools who thought they were there to teach, not to converse.

Contradictions of Schooling

Contemporary education is replete with contradictory demands. Here we touch on some of these.

Creativity versus Discipline

Perhaps the most tormenting question of contemporary education is how to reconcile two contradictory demands:

1. fostering inquisitive and creative minds eager to explore the unknown and solve unprecedented problems; and
2. training the same creative minds to become skilful, adroit and highly disciplined performers of particular, subject-specific, manual and mental tasks.

To a large extent, the lamentable rift between verbal and practical, hands-on learning, so deeply rooted in the established system of schooling, aggravates this contradiction. The contradiction is compounded when you consider the further problem of motivation, which has been moved to the forefront by all modern pedagogical theories.

Compulsory Versus Voluntary

Can you force a small child to play? Obviously, not. Children start to play only when they feel like playing. Equally, no teacher can force a student to learn actively and wholeheartedly unless they have a deliberate desire to do so.

Of course, we can, and often *do,* teach appointed subject(s) to students and make them learn quite successfully, judging by standard achievement tests, without any strong need and desire on their part. So, what is wrong with that?

The trouble with *compulsory* (that is, passive) learning is that while students appropriate a given piece of curricular content quite firmly, they all too often remain incapable of *applying* it to anything else besides right answers and getting high examination scores. As it happens, a student often cannot relate a newly acquired fragment of knowledge to other pieces learned previously, especially in other subject areas. Unable to connect recent acquisitions to what is already known, and to perceive the outcome as coherent whole, they can hardly be expected to transfer a powerful mathematical concept into a field of science in order to grasp the laws of physics and chemistry, or use the latter for better understanding of a living cell. It goes without saying that these disjointed chunks are even harder for students to apply to real-life issues outside school.

Schooling can bring forth truly substantial results only when coupled with inner motivation and self-propelled learning - in other words, when particular skill development is driven either by genuine curiosity, or by some pragmatic consideration as, for example, when seeking to find a clue to some intriguing riddle, or to solve a problem one has stumbled upon in a game.

We are back at our starting point. Is it possible for teachers not to compel and coerce, but to provoke, entice, or tempt students to embark on truly *active,* all-absorbing and penetrative learning? And, if so, then how?

There is strong reason to believe that ICT can help bridge the yawning gaps just described. First, however, it is worth recollecting that students generally *want* to comprehend a particular subject or master a methodological cornerstone of so-called classical schooling and.

Classical Hierarchy of Learning and Personal Responsibility

In medieval times, knowledge was a set of divine commandments transmitted from a teacher to a student, who was obliged to take them reverently and obedi-ently Later, Nature and its laws displaced the Deity, and the teacher's duty was to provide students with the knowledge of those natural laws, discovered by scientists, that would lead the human race further along the path of progress.

Three fundamental educational assumptions that date back to Socrates and later Descartes have until recently been taken as unquestionable:

1. Simple skills requiring little understanding are the easiest to learn and therefore easiest to teach the youngest or the mentally less capable.
2. There is a hierarchy of skills from simple to complex, and a hierarchy of performance from that requiring little understanding to that requiring abstract knowledge. To move up this ladder, the preceding rung must be mastered. In other words, Lesson One must be mastered before the student can successfully move on to Lesson Two.
3. There is a progression towards maturity that must be followed: the very young or the retarded cannot learn via abstract understandings and therefore must be taught by the route of simple skills and bits of information, which they eventually combine into large units.

Under this system of education, a team of workers or mental *agents* must manage learning activities, each performing a single, elementary function. This hierarchical organization is something like a tree in which the agent on each branch is exclusively responsible for the agents on the twigs that branch from it. It is easy to construct and understand such an organization because each agent has only one job to do: it needs only to *look up* for instructions from its supervisor, then *look down* to get help from its subordinates. Metaphorically speaking, these agents constitute something like a *machine* built purposefully to manufacture these particular, strictly specified products.

We do not doubt that there is room for teaching and learning certain disconnected, step-by-step accruing skills, required by many occupations, by this method.

But the great realization of the 21st century is this: no scientist, political leader or preacher knows for certain how to decide on this or that issue of global scale, nor what advice to give any of us on our daily cares, living in a world that is changing in all its facets at an ever accelerating pace. The destiny of mankind depends, rather, on decisions made (or not made) by each conscious and responsible person. It has become crystal clear that the long-established and respected ways of teaching in schools are not good enough. We must be concerned, not with adapting to a given world out there, but with making this world different.

The educational system of the 21st century must be oriented toward creating conditions that allow school students to act and learn freely in productive collaboration with their teachers, and also with their parents and other members of their community, local and global. In this, the application of ICT appears to be a necessity, as well as a pledge of success.

Old School as Organization

In the previous two sections, we describe basic relations and activities of learning, and expose certain basic contradictions of schooling. After investigating the limitations of what we call *old schools,* we outline the psychological background of possible changes that are occurring, and then proceed to the changes themselves.

Activities to Sustain

It is assumed that readers are familiar with how the *mass, standard, traditional* school works today. Let us call this the *old school.* To redesign such schools with the help of ICT, we need to take a fresh look at them as though we have never seen such enterprises before. We need to consider them anew and decide what to take into the future.

School-related activities can be broadly divided into two categories - internal and external - that the school as an organization is called upon to sustain.

Internal activities are carried out within the school's scheduled hours and inside the school walls. These core, central, obligatory and strictly formalized activities - one is tempted to say almost *sacred* activities - are the school's classes or lessons, comprising teaching and learning. Activities during intermissions are *profane,* and activities after scheduled hours are a mixture of the two. There are also internal activities of administration and supervision, and teachers' meetings, which are conducted without the involvement of students. All these activities imply an exchange of information, carried out through a number of channels, some established, officially approved, and highly formalized; the others, informal, weakly delineated, not always approved, often rebuked and prohibited, and thus covert, and even kept in strict secrecy. External learning activities, besides sports and clubs, are mainly homework. Students do their homework in an isolated, individual manner. The relation to internal activity is often through short assignment notes. Consultations with teachers, discussions with peers are occasional and irregular, as is cooperative work. External activities of school administrators are working meetings and consulting with superiors and colleagues from other schools, seminars, training sessions, and conferences.

The Learned Context of Learning

Neither organizational aspect of schooling should be neglected in relation to the use of ICT. As Penelope Eckert puts it:

> One of the greatest errors in education is to assume that the larger social context of the school is irrelevant or even secondary to learning....The social structure of the school is not simply the context of learning; it is part of what is learned. What a student learns in the classroom is indeed a very small other part... What the Burnouts learn in school is how to be marginalized... High school, therefore, is not simply a bad experience for these students - it teaches them lessons that threaten to limit them for the rest of their lives.

Writing about business organizations, rather than schools, managerial scientists often refer to *learning organizations.* Here is what one writer, Ronny Lessem, says in a paper titled *Linking artisan and scribe:*

Since at the present rate of technological change the problems to be solved differ from one day to the next, it follows that everybody in the organization, from those who frame the policies to those who manipulate the ultimate details of technique, must be endowed to the possible extent with the *means of learning*. One must ask here whether the school can evolve and change its structure and functions in response to the new challenges. Is the present school an organization that learns, or it is just a system, a machine, functioning according to predetermined and inherently closed programs?

School as a Social Institution

Lewis Mumford, an outstanding historian-philosopher of technology, described the new kind of religious, socio-political, industrial and military organization, invented during the Bronze Age under the aegis of the priest-kings, as a *mega-machine.* Being essentially coercive, undemocratic and hierarchical, such an organization paved the way to, and was inherited by, succeeding civilizations. Only recently was it questioned and challenged by a new vision of human progress based on other principles. Through this millennial old legacy, the school appears to be the social organization most resistant to change. In fact, it mostly strives to keep its basic structures and functions unchanged, including its information circuits, channels, and routes. Below, we examine typical approaches to channelling information, which, in turn, were determined by the traditional concept of so-called compulsory mass education. To make things clearer, however, we must trace the latter's origins back to three or four centuries ago.

There was no serious lack of quality as long as education remained a heavily guarded treasure or luxury, accessible only to a chosen few. Formal schooling was reserved exclusively for the high priesthood and aristocratic families, and denied to anyone outside the cloisters and castle walls.

School as an Invention of Industrial Era

The *classical school,* as we know it today, was invented at the dawn of industrial, mass-production-of-everything era. General education was claimed as the property of the people at the verge of the 17th and 18th centuries in Europe. Just and democratic at its inception, this path led in time to quite a different state of affairs. Historians and theoreticians usually say the school was first modeled after a printing-house - as Comenius announced in his 1657 book, *A Living Printery, or An Art of How Swiftly, Yet Informatively and Lightly to Stamp the Wisdom Not On Paper, But Upon the Minds.* It was not just a coincidence that schools were associated with the most advanced information technology of the time - the printing press with movable characters. The minds of pre-schoolers were considered a plain tablet or a blank sheet of paper upon which teachers could write anything they, or some higher authority, would think appropriate. In a short while, the thinking about what was appropriate to teach children was taken away from teachers and concentrated in the hands of those in political and economic power.

No less significant technologically and educationally was Gutenberg's concept of setting up a line of type by using separate letters cast in a uniform pattern in a mould: the origin of the standardized, replaceable part of ever increasingly automated machinery. It was only logical to apply the same principles to schooling, and since the mid-19th century, this approach has prevailed in most Western countries. A system was established where children and young people could learn different subjects from different teachers who, in their turn, could rely safely on a standard, ready-made curriculum and procedures designed by other specialists.

Information Routes and Flows in The Classical Old School

At the top of the said system, we see centralized pedagogical research institutions that design the curricula, instructional methods, textbooks and other materials, which, after having a stamp of approval from ministries of education, are distributed to schools and teachers. A teacher's duty is to read and follow closely the body of these materials in order to deliver it piecemeal to students, who are expected to memorize the content one chunk after another, and checking in to see if they succeed. The basic, though rarely announced, assumption is that teachers need not add a word to what has been given from higher authorities.

A principal and a supervisor receive from the higher educational authorities an approved bundle of curriculum-and-procedure materials and distribute these different packages among the teachers of particular disciplines. Each teacher subdivides the received package in accordance with the age grouping of students, the quotas of curriculum content to be assimilated daily, and the school timetable. Teacher-to-student communication is predominantly oral. Visual aids are usually illustrations taken from books. There is little hands-on activity with physical materials and tools on workbenches. The teacher is a lecturer, not a master of a craft (menial or mental). Little communication exists between teachers of different subjects on how to collaborate in making the educational process truly involving and exiting.

What Teachers and Learners do During Classes

Here is a brief list of what teachers and learners do in the traditional classroom of the old school:

- Teachers speak, learners listen.
- Teachers talk to learners, who listen to and supposedly perceive, understand and memorize what is said. Often, this is all that teachers do on a strictly formal, *technical-operational* plane.
- Teachers write letters, numbers, words and phrases on the chalkboard to help students hold facts in their short- and long-term memories.
- Teachers paste (clip) to the chalkboard, or hang on the wall, posters with pre-written (printed) letters, words and numbers, and then point to them with their finger or a pointer while giving explications, explanations and instructions.
- Teachers draw or use ready-made diagrams or images of certain objects or scenes related in some way to what they are saying.
- Teachers bring three-dimensional objects to illustrate lessons.
- Teachers manipulate these 3-D objects (other than to point to them or take them in their hands to show them to the class) in a transformative way, for example by using them in applied functions they are meant to illustrate. To show such manipulations and transformations of 3-D objects, teachers use workbenches.
- Teachers conduct spectacular experiments that excite students and which they remember all their lives.

In short, notwithstanding the content, the main tool and carrier of the teacher's message is the word, or, more precisely, the oral and, to a lesser degree, written speech. At the same time, we know that the additional activities are listed in ascending order of their supposed educational efficiency (and labour intensity).

In such classrooms, learners are not required or expected to:

- *do* anything besides follow a teacher's presentations and instructions expressed in oral and written words (texts) until they can assimilate and reproduce verbally the knowledge and skills required;
- *draw* in language or mathematics workbooks except perhaps for geometry, or drawing primitive diagrams for science (in most cases, learners are not taught to acquire drawing skills);
- *manipulate* or transform three-dimensional objects, other than, perhaps, paper, scissors, glue and pencils.
- *discover,* invent, design, and construct during classes anything of their own in relation to the curricular content; or
- *converse* with classmates on the content being taught.

This picture may be over-simplified, but it broadly reflects the features of the traditional school that are deeply embedded into organizational structures in many countries.

Rigid Timing

In a scheduled class period, the teacher delivers (orally, in blackboard writing, and by showing pictures) the assigned chunk of information simultaneously to all students in a monologue *broadcast* type of lecture. While taking in information coming from the teacher, students are obliged to remain silent and motionless until the teacher stops the delivery and asks them if everybody has clearly understood what was said. Then those who may not have understood can raise their hands and, after being granted the right to speak, say what escaped their comprehension. Teachers repeat an explanation twice or even three times, but often there is no time to clarify all problems, and there are always one or more students who dare not express their difficulties. Common sense prompts one to think that those who are in need might seek and find some help from their nearest neighbours in the classroom. Sadly, more often than not, such a common sense approach does not happen in *classical schooling.*

As everybody knows, communication between students during classes is usually frowned upon because it threatens to disrupt the very foundation of *classical teaching* (luckily, there are many good teachers brave enough to transgress this rule).

Monologue Lecturing

Information is constantly filtered downwards through the hierarchical system and no horizontal roots are stipulated. When a teacher gives a class an assignment demanding writing, calculating, or reasoning, each student is supposed to do the task individually and by themselves. No consultation with classmates is allowed, and any breaking of this rule is often punished. Consequently nothing even remotely resembling collaboration, productive discussion and teamwork is practised; neither are the corresponding skills being developed. As a result (and this becomes evident after some testing questions made by the teacher), not all students receive the full amount of curriculum information supposedly transmitted to them during class periods. Students do not have the channels, and nor are they encouraged, to exchange views and opinions about the curriculum. It is not surprising then that very few of them are motivated enough to discuss such things out of classes except to complain about it. Anyway, such behaviour is not anticipated or wanted in traditional curricula and procedures.

In such circumstances, one might conclude that most traditional school authorities would readily reject the idea of adopting ICT that would enable students to sustain autonomous information exchanges during classes.

Institution for Teaching Only

Because of society's evolving expectations of equal educational opportunity for all and the current emphasis on relevant and quality opportunity for all, the school system has developed into an increasingly complex organizational structure. This structure requires extensive and comprehensive administration and has enough problems sustaining stable and malleable conditions to put aside the problems of its transformative development. That is, to sustain the conditions that give teachers and administrators intellectual and emotional comfort, they naturally tend to see schools as exclusively teaching institutions. They have little time to think about schools as learning institutions and do not consider it a pressing priority. What are the consequences? Howard Gardner puts it this way:

We run the risk of investing incalculable resources in institutions that do not operate very well and that may never approach the effectiveness that their supporters - and for that matter their detractors - would desire. Moreover,...until now, we have not fully appreciated just how difficult it is for schools to succeed in their chosen task...We have not been cognizant of ways in which basic inclinations of human learning turn out to be ill-matched to the agenda of the modern secular school.

Disparate Subjects

The sum of what must be taught and learned, despite the charge to have it integrated and holistic, remains a collection of disjointed, isolated and unrelated subjects, struggling for allocated hours in the school timetable. No evident connection exists between corresponding activities or between actors *(functional agents);* no channels through which they can communicate and talk to each other; and no space for their mutual encounter and subsequent interaction.

Quite naturally, there is little information exchange between them precisely because subject matter in the classical school curriculum is impersonal, faceless and soulless. Neither teachers nor students can feel and see in such classrooms other living, willing, and acting personalities - those bearers of creative forces that had once brought into being all these areas of knowledge, mastery and expertise. No wonder they have little motivation to explore and develop the hidden inner potential of their own.

The Origins of Detechnicalized Learning

The mechanical-industrial syndrome is still felt in many areas of education, especially among the administrative staff. The vision of a smoothly run manufacturing plant with its driving belts and assembly lines does often eclipse the fact that school is (or at least, is said to be) a living entity, a society in miniature, a learning community of people, comprising some adults but mostly children drawn and bound together by extreme variegated needs, expectations, obligations, and responsibilities. To quote Seymour Papert who probably, more than anyone else, has helped us to understand the vast educational potential of computers:

The institution of School, with its daily lesson plans, fixed curriculum, standardized tests... tends constantly to reduce learning to a series of technical acts and the teacher to the role of technician. Of course, it never fully succeeds, for teachers resist the role of technician and bring warm, natural human relationships into their classrooms. But what is important for thinking about the potential for megachange is that this situation places the teacher in a state of tension between two poles: School tries to make the teacher into a technician: in most cases the sense of self resists, though in many the teacher will have internalized School's concept of teaching. Each teacher is therefore along the continuum between technician and which I dare call a true teacher.

The central issue of change in education is the tension between technicalizing and not technicalizing, and here the teacher occupies the fulcrum position.

Not since the printing press has there been so great a surge in the potential to boost technicalized learning. But there is also another side: Paradoxically, the same technology has the potential to detechnicalize learning. Were this to happen, I would count it as a larger change than the appearance on every desk of a computer programmed to lead the student through the paces of the same old curriculum. But it is not necessary to quibble about which change is more far-reaching. What is necessary is to recognize that the great issue in the future of education is whether technology will strengthen or undermine the technicalities of what has become the theoretical model, and to a large extent the reality.

In fact, institutionalized, compulsory education was turned into a machine (a mechanical production system), imparting its *products* with an inner program to proliferate the same pattern in all walks of life. Hence, the school became the model for the mechanization of society. Increasingly fragmented division of labour and specialization were, and still are, the key words. In fact, it was a cycle (or vicious circle) of mutual reinforcement that reached a climax in the mid-20th century.

At the beginning of the new millennium, this cycle came to a dead-end. To become alive again, we believe the school must transform itself from a machine for teaching into a *learning organization* more focused on creative experiments than on prefabricated detailed plans and checklists.

New Pedagogical Possibilities

Proposals for a radical reformation of traditional schooling are numerous. To explicate them all here would be a large task. However, we shall try to give instead a composite picture of the leading ideas that we deem the most promising, substantiated, and convincing. We start with basic notions, describing child personality and development, and with the question of how to measure them.

Intelligence and Intelligence Quotient

Dictionaries define intelligence as the power of seeing, learning, understanding and knowing. It is a mental ability. For example, we say, "He shows little intelligence" when we mean that boy is slow in understanding.

For a long time in the West, *intelligence* has been equated with the ability to think *rationally* and *objectively,* and to express one's thoughts and judgments in *scientifically based, quantitatively measurable, logically provable* propositions and assertions. Individuals were called intelligent if they were astute, shrewd, eloquent and quick in using words and numbers, especially in written form. In the Orient, by contrast, a man or woman who was well behaved and obedient to the supreme forces, respectful to the elders, deferential to traditions, or endowed with clairvoyance, was often referred to in terms that have been translated as *intelligent.*

Consequently, teaching and learning in Western schools were more concerned with transmitting and getting *detachable* and *distant* knowledge coded symbolically in oral and written speech, rather than with immediate interaction and participatory hands-on activities, experience and wisdom.

It was quite natural to establish a system of checking and testing both interim results and the quality of the end-products of this almost industrial-like manufacturing process.

At the turn of the 20th century, the French psychologists Binet and Simon were commissioned to research the possibility for *measuring intelligence.* From the start, the goal was to measure the sub-skills necessary for classroom success. Binet actually sat in a classroom, taking notes of students' answers to teachers' questions, and tried to construct rules for predicting who would fulfill the demands of the teacher best. Sampling school children's abilities to utter correct answers in many schools across France, Binet created the first intelligence test, later developed and corroborated by other researchers. With these tests, it became possible to estimate an individual's *intelligence* by processing the data of one's performance on a deliberately heterogeneous set of items, ranging from sensory discrimination of colours to vocabulary knowledge, and to calculate a so-called Intelligence Quotient or IQ.

What a magnificent epitome of the era of mass-produced education: now you could quantify how bright and stupid everyone is!

In pre-industrial epochs, people perceived each other as much more complex entities. Someone could be clever enough with words while incompetent in numbers; shrewd in business but poor in writing; incapable in abstract reasoning but masterful in crafts or apt in sports. It was only after the development of intelligence tests and what the statistician Spearman did with them that the construct of intelligence nested so firmly in the consciousness of educators and heads of Human Resource departments. Spearman found that all IQ tests that appeared after Binet and Simon's correlated highly with each other. He reasoned that they must have been measuring the same thing. Further, this cross-correlation could be explained by a construct he called *g,* for *general intelligence.* Some eminent critics disagreed, maintaining that human beings had multiple abilities, or factors of intelligence, but they were forced to admit that even these multiple factors had a high cross-correlation. Hence IQ tests became highly useful in the hands of busy school administrators eager to predict student scores and channel students according to their abilities. After all, that was how the administrators' own abilities would be measured and rewarded.

Eventually, all these tests, rather than measuring potential for achievement *became* the measure of achievement. More to the point, the tests that had been designed to sample education now came to determine what was taught. Large publishing houses began selling textbooks and other consumables to elementary schools with drill units that carried a remarkable resemblance to IQ subtests. Thus began a self-feeding, circular relationship.

Multiple Intelligences

For a while, there were voices arguing that intelligence was better conceived as a set of possibly independent factors. Later findings from AI (Artificial Intelligence) research, developmental psychology, and neurology, prompted investigators to put forth the view that the mind consists of several independent modules or *intelligences.* In the 1980s, Howard Gardner formulated his theory of multiple intelligences, in which he stated that people use one or more of at least seven (more recently eight and even nine) relatively autonomous, intellectual capacities to approach problems and create products. In many aspects, Gardner's views run against entrenched notions of pedagogical psychology. Gardner's seven intelligencies are:

1. Linguistic intelligence (as in a poet);
2. Logical-mathematical intelligence (as in a scientist);

3. Musical intelligence (as in a composer);
4. Spatial intelligence (as in a sculptor or flight pilot);
5. Bodily kinaesthetic intelligence (as in an athlete or dancer);
6. Interpersonal intelligence (as in a salesman or teacher);
7. Intrapersonal intelligence (exhibited by individuals with accurate views of themselves).

What is important to the present discussion is Gardner's stress on the fact that a particular intelligence cannot be conceptualized independently of the particular context in which an individual happens to live, work and play, and the opportunities and values provided by that milieu. For example, Bobby Fisher might have had the potential to be a great chess player, but if he had lived in a culture without chess, that potential would never have been manifested, let alone actualized.

The time has come for schools to incorporate a wider array of mental processes and activities into the learning process. Whereas traditional classes have been dominated by the spoken and printed word, the new classroom should practise a multisensory enhanced learning. Indeed, as long ago as 1920, Vygotsky's work showed that a child's cognition and thinking, to a great extent, relied upon the manipulation of material objects used as tools as well as societal surrounding.

Intelligence is always an interaction between biological proclivities and opportunities for learning in a particular cultural context. Vygotsky and Papert would agree wholeheartedly with Gardner; and Papert would especially emphasize the role of immediate surroundings, allowing and prompting the child to investigate and consciously transforming purposely its material, energetic and informational aspects and components.

Unfortunately, as Gardner and Papert never miss the chance to point out, the school system, which largely reflects yesterday's Western culture, teaches, tests, reinforces, and rewards primarily only two intelligences: verbal and logical-mathematical. These two intelligences are, of course, essential for effective functioning in a knowledge society, but so are all the other intelligences. Not only have the other kinds of intelligence been highly developed by gifted graphic artists, dancers, musicians and writers, they may also be pathways to learning for many poorly achieving students who do not learn in *legitimate* ways. For everyone, developing these multiple intelligences increases creativity, flexibility of thinking, and the broad cultural and humanitarian background that enriches living.

The resources for this enrichment are typically thought of as material artifacts like books, textbooks, and computer files. However, other individuals are part of one's distributed intelligence also. Most workers do not depend exclusively on their own skills and understanding; rather, they assume the presence of others in their work environments. This view is brought home vividly when one considers an office or a classroom that is being computerized and has access to the WWW

Testing Abilities

Another approach to the nature, structure and functions of intelligence(s) has been proposed by Robert Sternberg, who suggests three kinds of intelligence:

1. componential, which is assessed by many traditional tests used today;
2. contextual, which is the source of creative insight, and
3. experiential, which is the *street smarts* of intelligence.

Sternberg's latter two intelligences do not often show up on traditional tests, and are not always highly valued in the classroom, since curious and creative students and those who learn by doing tend to take up more of a teacher's time and attention. Such students are later valued in the adult world, however, as creative thinkers and process-oriented employees who often affect the bottom line in productive ways.

Sternberg feels that some people's major intelligence is in the traditionally tested/graded area of *critical thinking* (generating new innovative thought and connection), and that people who are able to make things really work for them out there in real life are *contextual thinkers.* Sternberg's theory is too complex to be elaborated here in full detail. One of its outcomes is the Sternberg Triarchic

Abilities Test (STAT), which is divided into nine multiple levels for different ages, and described as suitable for kindergarten through college, as well as for adults.

In contrast to conventional tests, STAT yields separate scores for compo-nential information processing (analytical ability), coping with novelty (synthetic ability), and (as a separate score) automatization and practical-intellectual skills. Equally important, the test puts more emphasis on the ability to learn than on what has been learned, and verbal skill is measured by learning from context, not by vocabulary. The test also measures skills for coping with novelty, whereby the examinee must imagine a hypothetical state of the world (such as cats being magnetic) and then reason as though this state of the world were true. In yet another example, STAT measures practical abilities such as reasoning about advertisements and political slogans, not just decontextualized words or geometric forms.

In fact, as Sternberg himself admits, STAT is not immune to prior learning, and nor is it *culture-free.* It is hardly thinkable to design a test that would satisfy all the considered demands. Intelligence is always used in some particular, usually rather restricted context, though it is highly desirable to have this context as wide as possible.

Sternberg's theory differs from Gardner's. However, the two theories are also highly complementary. Sternberg makes us strongly believe that intelligence needs to be seen as a broader and more complex construct than both authors declare, and the field is open to any experienced, thoughtful, and enterprising teacher eager to make her or his own contribution to the common educational cauldron.

Multiple Ways and Conditions of Learning

We must exploit universal features of the child's (and the adult's) personality to a greater extent. Children have a natural interest and curiosity about the internal and external world, and an eagerness to communicate and to play, making collections and ordering items, creating unexpected and aesthetically significant objects. The basis for human development - habits and skills for lifelong learning - should be established early in primary schools.

Appealing to Both Sensory and Symbolic Smarts

It is widely accepted today that it is not enough for students to understand and learn fragmented information. It is equally important for students to understand

Schools in Transition

The context, meaning, and gestalt of topics as well. The objective, sterile environment in many schools actually inhibits learning. Learning is also unlikely to occur when students harbour negative feelings about an instructor, peers, class work, or have difficult personal issues. The traditional classroom must be replaced by rich, stimulating, accepting, warm, and responsive surroundings. Sylvia Farnham-Diggory agrees:

> Both children and adults acquire knowledge from active participation in holistic, complex, meaningful environments organized around long-term goals. Fractionated instruction maximizes forgetting, inattention, and passivity. Today's school programs could hardly have been better designed to prevent a child's natural learning system from operating.

As most teachers know, students labeled *weak* or *slow* often turn out to be bright and skilful when confronted with something that is personally appealing or challenging outside the classroom. Though these students have difficulty learning in school, they often excel at making, fixing and operating tangible things: gadgets, bicycles, motors, electrical circuits, complex mechanical devices, arcade games, VCRs, various kinds of contraptions and even imaginary objects. These children are usually identified as having trouble with the *symbolic smarts* that form the core of schooling. It is not surprising that the traditional school focuses on what *weak* students cannot do, and does not see them as possessing virtuoso *sensory smarts* in some fields. Instead, it sees them as failing to perform, or not meeting the requirements. An ideal teacher will appeal equally to symbolic and sensory smart students with a view to bringing these two kinds of knowledge into active and fruitful collaboration.

For example, a computer with a Logo environment and LEGO extensions allows students to build working systems out of tangible blocks, using their hands as well as their *theoretical* mind, in the form of symbolic expressions on the monitor screen. When students are encouraged by teachers to reflect on and confront the differences and similarities that emerge as they move across materials, sensory modalities, and kinds of descriptions, it helps them to create mental bridges between *action knowledge* and *symbolic knowledge.* Previously hidden aspects of hands-on constructions are revealed. Children who build both real world and virtual world structures begin to see the resemblance among working systems. In making the resemblance explicit, they liberate and make easily understandable the basic principles that the working systems share.

Visual Cognition and Creative Thinking

Visualization of inner mental imagery and the outer graphic presentation of reality in pictures, drawings, diagrams, lists, and charts is a fundamental part of creativity, discovery, invention, and problem solving. The vital importance of visualization is affirmed by the fact that a surprisingly large proportion of the human cortex is devoted to vision and visual analysis, and that the bandwidth of the visual channel is greater than that of any other sense. In many instances, the eye, and those parts of the brain that process visual information, lay the foundation for enhancing conscious thinking, which in turn, grows from our preconscious mental activity.

To take full advantage of the capabilities of the eye, the goal of visualization should be objectification. This means that a phenomenon, inherently visual or not, should be represented as having form, colour, texture, motion and other qualities of objects. Inductive thinking relies to a great extent upon the human ability to visualize on this preconscious level. Major portions of the visual system including the retina, the structures ascending to the visual cortex, and parts of the visual cortex itself fall into the preconscious category. More powerful than a supercomputer, these functional entities relentlessly perform information-processing miracles, creating a three-dimensional, coloured visual environment that our conscious self exploits in a logical way to serve definite practical purposes. Our conceptual images are constantly being analyzed at a preconscious level, and produce useful data for establishing spatial relations, making conscious representations and building plans. In other words, the outcomes of these subliminal mental activities become the elements, tools, and procedures of rational thinking.

This is where computers make an enormous difference. When we visualize with the help of computers, video camcorders, and big-screen high-resolution projection, we restructure a problem situation so that more of it can be processed by the preconscious part of our brain - the visual system that is our silent partner. In this way, consciousness can be devoted to higher levels of critical analysis and synthesis. Especially interesting, are virtual worlds that model nothing but themselves, as do many games, chess among them. Nevertheless, by representing spatially the system of abstract relations between chessmen on a chessboard, a professional chess player can think in images. Similarly, it is also possible to visualize on a computer screen the spatial interrelations of elementary predicates and, consequently, to represent complex formulas of predicate logic

As a kind of modelling, visualization has many aspects. One is aesthetic-emotional. For example, nobody will deny that visualized mathematical objects and functions can be aesthetically beautiful. *Fractal* animated cartoons, capti-vatingly spectacular and shown on TV all over the world, have already inspired works of fine art (even if not eternal masterpieces). Beyond any doubt, it is precisely because of their aesthetic components that such themes as chaos, fractals, and the like, have become so popular in academic mathematical courses.

Another aspect of visualization-as-modelling is, as in the classical art of painting, selecting and making visible essential traits of the object or phenomenon depicted. By forcing us to pay attention only to what can be seen and perceived by the eye, visualizing helps to impart a meaning to a problem and makes it easier to find its solution. In the simplest case of a virtual constructor used to build interactive models of physical phenomena, we may get a picture of an ideal experiment, which is mathematically correct within a set degree of accuracy.

Using a similar learning environment under a teacher's guidance, the student can trace all levels of abstractions in modelling. For instance, there could be genuine physical objects and processes (say, a carousel on which children have a ride), material (LEGO-like) models, videotapes, computer simulations (virtual realities), graphical representations of processes' characteristics by co-ordinates and velocities within a set referential system, and symbolic modelling by algebraic and differential equations.

Changing Pedagogy

New pedagogy is based on the opposite of the traditional classical hierarchy -that is, a *heterarchy,* a term that depicts a system in which each working element or agent is equally ruled by all others. This means that, while learning, these agents communicate or talk to each other, exchanging messages filled with related information. In this system, there are no simple linear chains of cause and effect, but more and more cross-connected rings and loops.Behind the dazzling variety of new theories, methodologies, and working approaches to learning, one can detect several underlying patterns, or fundamental principles and practices that seem perennial. Re-christened in modern idioms, these principles are referred to as poly-sensory, experiential, project-oriented, constructivist, and connectionist.

Constructivism

Constructivism, a term introduced by Jean Piaget, asserts that the knowledge acquired by students should not be supplied by the teacher as a ready-made product. Children do best by creating for themselves the specific knowledge they need, rather than being instructed in what they must know. Seymour Papert later found that such things would happen especially felicitously when learners are engaged in constructing something external or at least shareable: a sand castle, a book, a machine, a computer program. These kinds of activities lead to a model of learning that involves a cycle of internalization of what is outside, then externalization of what is inside, and so on.

Connectivism

This mode of collaboration paves the way to *connectivism,* or *connectionism* or *connectivity of knowledge,* which Seymour Papert professed after many years clinging to logical step-by-step constructivism. According to his later views:

The deliberate part of learning consists of making connections between mental entities that already exist; new mental entities seem to come into existence in more subtle ways that escape conscious (i.e. step-by-step) control... This offers a strategy to facilitate learning by improving the connectivity in the learning environment, by actions on cultures rather than on individuals.

Papert asserts that conceptual connections between a given notion or phenomenon and a wide array of other notions and phenomena are often helpful in gaining a more substantial understanding of a subject under study. Rather than passively receiving ready-made facts, notions and opinions, students acquire advanced skills and knowledge by solving problems in their immediate surroundings that they consider personally meaningful and emotionally exciting. In the days of sweeping global changes, training for a particular skill or job must endow the trainee with an ability to be re-trained and self-retrained. It follows that we believe the concept of mass training to be short-sighted. Constructivist education must take command even in vocational and elementary schools, and a trainee must become a true learner. The priority is not the transmission of particular knowledge and skills from teacher to taught, but the development of the ability to acquire these by students on their own. All this, of course, is facilitated by new technologies of education.

For many decades, the polemics surrounding educational reform have vacillated between two points of view: those who favour a progressive, child-centred form of education, and those who prefer a return to a more structured, teacher-directed curriculum that emphasizes basic knowledge and skills. Today however, a growing number of educators adhere to an alternative trend, intended to reconcile these opposing stances. This latter view is the theory of a collaborative community of teacher and students, focused on a dialogue and co-construction of knowledge. Such an approach helps resolve the conflict between traditional *instructive* teaching and *constructive-connectivist* autonomous learning. In this, too, ICT are playing a key role.

Project Method: Learning by Designing

Among many proposals for revitalizing general education, the *learning projects* advocated and corroborated in the last century by John Dewey, Jean Piaget, Jerome Bruner, and Seymour Papert are among the most promising. The trouble is that such learning projects cannot be introduced in a form that the traditional school recognizes: as a ready-made set of precisely defined tasks or particular objectives, operations and procedures given in advance. Instead, these projects have to be found, discovered, invented, or designed in the course of a class.

To benefit from this project method, both teacher and student must acquire some generic skills rarely taught in an ordinary school. Different authors call these skills the *design mode* of thinking and looking at things, the *designer's approach* to problem solving, and *designerly ways of knowing.* Mastering and exercising those skills would eventually lead to the formation of *The Design* (or Third) *Culture,* mediating the much-lamented rift between the two cultures of C. P. Snow - the Techno-Scientific and Humanistic-Artistic.

We invite readers to take part in detecting, unearthing, and cultivating the elements and principles of design in learning. This involves conceptualizing its problem situations, generating options, making choices, conducting mental experiments, finding acceptable solutions, and evaluating probable outcomes before actually implementing them. From this standpoint, design can be seen as an innovative intellectual technology waiting to be converted into a powerful technology of education.

For a start, let us consider what makes, or might make, school learning really interesting, attractive, and successful for students and teachers alike.

True teachers do something more than just transfer information. In receiving any source-material, teachers make it a part of themselves by re-exploring, re-interpreting, and re-constructing its form and content in a personal way. Examining the phenomenon of inner speech, Vygotsky (1986) pointed out that a child, assimilating a certain notion, re-works it, and during the process of re-working, expresses the peculiar features of his own thought. V. S. Bibler, a contemporary Russian philosopher and educator, adds that in inner speech, an individual transforms the socialized and relatively static images of culture into a culture of thought, dynamic and personal. (Bibler 1996) Especially interesting is Bibler's remark that in such cases an inner speech becomes future oriented and serves as "the mould for *creating new, non-existent yet, but just possible* images of culture". We could say that true teachers act as designers of both the «images of subject-matter» to be presented in the classroom, and the tools to be used by students in order to transform given images into a personal culture of thought. In this way, they enable students to develop their own abilities to learn.

By initiating communication and interaction regarding the design of the learning process, a true teacher learns no less than the students, who, in fact, are teaching themselves and one another.

Teaching Students to Be Learners

If you are a devoted schoolteacher in the 21st century, what should be your essential mission, main professional calling, and foremost pursuit?

The answer is in the wind: to teach students to become good learners.

What does this mean, functionally, as well as structurally? We would argue that a good learner is someone who is always alert, attentive, perceptive, responsive, and ready to be pro-active in grasping, digesting or assimilating a knowledge, skill or competence. This is true from kindergarten, elementary, middle school and high school, through years in college or university, and in all walks of adult life. If you really devote yourself to raising and tutoring such characters on a daily basis, let us consider some necessary theoretical cornerstones, technical requirements, and organizational prerequisites.

To make a good learner out of every student in your class, you may pick up and try tentatively alternate trails, tools, and methods. However, we have good reason to believe that it is wiser to adopt the strategy of what might be called *the way of new schooling.* Here it is in a nutshell:

1 Find at least two or three (better five to seven) colleagues at your own or other schools, who share your strivings and are willing to collaborate either close by or far off (e.g. via email exchange) to develop a project.

   Teachers who wish to pursue such a mission must intermittently transmute themselves into part-time researchers, designers and constructors of the new educational technologies. The argument for collaboration is simple: there is no one who can instruct contemporary teachers authoritatively and unilaterally on what to do in all particular, unprecedented and unique circumstances. Therefore, teachers must think and act on their own while trying to weave a web of interconnectedness and mutual assistance with as many concerned and knowledgeable people as possible.

2. Show students a variety of optional activities from which each is asked to choose a few that are challenging, alluring, and suitable to them personally.

3. Provide a friendly environment, materials, and tools with which students can tinker freely, if only by imitating by example.

4. Encourage students by means of informal conversation and discussion to exercise playfully their explorative curiosity, adroitness, and inventiveness, coupled with developing an awareness of what they are doing in the broader cultural-educational context.

   At this preliminary stage, both students and adults learn that a teacher can be not only a mentor, tutor, or instructor, but also an older, experienced, skilful, and responsible playmate with whom it is easy to communicate and interact.

5. Introduce some simple and attractive structured games with strict, explicitly defined rules relevant to the topic under study, and invite the students to play to win.

   Now students learn that the teacher can initiate them into new kinds of competitive play and games that enable students to demonstrate their wit and mental adroitness.

6. Make students aware that their success in playing these goal-oriented games depends upon their willingness, and acquired ability to observe - not break! - conventional rules they have accepted by mutual agree ment.

In this way, students learn how to turn the limitations and restrictions imposed by these rules into a springboard for reaching higher levels of resourcefulness and ingenuity. They come to treat the teacher as a respected game-leader, whose mastery they are hoping to equal some day.

7. Devise a series of more complicated, project-oriented games that are related to the consequent themes, topics, and tasks in various subject matters and implying a collaborative rather than competitive approach to problem solving.

At this stage, the game has been imperceptibly transformed. In fact, it will no longer be clear to anyone whether it is still a game or a cognitive, productive activity of a serious kind. Students, in their turn, will become more and more involved in mutually supporting, intellectually and emotionally rewarding teamwork for exploration, research, designing, testing and implementing their discoveries, inventions, and solutions, while seeing the teacher as a partner in real business and a competent master of the craft.

Teachers as Master-learners

Schoolteachers must revise their positions, leaving behind the status of the omniscient one who has all the answers. Instead, genuine teachers will become advisers and learning facilitators. Influence and credibility will accrue to those who not only *instruct* but also *construct* and *connect* in front of the class, that is, by skillfully doing something they may really be interested in, prompting students to learn how to do it by their own minds and hands.

Possible learning projects are as diverse as assembling and operating model cars and toy trains, building and decorating puppet homes, writing and printing prose and poetry via a word processor and desktop publishing, turning out pop tunes with a synthesizer, drawing simple animated cartoons, or cracking the codes of mediocre computer games in order to make them more challenging.

The main goal of this construction and connection should be, of course, the acquisition of knowledge and skills required by the curriculum, plus the experience of being in control of one's own process of collaborative teaching and learning.

As a matter of fact, the authority of teachers can be re-established on the basis that they possesses three interconnected kinds of mastery:

1. *Mastery of Doing* - one can do a lot, but not everything, and can do more in cooperation with others.
2. *Mastery of Learning* - one is not the only source of information but can teach how to find alternative sources.
3. *Mastery of Collaboration* - one can multiply results by joint work with students and other teachers.

It is worth noting parenthetically that the word *mastery* has the double connotation of power to control one's surroundings, and wisdom to use it appropriately. Teachers of the 21st century are called to restore the dual meaning of mastery in its completeness.

References

Eckert, P. (1989). *Jocks and burnouts: Social categories and identity in the high school.* TeachersCollege Press, New York.

Farnham-Diggory, S. (1990). *Schooling.* Harvard University Press, Cambridge, MA.

Gardner, H. (1983). *Frames of Mind: The Theory of Multiple Intelligences.* Basic Books, New York.

Papert, S. (1993). *The Children's Machine: Rethinking School in the Age of the Computer.* Basic Books, New York.

Perelman, L. J. (1992). *School's Out: Hyperlearning, The New Technology, and the End of Education.* William Morrow and Company, New York.

12

Future of Learning and Teaching

The latest ICT allow radically new opportunities for human activities. How will education meet these challenges? Today, in the wider society, most people who need to add up a bill use a calculator. Most texts are written and read on a computer. However, such activities are not paralleled in our schools. Even in developed countries, most children use a calculator or a computer at school only occasionally (and calculators are used more often in science classes, than in mathematics lessons). We observe a digital divide, therefore, between the world at large and the schools teaching children to enter it. Of course, we do not underestimate a further digital divide between countries and between communities within a country. In the near future, it will be possible to turn to a mobile handset to answer most problems and questions on school tests, and to receive oral or written help or advice automatically (without even using a qualified expert) in a few seconds. What does all this mean for the future of education? What does it mean for the school finding itself in such circumstances?

New Possibilities

The fundamental error that many educators commit when they consider using ICT is to view them through the lens of their current practice. They ask, "How can I use these technological capabilities to streamline or improve what I'm really doing?" instead of asking, "How can I use ICT to do things that we are not already doing?" By their very nature, ICT call for innovation. It is about exploiting the full capabilities of technology to open new perspectives for both teachers and students.At the same time, it is unwise to ignore traditional styles and models of learning as well as ideas from the past that were not implemented in the mass school but were precious exceptions.Therefore, we need to start with things that we are already doing, but consider them anew.

Schools of Tomorrow

One way to introduce ICT into school education is to observe schools without computers and see what opportunities arise to facilitate various educational activities by using ICT. Starting from that point, we can recognize that schools without computers are different, and that different applications of ICT are possible. We discover that some teaching and learning activities can be advanced much more than others. Then we can reconsider how desirable different activities are from the point of view of educational goals for individuals and society. Eventually, we can discover, or imagine, certain new forms of learning beyond the reality, experience, and vision of past centuries.

Of course, it is an absolute requirement to begin in small steps experimentally and to have a program tested by broad practice before recommending it for others. Nor is it necessary for a school to have acquired all high-end ICT in order to feel the benefits and impact of ICT on practice. Every improvement in technology almost immediately finds its application in the practical work of some teachers in schools and broadens educational horizons (as we emphasize, not in just a technological sense, but in the sense of enrichment of human activities).

Oral Communication

Lecture

Let us start with an important general example of a traditional mode of teaching-learning - a lecture. In the classical model, the teacher speaks and students listen. As in other cases of oral communication, the teacher relies heavily on such extra-verbal components as the tempo of speech, voice dynamics, facial expression, gesticulation, and body movements. These *tools* of rhetoric are used to express something, to transfer information (including emotional and aesthetic), to hold the attention of students, to impress and to engage them.

Teachers control the situation by looking directly at students, tracking signs of interest or absence and other emotions, and using this (mostly non-verbal) feedback to tune up their part of the communication. Feedback from students can be oral or written (in the form of notes handed up to teachers). Depending on the teacher's rules, students have a chance to speak during a lecture or at the end of the lecture only. This communication is usually limited in time and form; students mostly ask short questions. Teachers can also pose questions to the students, sometimes expecting a non-verbal clearly visible response from all of them such as "Raise your hands, please, if you know who Newton is".

What makes the lecture an important and useful mode of learning and teaching are the following:

- One teacher addresses many students and this is economical for providing modern schooling to the whole population, not a selected elite only.
- Teachers can react to students' behaviour in a limited way by adjusting their talk, and individually in a more limited way, by addressing a short message to a specific person and giving other kinds of feedback.
- Within limits, students can solve problems of misunderstanding and unsuccessful communication by asking questions.

The disadvantages of the lecture model are that it:

- encourages passive learning;
- affords limited individualization; and
- allows limited extra-verbal communication with a limited use of the senses and channels of human perception.

What technologies are involved in the traditional lecture? And what extensions of these do we have, or can we expect in the future?

The major information channel for the lecture is the aural one. Of course there is human voice technology - you can be trained to project your voice to an audience of 100-200 people, or more. A special design of the auditorium can contribute to a lecture. Microphones, amplifiers, and other equipment can improve loudness and even acoustic quality of human speech. Students can also use microphones while asking questions. Installing audio equipment for a lecture in a large room or hall can be a sophisticated task that requires a professional. One of the important issues here is to place loudspeakers (the sources of sound) in a way that students get the impression the sound is coming from the lecturer - to amplify mutually two different channels of information, not to confuse them. Using a microphone requires proper positioning - not too far so you cannot be heard, and not so close that your voice is distorted. Surprisingly few people today manage to use a microphone properly, and so good sound in lectures is not so common.

Radio microphones are useful when it is desirable to move around in a room or to pass the microphone between discussion participants. An option of using small and light wearable microphones simplifies the problem of proper positioning but also requires simple technical knowledge. The loudspeaker is not the only option for amplification. We can supply every student (and the teacher, if needed) with headphones. Signals to headphones can come via wires or a wireless network. A popular application of headphones is in simultaneous translation, which is not widely used in schools, although often encountered at international meetings of researchers and others, and could be imitated in schools.

Visual Component of Oral Communication

The visual component of lectures is as important as in other cases of oral communication. At the same time, new ICT technologies are changing face-to-face lecturing. For example, in the case of bigger audiences, the speaker's face and figure can be captured by a video camera, magnified, and projected onto a screen.

In some subjects, an important component of the lecture content is given by visual images other than that of the speaker. Most lecturers traditionally use a blackboard or an overhead projector. In some subjects like mathematics, this appears inevitable. A broader list of typical visual components includes:

- key points of a talk indicated in a written form on a chalk- or whiteboard;
- the derivation of mathematical formulas, as well as mathematical formulas accompanying discussion of physical, biological, or economic issues;
- chemical formulas and other, less important formalisms;
- drawings and conceptual diagrams;
- all kinds of ready-made images (artistic paintings, photographs, book pages, technical drawings, maps) as illustrations; and

- real objects and processes (like experiments), if they are big enough to be seen by an audience.

ICT extensions of this communication are based on projection technology.

Now, a combined computer and projector open new possibilities and generate a new culture of oral communication accompanied by screen images.

In comparison with pre-computer lectures, this new technology allows the following:

- The speaker can combine pre-recorded images (including text) with images made during a lecture. Pre-recorded video fragments can be included accompanied by sounds if needed.
- Images of real objects obtained via cameras can be downloaded to a computer or connected directly to the projector.

This technology allows for clearer visualization, and saves time the lecturer needs to spend on writing. However, lecturers need to be aware of the following:

- Text on the screen should be economical.
- *Sans serif fonts* (like this) are easier to read on screen.
- Do not read the text from the screen; screen text is a tag to what you are saying.
- Leave a little time for an audience to absorb each slide.

It is often helpful to give listeners a printed copy of all slides from a presentation to take away with them (for example, these can be printed six slides per page).

The natural screen image of a lecture usually calls for two screens: one to enlarge the figure and face of the speaker, and the other for the visual-textual part of the speech.

Of course, digital video images can accompany transmitted and recorded lectures, placing the lecturer's face or figure on part of the screen, and surrounding it with other material, or simply using the lecturer as a background voice.

Communication between Teacher and Student

Today, teacher-student communication - whether face-to-face, live, synchronous, or online - is carried out within strict temporal and spatial boundaries. These boundaries are largely imposed by the school timetable with its:

- sub-division of the class period into a lecture or demonstration (sort of one-way broadcasting) and consecutive conversations with individual students that may or may not involve attention and participation from the rest of the class; and
- sharp divide between in-school and out-of-school time, where no direct communication is supposed.

Assuming the school's information space is digitized, these boundaries might be easily crossed, or broken down technically. However, to get there, we first must face two new problems. The first is how to weave a reliably functioning network, or a web of mutual interconnections between all persons involved. The other is to allow enough time for each network user to communicate adequately with other network users.

Communication Initiated by Students

A good teacher needs time and space to respond to students' questions, statements, raised hands, looking through the window, smiling, and other types of verbal and non-verbal behaviour, as well as to encourage their participation in group activities. This vital human component is not thrown out by the use of ICT. Indeed, we should think about elements of the teacher's role as being supported or automated by ICT. At the same time, ICT make possible new forms of teacher-student communication. As we know, email has revitalized letter writing, while voice mail and answering machine sometimes help when wanting to say something that is hard to do face-to-face.

Students' Speech

Microphones and screen presentations can help students even more than teachers. There are many cases where a student who is considered weak in oral communication develops eloquence, and even confidence, by using screen presentation support.

Answering Teachers' Questions

One of the drawbacks of teachers' questioning in the traditional school is that usually only one or two students are allowed time to answer during each class period. Computers, however, can record written and even oral answers by all students on the timeline.

Electronic Digital Lectures

Let us consider now the opportunities provided by modern ICT for broadcasting lectures with synchronous participation of learners. Synchronicity supports the organizational discipline mentioned above. A new opportunity provided by computer technology today is bi-lateral interactivity. Students can answer the questions teachers ask, and ask them questions, too, all in a written form, from wherever they live. Naturally, a CD and regular textbooks can accompany the course of such lectures.

In such situations, the major advantage of a digitized lecture is the breadth of the audience it can reach. The physical limitation here is the time zone. Of course, the number of actively participating students cannot be too big, but they do not all need to be in the same place.

For the teacher, the digitized lecture has other advantages. First of all, the lecture can be transmitted online (synchronously with the real event) to many places at once. Feedback is possible in the form of written notes sent by students. The teacher can show on screen the face of a student who has asked a relevant question. Other students asking questions that might be anticipated can receive standard answers generated by assistants or automatically.

The second option is to distribute a recorded lecture in canned form, recorded on DVD or videotape, or via the Internet. The advantages of these media are:

- mass distribution, multiplied audience;
- better quality text accompanied by pictures, and additional readings; and
- availability anytime, anywhere, at a learner's convenience.

ICT (printing and recording) make a considerable difference in delivering lectures. Nevertheless, certain advantages of new technologies can also be considered disadvantages. For example, the requirement to meet face-to-face at lectures at a given time is a discipline that organizes the process of learning. Sometimes, it is a welcome discipline for a professor! On the part of students, the obligation to make written notes provides additional support for concentration and memorizing through kinaesthetic activity and provokes online re-thinking of the content.

In some regions and communities, many people already receive general education by means of radio or magnetic recordings. Sometimes even a combination of radio transmission or playing a record and simultaneous face-to-face tutoring is used to good effect in general education. Many people learn foreign languages while driving and listening to audiotapes. The next step is TV and videotapes. These add something to the traditional lecture: you can see lecturers at their best time of the day, the voice is clear, the face is close, and so on. Eventually, we arrive at the HDTV and DVD era, with its picture-in-picture format.

Is it possible to learn using combinations of the abovementioned media? The answer is *yes.* Is it helpful to add to lecture text materials and video-audio records? Again, *yes.* In other words, the traditional lecture is not dying. It is in danger of becoming more interesting.

Reading

The lecture is not the only way to channel curriculum information to students. Students read textbooks and go to the library on the teacher's advice. They visit museums and art galleries, and take excursions to see natural scenic attractions, great architecture, and other monuments of historical and cultural interest. Each visit may bring them an enormous amount of information that helps them to assimilate, enrich, and enhance the knowledge they get from the formal curriculum.

ICT can be of great help in providing multimedia information on objects and sites of such kinds, especially those that are located too far away to be observed directly, or inaccessible for other reasons. At the same time, we should remember that understanding implies active participation on the students' part: the transformative inner reworking of content delivered. As Jean Piaget loved to say, to understand is to invent.

Reading is an important activity of the traditional school. Books contain not only written text, but also visual information. Good reading in the traditional sense implies, of course, good formal memorizing though this is becoming less important. It also means active reading - making notes, writing out quotations, and looking for and into other works referred to. Reading is part of the whole business of constructing a personal information space by the student. A process-intensive way of acquiring a particular piece of learning content can even help a student memorize it by heart.

Electronic Digital Textbooks

Let us consider the best possible canned (recorded) course of lectures. They have good video-audio quality, and may be accompanied by a printed text since the substitute of text-on-screen is not completely satisfactory today. Typically, lectures and accompanying textbooks can contain educational material of an advanced level or some optional information. In a lecture, this material can be relatively short and marked by a special introductory statement. In a textbook, it can be printed in smaller letters or placed in an appendix. In both cases, the options are limited, because of limits of material time and paper. In the case of electronic media, these limitations do not exist.

Modern electronic digital media such as DVD can accommodate hundreds of thousands of text pages. The digital lecture-textbook can thus be organized to display different levels of material, both in the sense of depth and breadth of subject matter and in the sense of how it is presented to the student. It can contain references or links to other related material whereas the lecturer has to point to the blackboard or show a slide again. The digital video textbook can also provide links to another part of the course, or to another course, or indeed to any piece of information available in the school library and beyond on the Internet.

Broadening the Range of Materials Used in Classrooms

ICT are making it increasingly easy for teachers and students to have access to a broader range of materials than they can use in the classroom. The simplest example is the copying machine, which allows teachers to make copies of articles, charts, or printed instructional materials from outside sources and to distribute these among students. Supplementary computer tools such as scanners or digital cameras allow teachers to bring in outside sources, enter them into a computer, and customize assignments. For example, teachers can bring a timely article from the morning newspaper into class, scan it in minutes, and have their students work on rewriting, editing, or adding other research material to the story on the same day. Encyclopedias, art collections, atlases, and other reference books in a less expensive, and less space-consuming electronic format will be of everyday use in classrooms.

Already, in many schools, students can browse interactively or conduct electronic searches in CD-ROM databases, encyclopedias, or other reference work. Thus, the new technologies allow access to a broader range of instructional resources. They also offer students the opportunity to learn how to use electronic tools to access information and develop research skills in solving problems.

Web Learning

Learning on the Web is one of the most promising and rapidly developing areas of ICT in education. At the same time, it is one of the most complex psychologically and socially controversial fields. There may be problems for some students with sensitive topics like sex education, narcotics, and political or religious extremism. Some voices are calling for compulsory technical restrictions imposed on accessing objectionable sources of information.

There are also hybrid situations where content can be pre-loaded onto a learner's computer and integrated with other dynamic environments on the Web. Automated and human responses can be mixed.

WRITING

Speed of Writing

Most people, and especially children, can type faster than they write, and they can learn to type faster than learning to write. For smaller children, writing in clear calligraphy is a major problem. ICT allow students to learn communicative skills independently of the kinaesthetic ability to write. Writing in a clear script is important, but this can be trained separately, while students get on with the excitement of communicating.

Writing as Designing and Constructing

Two Russian proverbs reflect the irreversible character of some oral and written communication:

> *A word is not a sparrow - you can't catch it after it has fled.* Nearest English equivalent: *A word spoken is past recalling.*
>
> and
>
> *What is written with a pen cannot be cut out with an axe.* Nearest English equivalent: *What is writ is writ.*

In oral communication, this reality will probably never change. However, one of the beauties, and the banes, of the modern computer is that you can change whatever you want at any time. Moreover, changes are reversible. You can keep all versions of a paper or manuscript, and changes are traceable. In other words, the written object is close to the ideal in its flexibility. Indeed, perhaps for the first time in history, it takes less time to make a change than to think of it.

In education, this means that students are free of the horror of fatal errors. They are in a more adult position: if you, the Teacher, do not like it, I, the Student, can change it. As a result, the whole culture of writing in school is changing.

In the traditional school, the student writes an essay and the teacher offers corrections and advice. The student often pays little attention to these corrections and even less to the advice. In a very few cases, the student may argue with the teacher but there the story ends. In this new model, students with a little effort have a chance to improve the text, rewriting part or parts of it, and resubmitting it to the teacher for comments, and then taking these into account. The resulting evaluation of their work will take into account the efforts to improve it. A student's work can be reviewed, and undergo formal and informal evaluation, by peers and also by different teachers like the science teacher, the language arts teacher, or the ICT-coordinator, all at the same time.

The process of producing written work can be sub-divided into three main phases: *prewriting, writing,* and *postwriting:*

1. Prewriting includes deciding on a topic to write about, brainstorming one or more topics, reminiscing and selecting the most significant aspects, and gathering and organizing thoughts about how the writing is to be structured.
2. Writing is the creation and the online reading and editing of an emerging text.
3. Postwriting comprises rewriting, stimulated by immediate editorial feedback from the teacher (and classmates), then meticulously checking for spelling and grammar, correcting the syntax, revisiting and changing word sequences. It also may include any other editorial and publishing work down to physical manufacturing the book with stitching, sizing and binding. Students write better when they have a real audience for their written work and when the teacher offers them convenient channels and mechanisms for reaching a wider reading public via, for instance, the Internet or school newsletter.

The writing process described above is not confined to fiction or non-fiction literature. It is archetypal for all kinds of activities related to design and implementation of any project - be it erecting a skyscraper, establishing a bank, or writing and debugging a computer program. Above all, this circular procedure is a powerful conceptual tool for truly efficient perception, thinking, cognition, and learning. By its very essence, it implies discovering, inventing and creating meaning, which can be expressed, presented and embodied in fleeting spoken words, in corporal movements, gestures, and postures, in graphic symbols, in hand-made articles, or in heavy-duty mechanical devices.

In general, writing in schools today is becoming closer to other types of design and construction activity, including top-down planning using outliners, using pieces of old work, and different stages of finishing.

Spelling

Another feature of ICT that is changing radically the art of essay writing is spelling. What once took considerable effort has become a trivial task with automatic spelling checkers. The immediate adoption of spelling checkers would be too radical perhaps for the school system in certain countries. However, to ignore them means adding one more item not of direct use to academic knowledge to be acquired. Therefore, we should rethink the goals and values of education, and place more critical thinking, perhaps more language construction, and more teaching about computer tools into the writing process.

Hypertext

What distinguishes inner speech from outer speech in oral or written form is its non-linearity. Thinkable objects are not linear, but a network of associations. This is reflected in the hyper-structure of texts, which with printed-paper, can be represented in the form of footnotes, endnotes, and bibliographic references. To teach children hyper-writing is not difficult because for them it is more natural than it is for adults who have learned how to linearize and discipline speech.

Multimedia

The multimedia information object is a much more natural thing in a child's inner world than a text. ICT provide tools for making these objects visible on paper and on screen, on the Internet, or for a classroom performance. After students make multimedia objects, by writing texts, collecting information from the Internet and encyclopedias, inserting drawings and photographs made by themselves, adding speech and sound, it becomes natural to share it with other students and the teacher. This hybrid activity can be important for mastering cognitive skills.

Cooperation and Sharing

Students sitting together in the same classroom, or communicating over a longdistance network, can do cooperative writing. This is important, first, as practice for joint work and, secondly, for life, but is generally neglected and sometimes even suppressed in the traditional 20th century school.

The ability to copy and email information objects like essays, pictures, and presentations gives students the opportunity to share information easily with, and receive comments from, others outside the classroom. These other audiences could be teachers of different subjects, other students and friends, parents and relatives, local community, a pen pal, or (by posting it on a website) others in the world.

Essay Writing and Citation

There is a downside when it comes to the influence of ICT on essay writing, as many teachers have discovered. Essay writing on different subjects and topics became more and more popular as a reaction to standardized tests in the 1990s just as the Internet was becoming easier to use. Within a few years, teachers found they were reading more and more identical essays submitted by students. Students had discovered a new, easier way to *write* an essay - find it on the Internet.

This kind of cheating led to a whole system and even a commercial business of counter-measures to provide teachers with tools to detect copying. Are these countermeasures good or bad? There is no question that copying without acknowledgment is bad, but the solution is not to police minute phrases that might be parallel. There is an opportunity here to introduce students to appropriate ways of citing the work of others, which after all is the basis of scholarship. What teachers should look for is independence and originality of thought. The reaction to a discovered case of copying without citation should not be that this is a deadly sin but rather "Good for finding some relevant information. Now tell me what YOU think about this topic and include a correct reference link, please". A disagreement over the printed word is rewarded and becomes a basis for critical thinking and evaluation.

Transforming Oral Speech into written Form

The classical work of taking dictation can be radically transformed as well by ICT. A teacher may ask students to use their computers to make a sound recording of their oral text, recited as normal speech, and then to transcribe it. Each student may play the recording back while listening through individual headphones as many times as they need to write down every word. The advantages of such dictation are obvious:

- All students work at a pace that suits them best.
- A teacher can trace the progress of each student in detail by simply connecting to the screens of students' computers.
- When teachers see a student finish a task, they can provide more oral text, either as live dictation through a microphone, or as a pre-recorded sound file. In this mode, every student in a classroom can move along at their personal pace, not interfering or competing with other students for the teacher's attention and time.

The next stage would be to give the class an assignment to make an abstract, or synopsis, of the teacher's oral text. The major difference here is that students themselves choose the object of transcription. It can be a TV discussion or a movie segment, a political leader's speech or, in the best case, something recorded by students themselves - a teacher's introduction, a street interview on the environment in the school area, or Grandma's story of her childhood. Digital technology provides a comfortable environment for this activity: to slow down the tempo, segment and mark the texts, see the speaker, and so on.

Group Discussion

In the new paradigm, there is much more space for class discussion with many students participating. Such discussions can start with a text or a hypermedia piece presented by teachers or students. The major points expressed by the participants can be recorded and presented on screen. Thus, the evolving discussion is visualized. Moreover, short video-clips of speeches can be made and presented on screen in the form of icons. The teacher can participate as moderator. The discussion is not limited in space and time: it can go on the Internet as live chat or be delayed. Prerecorded and recorded discussions can be sent as an immediate-to-all or delayed message. At the same time, screen-written images help to make discussion more systemic, effective and disciplined.

Teachers' Notes

Notes can help teachers say what they intend to say. Teachers can even prepare the whole text of a lecture in written form, though this is usually less effective than a lecture without notes or with a limited use of them because it narrows the channel of communication (including eye contact) and misses out on feedback. At the same time, short notes in the form of key points or key words presented to the audience beforehand can make a lecture easier to follow.

Students' Notes

Notes made by students can help them remember information provided in lectures. What can ICT add to this situation?

- Notes can be taken by students on computer unless it is too noisy to type during lectures.
- Notes can be made before the lecture by teachers and distributed to students with extra space to add hand-written notes, or notes in electronic form.

Autonomous Automatic Recording

Finally, an entire lecture may be recorded on camera.

Working with a recorded lecture, students can produce written text with the needed level of detail and additional links, screens of the presentation placed properly, a still image of teacher's face, or audio-video fragments at the most dramatic points.

With ICT, no teaching and learning activity need be left without audiovisual, graphic, and alphanumeric documentation, including students' work, comments, drawings, and written reports. Instant access to these records allows prospective students to discover that they can master these new conceptual tools and to control and improve their own work performance. The earlier they begin, the better.

From an educational point of view, writing priorities have changed in all aspects, including calligraphy, spell-checking, and oral input.

- Writing is not textual: it is now multimedia composing.
- The products of writing can be made accessible to a large audience, including, by means of the Internet, anyone in the world who might be interested.

- The process of writing can be collective, involving the author's classmates, students from other schools, editors, and many others.
- Text is not static, but in constant development.
- Computers can help in speed and quality of writing.

While acquiring basic writing, reading, and communication skills, students become accustomed to various ways and means of acquiring, transmitting and using information and knowledge needed to achieve concrete goals. Presenting one's thoughts and collected information to other people can be the final stage, for instance, of a history or science project, or the major part of a journalistic activity, or an initial part of a fund-raising campaign.

Science Experiments and Observations

Certain fundamental concepts of mathematics and science are given to visual realization (modelling) that ICT are well suited to reproduce. In such cases, students can freely manipulate objects representing these concepts on a computer, experiencing in different ways the dynamic relations between their actions and the visible behaviour of the model.

For example, by connecting to a distant sensor, a computer can display a graph showing the measured distance from the sensor to a moving body (for instance, the body of a student walking back and forth along a wall in the room). In this case, the walking student can see the correlation between their moves and the graph. They can follow a given graph pattern or explain in words what was happening at this or that moment previously recorded and seen on the screen. Or they can tell what one should do to produce some particular pattern on the screen. Then, they can command or advise another student or the teacher how to walk with eyes closed.

For another example, the concept of thermo-conductivity can be demonstrated and explored using a temperature sensor and thermal perception of the human skin.

In the world beyond school, computers automatically collect data and control real three-dimensional material objects and processes. Similar applications can be exciting and educational in school contexts as well. Children's construction kits can include interfaces, input sensors, and output devices such as motors and lights. A computer program can control a model constructed by a child. Even more importantly students can write the computer program. Furthermore, there is a *programmable brick,* which has input connectors to which sensors can be attached. This piece of integrated hardware and software also has output connectors to which motors, bulbs, and sound signals can be attached. One can input a program into the brick memory. The program is written on a regular computer and then transmitted to the brick by wire or infrared ray. The student can design a robot, for example, and plan its behaviour in a chosen environment. Then the robot is made out of LEGO blocks and the description of the robot's behaviour, in the form of a computer program, is put into the brick's memory. Modern bricks can interact with each other and also with computers via infrared connection.

Of course, this needs software support to provide interfaces between input-output devices and the computer, as well as between computers and human beings. This software can include algorithms for data processing and visualization. The computerized science lab combines many types of sensors with software to collect, store, analyze, and graphically present data. The sensors can be wired to computers or transmit data wirelessly; data can also be accumulated on a small device called a data logger for later transfer to a computer.

School Use of General and Professional Applications

As the experience of schools tells us, many students are ready to use conventional application packages. With them, students can tackle tasks similar to those facing adults; they can write, draw, edit, make a database, and create a spreadsheet or screen presentation.

We note several special types of software that have clear and productive use in schools (even elementary schools):

- CAD (Computer Aided Design or Drawing).
- GIS (Geographic Information Systems).
- Data analysis packages.
- Project planning software.

Needless to say, professional applications of CAD are too complicated for beginners. Moreover, since they offer a broad spectrum of ready-made tools and instruments, they make it impossible for the student to create a tool for a particular task - an activity that is immensely rich and valuable from an educational point of view. However, there are school versions of these applications that have special features that allow for more simplicity and openness of use.

GIS allow a student to use existing maps and to put more information on them in the form of a word, picture, or hyperlink. The teacher can use the map, without accompanying text, to check students' memorization of geographic names. There are software products, called *timeliners,* that can be used in learning history in much the same way that digital maps help in learning geography.

The computer as an instrument for data collecting, analyzing and presenting in visual form is an important tool to balance technicalities of paperwork upon data (e. g. environmental or social) and understanding their meaning.

Project planning software is another way to visualize, in this case the process of design and implementation of a student or team activity, including a learning activity.

Virtual Laboratory

In a computer-run virtual laboratory, we can stage experiments that imitate real ones. A student or teacher can construct shapes, choosing, pointing, moving, indicating numerical parameters by sliding an indicator, or by direct input. They can also change settings easily. The student or teacher then simply pushes the START button and the experiment begins. The parameters' values can be organized in tables, and their data can be presented on graphs. In solving algebraic equations, students can use graphs to verify their calculations and transformations of the formula. In models of atomic and molecular structures that simulate individual particles' interaction, students can track emerging phenomena such as temperature, pressure, states of matter, phase change, absorption, latent heats, osmosis, diffusion, heat flow, crystals, inclusions, and annealing; chemical phenomena such as exchange energy with bonds, chemical equilibrium, heat gain and loss in reactions, explosions, stoichiometry colour, spectra, florescence, and chemiluminescence, plasma, surface tension, solutions, hydrophilic and hydrophobic molecules, conformation, binding specificity and self-assembly.

Working with microworlds can help a student to construct knowledge of real world subjects (physics, geometry, economics, environmental studies) as well as of abstract mathematics. The applications in secondary schools have been very successful, especially in geometry and physics. *Geometer's Sketchpad,* for instance, is a computer environment in which students do their own mathematical research, set up experiments, state hypotheses, and prove or refute them. This software has radically changed the perspective of how to treat a school subject that has remained fundamentally unchanged for 2000 years. A similar product for teaching physics is called *Interactive Physics.* There are algebraic manipulation packages of a similar kind. Aimed at learning geometry and physics in middle school, these programs are successfully used for preparatory purposes in primary education as well.

New software allows children to construct any combination of simple machines, which helps in the development of reasoning skills, including spatial, causal and design thinking. Another important class of microworlds is tutoring environments for typing, spelling and foreign languages. Mathematics teaching today is in a paradoxical situation in that every mathematical problem can be solved by a personal computer. Therefore, as in other subjects, we are forced to rethink how and why we teach the subject. At the same time, ICT are a boost to experimental mathematics, allowing students to draw graphs of functions, and check relations in geometrical configurations in which parameters as a point position can be changed by dragging a mouse.

Organization of the Learning Process

Guided Learning

A software program can incorporate a teaching strategy, which gives pieces of information and tasks to students and interacts with them. The simplest versions of this approach are referred to as drill and practice. In some cases, this works quite well - for example, typing tutors. In other cases, a large investment is required to produce a quality product (as in foreign language teaching). Nor are all products equally effective or appealing to students' imagination.

Tests and Examinations

Taditionally, testing (assessment) gives teachers and students feedback and serves as a basis for certification of learning and teaching as well as a gateway to further education or a job. There are obvious reasons why testing procedures should be simple in a technical sense (so as not to require much time from the person who conducts it) and objective (in order not to depend on the test-giver's attitudes, views and conditions). This has led to so-called multiple-choice tests, which can be extended in new ways by ICT.

What are the advantages of such tests? Clearly the procedure is quick and objective; results are stored automatically in the computer and are available via a network. Problems can be chosen from item banks, and even generated randomly as specific cases of a generic parametric problem. The problems themselves can be presented in a multimedia form. Extensions of multiple-choice tests are possible, for example, including blind-maps, grammar exercises in the form of filling in blanks, and written dictations. Computers now recognize oral speech, so they can check the answer to a foreign language exercise, for example. What more can an automated testing program do? A computer can certainly record all interactions with students. To make it economical, we can limit this recording to all text inputs and some oral (through microphones) and kinaes-thetic (with a mouse) inputs. The problem, then, is how to evaluate these moves and how to react to them.

There is a big temptation to automate the process of interaction. This is a model of so-called *programmed learning,* developed long before computers came into existence, and then revitalized in the form of *Computer Aided Instruction* (CAI). In some cases like touch-typing, this works perfectly. It can work also in the process of learning technicalities of certain ICT environments such as text editors, CAD packages, or search engines. Open inquiry technicalities can be learned in the same way by, for instance, varying structural parameters of a system under experimental investigation and registering the changes in its functional behaviour.

Can the inquiry itself be monitored and controlled along similar lines? This is the Philosophers' Stone, sought for years by researchers and prophets of ICT in education. A definitive answer has yet to be found.

Nevertheless, it is clear that automation of much of a teacher's work is possible. We can outline some features of a system that supports interaction between student, teacher, and information environment:

- Scripts of interaction are available, understandable, changeable and able to be constructed by educational researchers, textbook writers, willing teachers, and students (the most controversial and the most exciting opportunity). Records of interaction are also available in an understandable and structured format.
- The system of script writing and use can be integrated into general school information space, and into specialized learning environments used by a student or teacher. The system can monitor and control a student's use of tools, resources, search and observation instruments.

Students can thus be restricted in using calculators, spell checkers, equation solvers, historical databases, Internet space, looking inside living organisms and chemical molecules. Strictly enforced, this can make learning in a rich ICT environment similar to the 20th century school.

- The system provides tools for organizing usual and complementary educational activities, including classwork and homework, essay writing and submitting, word-problem solving in mathematics and physics, conducting virtual experiments in the setting provided by a textbook or a teacher, or constructed by a student.

Elements of this complex information system are already in use in schools worldwide. While they are not the final solution for everyone, they may be useful in almost any school. For example, any school can use a computer to record test scores, to place individual assignments on a school website, or to collect students' works via email.

Diaries and Portfolios

A prerequisite for success and progress in learning is keeping diaries of the learning process, as well as portfolios of texts, drawings and other artifacts produced in the class or workshop. Teachers and students should make their diaries and portfolios as encompassing and detailed as practicable.

Furthermore, because innovative pedagogical proposals are always restrained by a lack of time, diaries and portfolios save a great amount of time that would be spent gathering information, or on labour-consuming routine operations. In general, as we have seen in other areas, ICT allow teachers and students to achieve their particular educational objectives within the standard school time periods, or even faster.

Information Resources for Education

We can summarize the categories of components and activities that are integrated in the school information space. These are:

- Information sources
- Information instruments
- Control tools

Individual pictures, texts, sound recordings, maps and other information objects, and their collections constitute *information sources.* They can be properly described and open for use by all students, teachers, and textbook authors. They are numerous - currently millions of items are organized for education.

Information instruments are much less numerous. There are dozens, not hundreds of them. Most are produced in the long process of labour-consuming programming, debugging, testing, and revising; some were developed in the form of code open for further improvement by anyone interested.

Control tools for the learning process implement specific content and didactics in school practice. Many of them are made with the help of certain generic instruments.

Complex Educational Events

In this section, we consider more complex educational events and how ICT can be used as successful learning tools for these.

Approaching the New Literacy

Literacy is the ability to vocalize a written text, or, conversely, transcribe an oral text. This skill is overvalued in the same manner as mechanical numeracy - the ability to do calculations mentally or with a pen and paper - because often we measure overall learning success of students by the speed of their oral reading or mental calculations. ICT can do these operations much more quickly and with better quality anyway. At the same time, higher-level competences are becoming more and more important. Priorities are changing. The new literacy - the system of basic linguistic, logico-computational, and communicative skills and competencies, needed to deal with internal and external technology - is a latchkey that opens the doors of subsequent stages of organized teaching and learning. An introduction of ICT in schools gives students an impetus to learn, unlocking many doors of perception and cognition.

We now discuss the roads by which young learners can approach the new literacy and the role of ICT.

Oral Language Learning

The first, and in many cases the best, teacher is a child's mother and other family members. Different processes are involved in learning the mother tongue, like imitating, asking questions and claiming help. A child also learns a lot just by moving, seeing, listening, smelling, and falling. An adult's presence and interaction is not always critical. Interaction with the physical world, observing and imitating an adult's behaviour, can sometimes be enough. Usually a computer cannot add much to, or substitute for, the development of this process of understanding physical reality. However, it can provide a considerable part of what an adult does in connection with a child's learning activity. Every object on a screen, for example, can pronounce its own name when touched. If an action or an event is occurring on the screen, the participants can explain what they are doing. Today's computers can even ask questions, hear and correct answers.

Student Universe

The simplest and most convincing application of ICT in school occurs on the very first day, when students tell a computer (with the teacher's help) their names. Now it happens in written form by typing: in the near future, it will be done aurally, in combination with keyboarding. The computer will memorize the names and even print out corresponding name badges. The badges are given to students (teachers and other adults at school have the same kind of badges), who can now read their teacher's and each other's names. Reading becomes practically important!

The computer then prints out a series of pages. If you cut and bind these together, you will have your first address book containing the names, addresses, and telephone numbers of all your schoolmates.

At some point, you start to collect your family memoirs - photographs, stories, letters, and combine these with additional findings in electronic archives. This kind of project may be extended indefinitely.

Written Language Learning

Learning how to write a language is a combination of learning to:

- produce letters and their combinations - words on paper with brush, or crayon;
- write words in the correct spelling;
- write down oral speech; and
- generate a text based on your understanding of what you are going to say.

Traditionally, children learn these activities sequentially. In fact, the last step usually comes too late and the natural urge of the child to communicate freely is thwarted (mostly by grammar exercises). Eventually this delay reduces students' interest in oral communication as well.

Many-faceted texts. Evidence shows that young children do not think of texts or writing strictly in print-linguistic terms. Given their first notebooks in school and let loose to do their own thing, they draw pictures and invent symbols; some write letters, some make their names, words, even phrases. Almost all declare they can "write and read already".

At the same time, modern children are bombarded visually by many other *written texts* that actually have many facets not reducible to just words. Among these are labels, trade marks, colour codes and graphic instructions on cereal boxes and candies, table games and hi-tech toys; traffic signs, comic strips, TV-station and car logos, mailed advertisements, and many other impressive things of similar kind, which children can perceive, bring with them into a classroom, and reproduce here and there on paper without much hesitation. All these are part of a child's communicative world and cannot be cast aside and ignored as anomalies of no interest to educators. Small children are especially inventive and productive when given a computer with a multimedia (text/graphic/sonic) editor. Very often they produce dynamic pictorial presentations and even animated stories with a soundtrack of an oral enactment, with photos or drawings of the main characters, and with commentaries on their action and behaviour. More often than not, picture drawing precedes writing, and the accompanying oral commentaries are usually more complete and elaborate than a fragmentary and abruptly written text. However, once all this is done, a teacher can ask students to transcribe their spoken words using the keyboard, or just picking up needed letters from the alphabet shown on the screen. Even if the first attempts do not produce real outcomes, students can always try again, and in time make small, noticeable improvements. *Nomination*. An important part of learning a mother tongue and the world is students' creations of their own language. In a more scientific way, we can say that giving names corresponds to the elementary act of cognition through discovery, as well as gaining control over what has been named. While teaching names of objects, letters should not necessarily be written in calligraphy; they can as well be handled as pre-fabricated units and posted beside, above, or underneath the drawn images. Students can be encouraged to *read* their texts in both a sequential and non-linear *omni-direc-tional manner*.

As soon as students start writing in this way, it ceases to be something non-situational and isolated, taught compulsorily and out of context (the plague of so many elementary grammar classes). It becomes storytelling, re-enacting of the plot of a play, a thought made visible, and a communication of created meaning to others - activities already familiar and pleasant for all children. The itch to read aloud what has been written amid this enthusiastic exchange occurs immediately, providing powerful motivation to continue this joyful and collaborative learning-by-doing.

Virtual Reality of Words and Meanings

Let us reminisce for a moment about how the ABC is typically taught in an ordinary school or kindergarten. The teacher typically demonstrates a set of different large-sized characters, usually paired with pictures of objects designated by the words that start with the same letters. Then, the teacher writes them on the blackboard, or parades three-dimensional plastic or wooden items taken from a bag and places them upon a desktop. The student composes them into a scrabble-like series of two-and three-letter words *(on, at, or, dad, mum, boy, sun, sky),* and reads each word aloud. After the demonstration, each student is given assorted cardboard printed or wooden block characters with an assignment to build and, hopefully, write the same words on the paper. As any teacher knows, this is by no means a simple enterprise, if only because of the physical obstacles involved.

The teacher's immediate objective is to keep 25 or 30 students' attention. In practice, only the children sitting close to the teacher's desk perceive the intended message in its entirety. Those in the back rows inevitably miss relevant points, shades, and nuances. They also are more susceptible to distractions and deviations, ambient sights and sounds, the temptation to whisper with one another, or just falling into a daydream. Now and then, a boy or a girl may start to scream desperately and appeals for help because something went wrong. In coping with these encumbrances, teachers strain their voices and exaggerate their gestures, and periodically call by name the students who need to be woken up. And teachers barely have time to look over their shoulders at what students are scribbling in their workbooks, and they have even less chance to consult with or instruct the more confused and perplexed ones.

When it comes to evaluate their progress, teachers can hardly summon each student to the blackboard before the class is over. The rest are inevitably relegated to the daily homework of copying letters - an assignment requiring mechanical repetition and devoid of any cognitive effort or emotional reward.

Now assume you are giving the same lesson in an ICT-networked classroom. Each student's desktop is supplemented with an enveloping VR-helmet, gloves and other paraphernalia, which these pre-literate children have already mastered technically by playing computer games. This time you invite them to put on the gear for an adventure in *The First Grader's Grammar Cyberspace.* In a moment, students see and hear via their private high-resolution multimedia displays the image of a teacher sitting or standing in equally close proximity to each student. There is a *live,* synchronous, or online digital closed-loop translation of what you actually do on the black or white (magnetic) board, or upon your desktop with three dimensional characters as you compose words and read them aloud during the aforementioned letters and words demonstration.

If students do not comprehend or miss something, they can raise their hand and ask the teacher to explain or repeat it once more. All the other students can hear and see the question and the teacher's response. After the introductory stage, the teacher can decide whether or not to continue the explanation individually.

When the demonstration is complete and an assignment is understood, all the students see and hear the teacher offering a set of characters to compose and copy the exemplars. This time you switch from *live* online communication to a prefabricated program. Now the children have the visual, aural and tactile impressions of dealing with genuine material objects, which are in fact only interactive virtual realities. Each student starts to work independently offline and soon discovers that the characters encountered have some intriguing features. When touched, perhaps they spell their own names; when two or three are joined together, they pronounce the word (if rightly composed), or emit a protesting sound (if the combination is wrong). When students place two, three, or more words in a row, they hear them pronouncing the whole sentence. The students do not need to ask a teacher whether a word or sentence is right or wrong, the program makes this clear, and students can move on to the next part of the assignment - practising writing the words they have formed by manipulating tangible characters. The students see a virtual sheet of paper and a pen or pencil-like stylus, which they grasp, and start to write, seeing scribbles appearing instead of expected letters.

Everything written on VR-paper with a VR-stylus is instantly erasable (though it is actually being saved as backups for later evaluation). Thus a student can have any number of tries until a more or less satisfying result is reached. Students can address a teacher orally or have an online conversation to share their doubts, troubles, feelings, and thoughts concerning the task, without disturbing classmates. The teacher, meanwhile, can watch on a multi-screen display what is happening on each student desktop simultaneously. If you want to focus on Mary's or John's desktop, you can enlarge their particular screen. You can whisper in their ear something encouraging, soothing, reproaching, or enlivening, as well as giving them a helpful hint while remaining unheard by anyone else. You can also point with your finger to this or that character or word, even grasp it with your hand to change its position.

If you think it desirable, you can address the whole class and draw everybody's attention to a typical or rare and interesting problem under consideration, and then let them return to their individual work. At the end of a class period, the teacher has the full records of every student's activity, and thus will be able to track and evaluate what they have accomplished.

Learning Oral Speech by the Deaf

The visual and tactile representation of speech patterns can be instrumental in teaching deaf-mute children to speak. Students are given a visible or tangible sample pattern of a particular vowel, consonant, syllable or word. They are asked to articulate corresponding sounds while watching on the display what is being actually produced by their vocal apparatus. Next they are requested to compare and evaluate achieved results against a sample. If considerable discrepancies are detected, students are asked to repeat the procedure in order to improve their articulation until it is as close an imitation as possible of the sample.

Foreign Language Learning

As is well known, the most effective method of learning a foreign language is to live in the country concerned. This is the basis for a natural approach to learning languages even when one cannot be physically there.

A pre-ICT version of this approach was called *immersion* and consisted of a series of role-play games controlled by a qualified teacher. CD-ROM versions provide similar simulated interactive environments with sounds and images. The ability to have written, and, sometime in the future, oral interaction is the principal element of this concept.

The Internet can provide different levels of presence, starting from email communication to virtual museums and videoconferencing to (in the future) online virtual reality where a large number of students will be able to collaborate on global educational projects, where foreign language learning will be combined and supported by on-screen automated translation.

Design and Construction in Learning

Here are the main stages of a designing-constructing cycle:

- defining needs, goals, requirements and limitations of a design;
- building up teams, defining working plans;
- writing down specifications and drawing first sketches and blueprints;
- making models and prototypes;
- checking and verification of specifications; and
- making the final model.

In a school setting, ICT are a base for a simplified CAD/CAM (Computer Aided Design/Computer Aided Manufacturing) system, in which a technical drawing on a computer screen can eventually be transformed to a real object made of material that is simple to process, but we extend the design concept well beyond this and so we continue with some other representative examples.

Microworlds

Agents to be Taught by Students

As we have emphasized, the computer is a universal information-processing machine. In particular, a computer with adequate software can simulate and present on screen different real or imagined settings and environments. These are sometimes called *microworlds.* Microworlds are helpful in different applications.

First of all, microworlds are effective and popular tools for learning fundamental aspects of computer programming, especially structural programming. Ideally, they establish a direct connection between a student's semi-formal planning of activity in the microworld and its implementation. The link between the two is called a special *Agent* or sometimes *Executor.*

An Agent is capable of performing a set of commands given by a child - for example, to move across the screen, make turns, and leave a trace of its movements. In a sense, the child is *training* the Agent to perform quite complex tasks. A specific example is the *Robot-in-Maze* microworld. The maze is a labyrinth usually within the boundaries of a rectangular grid. An Agent called Robot has a limited set of elementary sensors such as the ability to *see* or *feel* a wall in front of it and a repertory of predetermined actions like, for instance, *head North.* A large set of tasks can be given to the student. The first tasks begin simply with, for example, the maze as an empty rectangle. Further tasks can bring a student to sophisticated issues of structural algorithm design. Students can immediately see the execution of their plan on the computer screen.

Another well-known example is the *Turtle* microworld. An Agent called, and looking very much like a, Turtle can move forward any specified distance, turn to any specified angle, draw geometric figures, and change shape and colour. The most important example of a Turtle microworld is the Logo family. In fact, some of the Logo languages combine the idea of microworlds with general applications components (text, graphics and sound editors) and general office applications.

Being in Command Motivates Learning Activity

A teacher begins by showing students how an Agent can be made to move by typing commands at a keyboard or by clicking pictorial icons and setting sliders, determining kinds, directions and parameters of the Agent's movements. For example, typing FORWARD 100 makes an Agent move in a straight line a distance of 100 Agent *steps* of one millimetre each. Typing RIGHT 90 causes the Agent to pivot in place through 90 degrees. Typing PENDOWN causes the Agent to lower a pen in order to leave a visible trace of its path while PENUP instructs it to raise the pen and leave no trace. Students need to explore a great deal before gaining mastery of these steps but the task is engaging enough to carry most children through this stage of learning.

Since learning to control the Agent is like learning a language, this activity mobilizes the student's expertise and pleasure in speaking. Since it puts the student in charge, it also mobilizes the student's expertise and pleasure in commanding. To make an Agent trace a square, you walk in a square yourself and describe what you are doing in the language of programming. And so working with the Agent mobilizes as well the student's expertise and pleasure in motion. It draws on students' well-established *body-geometry* as a starting point for the development of bridges to formal geometry.

Students' first goal in this microworld is not to learn formal rules but to develop insights into the way objects move in space. These insights are described in the Agent's *language* and thereby become *programs* and *procedures* for the Agent. For example, suppose a child wants to *teach* the Agent to draw a house. First of all, it is necessary to make an Agent draw a square, then a triangle on top of it. A teacher may provide helpful hints on how to write a proper command. A more complicated problem arises when it comes to making an Agent that can move only along straight lines draw a circle. A teacher does not provide answers, but rather introduces students to a method for solving, not only this problem, but a large class of others as well. This method is simply to *play the Agent* - that is, for students to move their body as the Agent would move on the screen in order to draw a desired pattern: when you walk in a circle, you take a little step forward and you turn a little, and you keep doing this until the full circle is completed.

It is worth noting than such geometry is not insignificant. Thus, students are led imperceptibly to an intuitive grasp of physics, calculus and mathematical modelling that is used in many other areas of contemporary science, technology, and humanities alike.

Building Learning Aids

No less important, by *teaching* the microworld's Agents, students learn to design and construct their own software tools and aids to be used in learning the *hard* items of the standard mathematics curriculum and other subjects. The first project of this kind was successfully implemented in the mid-1970s, and the corresponding methodology has been used ever since. The story is described by Seymour Papert in his book, *Mindstorms* and goes something like this.

A class of fourth-graders had just started to study fractions and, as often happens, many appeared to be rather slow in grasping the issue. Taditionally, in such cases, the backward ones would have been given additional instruction and tuition. Now, instead, they were equipped with Logo microworlds (already familiar to them) and invited to find and develop some means for explaining and teaching fractions to themselves and others who needed help. They were also provided with seed ideas on how to think of themselves as collaborators in the project and its data collection, processing and reporting.

Each day, before going to the computer, the students spent 5 to 7 minutes writing their plans and drawing their designs for making, comparing and analyzing fractions, presented as graphic objects in their personal designer's notebooks. Then they worked at computers for 40 to 55 minutes individually or in groups, having full freedom to choose which concepts they wanted to teach, what the sequence of their lesson should be, and what instructional games, quizzes and tests to include. The amount of time spent at the computer was limited in order to fit the project into the schedule of the class and of the school. Over the course of four months, the class had developed several programs on teaching fractions that were diversified conceptually and quite useful in classroom practice. Judging by pre- and post- tests, students' ability to work with fractions, as well as with the microworld proper, had increased considerably. They had not only discovered that *fractions are everywhere* and can be easily explained in their *becoming,* but also acquired fluent ability to do other problems by manipulating fractions. The very integrating of mathematical concepts, drawing, constructing and writing made these disciplines mutually supportive.

The possibilities of microworlds in education are limitless. Supplemented with specialized tools, they enable students to create environments for the entire range of learning activities, from producing animated cartoons on central themes of literature and history to conducting scientific exploration and constructing advanced industrial machinery. Above all, they enhance students' general competence and confidence in active learning.

Artificial Life Experiments

Students can make working models of living organisms using blocks from construction sets that have motors, gears, wheels and sensors. After connecting their artificial creatures to a computer, they can write computer programs to control the behaviour of their animals. As mentioned above, the programmable brick -a special microprocessor included in the construction set - allows the model to function and move independently of the desktop or notebook on which the controlling program was written.

Such systems allow the images on the computer screen to be realized in three-dimensional, tangible form. Through these activities, primary school children can explore and discuss some of the central themes of Artificial Life research. This is not merely a scientific and technological topic, but a set of extremely powerful ideas that include emergence, bottom-up design, and system-oriented thinking. Giving children access to the forefront of modern science is, in general, an effective learning strategy. When children sense that they are involved in a new and dynamic adult enterprise, they eagerly invest themselves in the process. This project on artificial life can proceed in three-dimensional physical modelling and computer-screen versions. The students start with simple, easily understood rules or units, and study how complexity emerges from interactions among elements. Moving from simple to complex, from concrete to abstract, is just how children learn in everyday playful surroundings. Furthermore, they learn best when they are building and inventing things that they believe in and care about (which is why living things are useful at this stage).

For example, a youngster might program an animal like the screen turtle to move toward a light, but change direction if it bumps into any obstacles. Children can explore how artificial organisms behave in different *habitats,* and how they interact with other creatures. In addition to changing an animal's program, students can change its habitat. For example, a student might try adding more lights, or making the lights flash, and then wonder whether the animal will behave differently in the new environment. Which light will it seek out? Why? Children can also change the hardware or software of the animal and see the difference in its behavioural pattern. In many cases, such experiments pose a question of basic similarities, as well as distinctions, between organic and mechanical organization.

By the same token, students are not restricted to artificial animals: they can also build and program various machines, from vehicles to robots. This system-oriented approach influences the way children think about systems of all kinds: physical, political, and economic. But the most important thing is how this process influences the way students think about themselves as human beings who create systems, not the other way round.

Basic Music Composition

Let us consider an example of a design and construction activity in music. Traditionally, music classes in elementary school concentrate on performing and not on composing. On the other hand, children aged 7 and up, with no knowledge of formal musical notation, can learn how to create simple melodies in one or two years by operating a computer with an audio synthesizing and editing microworld used as a medium and tool for structuring and shaping the *material* of sound. A microworld of this kind provides a choice of musical notes in the range of seven octaves and commands that set a desired pitch, volume, and duration to consecutive strings of sounds (and pauses). Further, the sound can be given the coloration of any particular instrument and be made to simulate the sound of an ensemble of several instrumental voices.

The first stage is indiscriminate exploration: each student produces various sounds for the sheer pleasure of it and without paying much attention to their quality. After a while, they limit themselves to playing with low or high sounds, with an emphasis on the duration of the sound. Then students can start to build small melodies that lack formal structure since they are chosen at random. At this point, they are usually more concerned with the duration of the melody than with the actual sounds. At the end of the first stage, students select the sounds they like most, name them, and create melodies based on these sounds. In this way, they learn to program the sounds and melodies in a natural way, because they have a need to do so. They start to exercise auditory perception and to pay more attention to pitch than to duration.

In the second stage, students usually discover short sounds by chance and they start to glimpse the effects of sounds' parameters (pitch and duration). Thus begins a period of discriminate exploration of the musical microworld as they reflect on each sound's qualities. The sounds are not chosen at random anymore. Duration is the most prominent sound quality at this stage. The development of sound appreciation is apparent in the expanding selection of meaningful words that students use to name, not only sounds, but their created melodies as well. Once students begin to play with short sounds, they then tend to regulate the quantities of sound. For example, they discriminate between long and short sounds, while associating them with numbers; they combine closed notes, or make repetitions of two or three sounds, which results in sketches of a more formal organization where, for example, the first and last sounds are the same.

The third stage brings mastery of this particular music microworld. Here, students match the commands of sound qualities with desired pitch and duration. They become capable of anticipating a sound in their minds and generating it with the computer to produce more elaborate combinations leading to more complex musical patterns. From this point on, students are aware of what they can do with this programmable instrument by setting a goal and carrying it out. There is an evident tendency toward perfecting the musical sentences and making them more expressive. The students are trying successfully to compose music they can dance to or sing, and to depict aurally some simple scenic actions and characters.

Scientific Research

Students at all grade levels and in every domain of science should have the opportunity to use and develop the ability to think and act in the ways associated with empirical inquiry, including asking questions, planning and conducting investigations, using appropriate tools and techniques to gather data, thinking critically and logically about relationships between evidence and explanations, constructing and analyzing alternative explanations, and communicating scientific arguments. The general model of scientific research and the qualities required of a researcher have many things in common with the models and qualities described above as important for most social roles, far beyond the purely intellectual one.

Stages and types of research activity in school education are:

- formulating goals and research hypotheses;
- finding basic information, known experiments and results from the Internet and other sources;
- contacting experts, group discussions, carried on during face-to-face meetings and via telecommunication;
- overall planning of a project, correcting plans in progress;
- designing and constructing the investigation setting;
- running experiments in hands-on, automatic, and distant mode;
- analyzing and presenting data using mathematical models and means of visualization;
- discovering patterns, finding connections, making explanations and conclusions, verifying hypotheses and producing new ones; and
- conducting group discussions of results in classrooms and producing reports, presenting and publishing results via the Internet, screen, and text formats.

Based on the previous discussion, we can compile a list of hardware and software instruments to support these activities. Of course, special types of research may require special tools. These tools include:

- general office applications with text and graphics editing;
- lab equipment including computer-based testing and measuring devices; and
- tools for numerical and algebraic computations, spreadsheets, graphing, and statistical analysis.

Research in Social Sciences and Humanities

Research in the social sciences and humanities has much in common with research in the natural sciences, as well as with artistic projects. Moreover, interesting educational results can be achieved in combination with different activities by, for instance, interviewing people for their opinion on a specific scientific fact or on the environmental consequences of an industrial process, or making pictures or drawings of local streets. In this field, a research scenario might call for students to collect personally relevant information on their neighbourhoods, starting from their own files. It is conceivable that students start with the history of their family and expand it to a nation, and then to all humankind. Organizing and presenting information, the creative and artistic recording of human impressions and transcribing interviews are some core elements of artistic and social science projects. In many cases, a project does not necessarily include every stage.

References

Papert, S. (1981). *Mindstorms: Children, Computers, and Powerful Ideas*. Basic Books, New York.

Rhodes, J. (1991). *Conceptual Toolmaking: Expert Systems of the Mind.* Basil Blackwell, Oxford.

Rieber, L. P. (1995). A historical review of visualization in human cognition. *Educational Technology Research and Development*. 43 (1), 45-56.

Sternberg, R. J. (1986). *Intelligence Applied: Understanding and Increasing Your Intellectual Skills*. Harcourt, New York.

Sternberg, R.J. (1988). *The Triarchic Mind: A New Theory of Intelligence.* Viking Press, New York.

Toffler, A. (1970). *Future Shock.* Random House. New York. p. 6.

UNESCO. (2003). *Performance Indicators for ICT Use in Education.* UNESCO, Bangkok.

Bibliography

Adams, A. & Tulasiewicz, W. (1995) *The Crisis in Teacher Education: a European concern?* London: Falmer Press

Anderson, J. (1993). *The New Literacy and Technology*. Keynote address to the International Reading Association Convention, San Antonio, Texas, April 1993.

Bederson, B., Shneiderman, B. (2003). *The Craft of Information Visualization: Readings and Reflections.* Morgan Kaufmann Publ., San Francisco.

Berliner, D.C.. Learning about and learning from expert teachers. *International Journal of Educational Research*, 35(5), 463-483.

Biggs, J.B.. *Student approaches to learning and studying.* Melbourne: Australian Council for Educational Research.

Boaler, J. (1999). Mathematics for the moment, or the millennium? *Education Week* 17(29): 30–34.

Bonta, P. (1990). *Building on Intuitions: Music Composition in a Logo Environment.* In Idit Harel (Ed.). 1990. *Constructionist Learning.* MIT Media Laboratory, Cambridge, MA.

Caldwell, B. *Re-imagining educational leadership.* ACER: Melbourne

Card, S.K., Mackinlay, J.D., and Shneiderman, B. (Eds). (1999). *Readings in Information Visualization: Using Vision to Think.* Morgan Kaufmann.

Carlsen, W. S.. Effects of new biology teachers' subject matter knowledge on curricular planning. *Science Education*, 75, 631-647.

Castells, Manuel (1996): *Information Age: Economy, Society and Culture,* Volume I: The Rise of the Network Society.Blackwell, Oxford.

Collins, J. *Good to great and the social sectors,* Random House: London

Coombs, Philip H. (1968): *The World Educational Crisis: A Systems Analysis.*Oxford University Press, Oxford.

Davies, C. (1995) *Gender and the Professional Predicament in Nursing* Buckingham: Open University Press

Dede, C., Korte S., Nelson, R., Valdez, G., & Ward, D. J. (2005). *Transforming learning for the 21st century: An economic imperative.* Naperville, IL: Learning Point Associates. R

Dede, C., Korte, S., Nelson, R., Valdez, G., & Ward, D. (2005). *Transforming education for the 21st Century: An economic imperative.* Chicago, IL: Learning Point Associates.

DES [Department of Education and Science] (1984) *Initial Teacher Training: Approval of Courses Circular 3/84* London: DES.

Dewey, J. (1938). *Experience and education.* New York: Simon and Schuster.

Doppelt, Y. (2003). Implementing and assessment of PBL in a flexible environment. *International Journal of Technology and Design Education* 13:255–72.

Downes, S. (2007). *Emerging Technologies for Learning.* Coventry, U.K.: Becta.

Downes, Stephen (2006): *Learning networks and connective knowledge.*http://it.coe.uga.edu/itforum/paper92/paper92.html, accessed 17 November 2006.

Eckert, P. (1989). *Jocks and burnouts: Social categories and identity in the high school.* TeachersCollege Press, New York.

Elmore, R. *School reform from inside out.* Harvard Education Press: Cambridge

Entwistij, N. & Ramsdkn, P.. *Understanding undent learning.* London: Croom Helm.

Farnham-Diggory, S. (1990). *Schooling.* Harvard University Press, Cambridge, MA.

Field, John (2006): *Lifelong Learning and the New Educational Order.*Trentham Books, London.

Friedhoff, R. and Benzon, W. (1989). *Visualization: The Second Computer Revolution.* Harry N. Abrams, New York.

Friedman, T *The world is flat: a brief history of the 21st century.* Farrar, Straus and Giroux: New York

Fullan, M. "Professional learning communities writ large" in Dufour, R. & Eaker, R. (eds) On common ground: the power of professional learning communities. Solution Tree: Bloomington, IN

Gardner, H. (1983). *Frames of Mind: The Theory of Multiple Intelligences.* Basic Books, New York.

Geier, R., P. C. Blumenfeld, R. W. Marx, J. S. Krajcik, E. Soloway, and J. Clay-Chambers. (2008). Standardized test outcomes for students engaged in inquiry-based curricula in the context of urban reform. *Journal of Research in Science Teaching* 45(8): 922–39.

Goleman, D. (1996). *Emotional intelligence: Why it can matter more than IQ.* London: Bloomsbury.

Gultekin, M. (2005). The effect of project based learning on learning outcomes in the 5th grade social studies course in primary education. *Educational Sciences: Theory and Practice* 5(2): 548–56.

Heineke, W.F. and Blasi, L. (Eds). (2001). *Methods of Evaluating Educational Technology.* Information Age Publishing, Greenwich, Connecticut.

Hough, M., Paine, J. and Austin, L. *Creating quality learning communities.* Macmillan Education: South Melbourne.

Karoly, L. A. (2004). *The 21st century at work: Forces shaping the future workforce and workplace in the United States.* Santa Monica, CA: RAND Corporation.

Lave, J., & Wenger, E. (1991). *Situated learning: Legitimate peripheral participation.* Cambridge: Cambridge University Press. Brown, op. cit.

Lawton, D. (1980) *The Politics of the School Curriculum* London: Routledge & Keegan Paul.

Luft, J. (in press). Beginning science teachers in different induction programs: The first year of teaching. *International Journal of Science Education.*

Martin, E. & Bai.ia, M. An expanding awareness: How lecturers change then-understanding teaching. *Research and Development in Higher Education, 13,* 298-304.

Mortimer, E. & Scott, P.. *Meaning making in secondary science classrooms. Philadelphia*: Open University Press.

National Research Council. (2001). *Knowing what students know: The science and design of educational assessment.* Washington, DC: National Academy Press.

Papert, S (1993): *The Children's Machine: Rethinking School in the Age of the Computer*. Basic Books, New York.

Perelman, L. J. (1992). *School's Out: Hyperlearning, The New Technology, and the End of Education.* William Morrow and Company, New York.

Perry, W. G. Jr. (1981). Cognitive and ethical growth: The making of meaning. In A. W. Chickering (Ed.). *The modern american college* (p. 79). San Francisco: Jossey-Bass.

Reeves, T. C. (2006). How do you know they are learning?: The importance of alignment in higher education. *International Journal of Learning Technology*, *2*(4), 302–304.

Rhodes, J. (1991). *Conceptual Toolmaking: Expert Systems of the Mind.* Basil Blackwell, Oxford.

Rieber, L. P. (1995). A historical review of visualization in human cognition. *Educational Technology Research and Development.* 43 (1), 45-56.

Siemens, G. What does it mean to know today? *Education Review* 16(08),13.

Sternberg, R. J. (1986). *Intelligence Applied: Understanding and Increasing Your Intellectual Skills.* Harcourt, New York.

Sternberg, R.J. (1988). *The Triarchic Mind: A New Theory of Intelligence.* Viking Press, New York.

Taylor, C.. Assessment for measurement or standards: The peril and promise of large scale assessment reform. *American Educational Research Journal, 31,* 231 262. TRICAVIUT, K. & PROSSHR, M.. Towards an understanding of individual acts of teaching and learning. *Higher Education Research & Development, 16,* 241-252

Toffler, A. (1970). *Future Shock.* Random House. New York. p. 6.

UNESCO. (2002). *Information and Communication Technologies in Teacher Education: A Planning Guide* (Ed. P. Resta). UNESCO, Paris.

UNESCO. (2002). *Information and Communication Technology in Education: A Curriculum for Schools and Programme of Teacher Development* (Eds J. Anderson and T. van Weert).UNESCO Paris.

UNESCO. (2003). *Performance Indicators for ICT Use in Education*. UNESCO, Bangkok.

UNESCO-IBE. (1995). *Teacher Training and Multiculturalism: National Studies*. IBE, Geneva.

Veenman, S, & Denessen, E.. The coaching of teachers: Results of five training studies. *Educational Research and Evaluation*, 7(4), 385-417.

Vygotsky, L.S. (1978). *Mind in Society*: *The development of higher psychological processes*. Harvard University Press, Cambridge, MA.

Wenger, E. (1998). *Communities of practice: learning, meaning, and identity*. Cambridge University Press, New York.